SKILLET LOVE

SKILLET LOVE

From Steak to Cake:
More Than 150 Recipes in One Cast-Iron Pan

ANNE BYRN

PHOTOGRAPHS BY DANIELLE ATKINS

GRAND CENTRAL
PUBLISHING

NEW YORK   BOSTON

Copyright © 2019 by Anne Byrn

Photography copyright © 2019 by Danielle Atkins

Food styling by Teresa Blackburn & Anne Byrn

Prop styling by Jessie Pickren

Cover design by Claire Brown. Cover photograph by Danielle Atkins. Cover copyright © 2019 by Hachette Book Group, Inc.

Grand Central Publishing
Hachette Book Group
1290 Avenue of the Americas
New York, NY 10104

grandcentralpublishing.com
twitter.com/grandcentralpub

First Edition: October 2019

Grand Central Publishing is a division of Hachette Book Group, Inc. The Grand Central Publishing name and logo is a trademark of Hachette Book Group, Inc.

The publisher is not responsible for websites (or their content) that are not owned by the publisher.

The Hachette Speakers Bureau provides a wide range of authors for speaking events. To find out more, go to www.hachettespeakersbureau.com or call (866) 376-6591.

Print book interior design by Gary Tooth / Empire Design Studio

Library of Congress Cataloging-in-Publication Data

Names: Byrn, Anne, author. | Atkins, Danielle, photographer.
Title: Skillet love : from steak to cake : more than 150 recipes in one cast-iron pan / Anne Byrn ; photographs by Danielle Atkins.
Description: First edition. | New York, NY : Grand Central Publishing, Hachette Book Group, 2019. | Includes index.
Identifiers: LCCN 2019014326| ISBN 978-1-5387-6318-6 (hardcover) | ISBN 978-1-5387-6317-9 (ebook)
Subjects: LCSH: Skillet cooking. | One-dish meals. | LCGFT: Cookbooks.
Classification: LCC TX840.S55 B97 2019 | DDC 641.7/7—dc23
LC record available at https://lccn.loc.gov/2019014326

ISBNs: 978-1-5387-6318-6 (Hardcover); 978-1-5387-6317-9 (ebook)

Printed in the United States of America

LSC-W

10 9 8 7 6 5 4 3 2 1

To iron skillets and good friends—
both get better with age.

CONTENTS

INTRODUCTION
A Timeless Classic

"Trapped within the iron confines of these skillets…are the scents
and secrets of a family's culinary history."
—JOHN T. EDGE

"Things of quality have no fear of time."
—UNKNOWN

"Fashion changes, but style endures."
—COCO CHANEL

MY LOVE AFFAIR with cast iron did not begin forty years ago when I bought an old 12-inch Griswold at an Atlanta estate sale. Someone had cared for that ebony-black skillet. Someone had fried chicken in it. Made cornbread, too. It was shiny and smooth, with no hint of rust or neglect.

I adopted it into my family of pots and pans, and it moved with us from Atlanta to Nashville, and in between was crated and shipped to and from England, where it roasted lamb and potatoes for friends. No matter the kitchen, and no matter the occasion, my skillet fit in, segueing from anniversary dinners of seared salmon to Saturday pancakes with kids.

And yet, I never showered it with praise. That was reserved for the French copper pans I brought back from cooking school in Paris. You could say that this humble iron skillet with the perfect patina had been like a relief player, waiting for the one recipe to get my attention.

Then one July afternoon two years ago, I grabbed the skillet on a whim and poured in a favorite pound cake batter. That cake rose to a glorious height. The crust on top was golden and crackly, and the interior crumb was even and smooth. I had never baked such a perfect pound cake. My skillet, practiced and ready, performed like a seasoned pro and knocked that cake out of the park. In that instant, I fell in love. Yes, in love with my skillet.

It should have been sooner, because I was made for the efficiency of cast iron. Give me a sharp knife and a decent cutting board, and I am ready to cook. I prep many recipes with just a bowl and a wooden spoon. The cast-iron skillet is that same sort of basic tool.

Plus, raising children and being concerned about their health as well as my own, I should have given the iron skillet credit for being naturally nonstick. Unlike the artificial nonstick surfaces on many pans that cannot be placed over high heat lest they impart harmful chemicals into our food, the iron skillet begs for high heat. It is iron, for goodness' sake, forged at extreme heat so you can safely crank up the stove or oven and let the pan get seriously hot to sear, sizzle, roast, fry, blister, bake, braise, and caramelize, introducing big, bold, restaurant-quality flavors in the process.

I've spent a lifetime reading about, listening to, and interviewing famous chefs. I have quizzed them on the little details that make a recipe better. I remembered Lydie Marshall's suggestion in a cooking class decades ago when she advocated cast-iron skillets instead of copper. While writing this book, I tracked down Lydie in the South of France and asked her via email why someone so knowledgeable about French cooking chose iron over copper. Her answer was simple: Cast-iron pans are more affordable.

And therein lies another attribute: The cast-iron skillet is the pan of the everyday. You might desire copper or stainless steel, but you can afford cast iron. It is no-frills and authentic. It is for starting out and paring down. It is the only pan you ever need. And it works with you wherever you are on the timeline of life because it is wonderfully vintage and also modern and relevant. It bakes fruit pies, crostatas, cobblers, and pound cakes with rustic beauty. It sears tuna to perfection. It roasts mussels, corn on the cob, even cashews. It produces crisp-sided no-knead breads and pizzas that taste as if they were baked in a wood-fired oven. And on weeknights, it is a time saver because you can pile the entire meal into it, leaving only one pan to wash.

This book, *Skillet Love*, is my salute to the timeless, sustainable 12-inch cast-iron skillet. I'm not alone in my adoration, as there are collectors and devotees around the globe. But this is my deep dive, and I share recipes, advice, discoveries, and musings in the hopes you will pull out your skillet right now and not wait forty years to fall in love with it.

THE TEN PRINCIPLES OF CAST-IRON COOKING: UNDERSTANDING THE MAGIC

People might have originally cooked with cast iron because it was the only pan available, but today we have options. I wanted to understand why this skillet makes our food taste good so that we can be intentional about cooking with it.

If you take away one thing from this book, it should be that the cast-iron skillet allows you to cook boldly. Big flavors are achieved by a number of techniques and tricks, but the most important is high heat. The next time you dine out and look into the open kitchen at your favorite restaurant, you will likely see fire and flame. You will hear sizzling, and you will smell char. In the world of food science, that means flavor.

When steaks, fish fillets, or pork chops hit a hot pan, their proteins immediately stick to the pan, but after a while, the food releases and reveals a crust. That crust seals in flavors. It's the same principle in baking. The crisp exterior of a cake baked in iron allows the inside to be delicate and tender. High heat and hot sears are made possible with cast iron because the skillet can be heated dry without cracking, warping, or burning. It loves heat.

Here are my ten discoveries about why food cooked in a cast-iron skillet tastes so good:

1. The Hot Sear: Steaks, Chops, and Fish

When you cook a steak or chop, let the skillet heat up on the stove or in the oven before you add the meat. That way, the skillet soaks up all the heat and retains it so that when the food hits the pan, it sears.

Let's be honest—cast-iron skillets are not the best at heating evenly. That's because the thermal conductivity, or how it transfers heat within the pan, is low. But these skillets *are* the best at retaining heat—better than carbon steel pans—so even when cold steaks are added to the hot iron pan, the skillet temperature stays hot enough to sear. You just need to preheat that pan on top of the stove or in the oven. Use the heaviest iron skillet you've got, because it retains even more heat. And if you are really serious about searing, heat two skillets for steak: one to sear the first side, and the second hot skillet ready to sear the second. It's important to leave the food untouched for several minutes while it sears. This allows the juices to be locked in and the seasoning on the outside to char.

That's it!

Well, one more thing: Searing in cast iron is a little like Cinderella going to the ball and needing to be gone before the stroke of midnight. When your gorgeous steak is perfectly seared to doneness and doesn't need further cooking, you've got to quickly sweep that steak out of the pan and onto a plate or it will overcook from the skillet's residual heat—what remains after the stove is turned off. Use this remaining heat in the skillet to simmer a quick pan sauce to pour over the steak on the plate. More on that in discovery #10.

2. Stir-Fry: Just Like a Wok

Cast-iron skillets can be used to replicate Chinese takeout in your kitchen, so choose a skillet with the deepest walls. You will need the pan depth to toss around ingredients and keep them moving so they stir-fry (thus, the name). Stir-fry works in cast iron because the skillet can get hot enough, needs just a tablespoon of oil, and the ingredients cook quickly.

To begin, prep all your ingredients, making sure they are chopped about the same size so they cook in about the same amount of time. Heat the skillet over medium-high heat. Add about a tablespoon of peanut oil, which has the highest smoke point of the oils, or your favorite neutral vegetable oil. Add your seasonings, like grated fresh ginger or minced garlic. Keep everything moving by stirring so it does not burn. Add the veggies and stir-fry, then remove them and add your protein—shrimp, scallops, thinly sliced chicken, lean pork, or beef, or tofu cubes. Stir-fry no more than 12 ounces at a time so the food fries but does not steam. Remove the protein, add the sauce and let it cook down a bit, and then throw everything back in the skillet for a good stir.

The benefits of stir-frying regularly are a happy family, a healthy diet, and a skillet with a deep, black, well-seasoned glow.

3. Dry-Roast: From Nuts to Pizza

When you heat the skillet and then add food without any fat, you are dry-roasting. This is the method used by the wives of the Brittany fishermen hundreds of years ago to cook fresh mussels. It also works for roasting nuts of all types—cashews, pecans, walnuts, and even peanuts in the shell.

Dry-roasting also improves the crust on pizza and breads like English muffins. In the case of pizza, you first dust the hot skillet with a little cornmeal before adding the dough. This is a bread-baking trick used in wood-fired ovens. If the cornmeal turns golden brown when it hits the pan, the pan is hot enough to add the pizza dough. The pizza bakes crispy on the bottom and is done in 12 to 15 minutes.

Another benefit of dry-roasting is that there is little cleanup. In most cases you can simply wipe the skillet clean with a damp paper towel.

4. Roast with Oil: Bring on the Vegetables

Anyone who uses their skillet day in and day out to feed the family has most likely roasted with oil. You heat up the skillet, add a little olive oil and some chopped vegetables or meat, and place the pan in the oven. It couldn't be easier or more successful.

The process works because the oil acts as a barrier, at first preventing the food from sticking to the skillet. As the heat of the oven extracts moisture from the vegetables or meat, they begin to stick to the skillet, and this becomes that delicious seared flavor.

I can't think of a vegetable that isn't improved by roasting in oil in cast iron. Before serving, sprinkle on your favorite salt and freshly ground black pepper, or maybe a handful of chopped fresh herbs, or a teaspoon of grated lemon zest. You taste the vegetable, you get these amazing compliments, and you know it was the skillet that did the work. You can also roast cubes of chicken or fish for salads or curries, or slices of steak for paninis. Again, heat the pan first, add the oil, and then add the food.

As to what oil is best, use olive oil or the vegetable oil you like best for cooking. But beware of butter, for it will burn and can taste bitter. Ghee—or clarified butter—is a better choice.

5. Sear, Then Braise: Create a Skillet Supper

Using the skillet as the one pan that cooks it all might seem new, but it's really an old and trusted technique of searing and then braising. Your grandmother knew it would gently cook tough but flavorful cuts of meat. Today, we apply this method to cooking most anything. You heat the skillet, add a little oil, and first sear your proteins that need some time to cook, such as bone-in chicken, steaks, or fish fillets, then remove them. The exceptions are foods that cook quickly, such as shrimp or scallops—they are instead added near the end of the process.

Then you add flavors to the hot pan, like onion and garlic and ginger and let them cook. Next, you deglaze and scrape, adding wine, beer, or stock to the skillet and scraping up the bottom of the pan to release the bits of cooked food and flavor. Next, add your veggies, like fresh or frozen peas, chopped green beans, asparagus spears, or zucchini strips, and let them cook. The protein is then returned to the skillet—or, in the case of shrimp and scallops, everything in the skillet is moved to the side to make room for them to cook on their own in a bare area.

You can get a lot more elaborate and braise shanks of lamb, thick pork chops and roasts, and whole chickens. But you will need a lid for these longer-cooking recipes—either tempered glass or cast iron.

6. Fry: Why Grandma's Skillet Still Looks Good Today

It's no secret how the black patina developed on an heirloom skillet. It fried chicken! Oil is the best friend to the skillet. It keeps it protected, impervious to any moisture that might cause it to rust. Think of oil on a skillet like moisturizer on your skin. Frying is the direct route to a gorgeous jet-black skillet. Heat plus oil builds the patina and makes your skillet naturally nonstick.

And while health experts say we should not exist on a diet of fried food, treats such as skillet-fried chicken or homemade doughnuts are worthy splurges. The chicken I fry in cast iron is life changing. I don't fry it every day, nor even once a week. But when I do, my husband smiles. It is the fried chicken he remembers from childhood. With just one bite he is instantly transported back to his mother's kitchen in Chattanooga.

The iron skillet is able to fry so well and create these strong memories because it is heavy, retains heat, and is durable. You don't need an electric fryer. You just need your skillet, oil, and heat.

7. Bake: From Sticky Buns to Tarte Tatin

It was a pound cake recipe that opened my eyes to the possibilities awaiting us with the iron skillet. You, too, can adapt your favorite cake, bread, and pie recipes to the 12-inch skillet, and it's a fun process.

The easiest cakes to adapt are those that are sturdy. The Cast-Iron Pound Cake (page 201) and other cakes with structure and substance can bake to doneness inside while the outside

Georgia Burnt Caramel Cake, page 211

INTRODUCTION: A TIMELESS CLASSIC

develops a delicious crust. You can serve them right out of the skillet, or in the case of the Brown Sugar Birthday Cake (page 202), unmold, pour over a quick icing, and light the candles. And then there is Fresh Pineapple Upside-Down Cake (page 213), the most famous cake cooked in cast iron. It works because the flavors of brown sugar and pineapple caramelize on the bottom of the skillet; when inverted, this canopy of flavor trickles down into the moist cake underneath. Before they were called upside-down cakes, they were just known as skillet cakes.

When ovens were fueled by wood fire and later by coal, it was the skillet that was tough enough to withstand the heat. Our thin metal baking tins didn't come along until electric and gas ovens had modernized the baking process. A relative newcomer recipe to skillet baking is a large chocolate chip cookie popularized in restaurants and now fun to make, bake, and serve piled with ice cream at home. Sticky buns and other sweet rolls, as well as coffee cakes, pies, and crisps, can all be baked in skillets.

8. Caramelize: From Onions to Fruit Pies

As I mentioned, the magic of the pineapple upside-down cake happens when the sugars in the pineapple caramelize in the heat of the pan. The retained, constant heat of the skillet allows fruit—whether pineapple, peaches, cranberries, apples, or bananas—to give up its juices, and those juices evaporate until what is left is a syrup of condensed fruit and caramelized sugar. This makes for the beginning of wonderful pies, cakes, and condiments with rich, deep flavor.

Caramelization also happens when you slowly cook down onions until they're deep brown and sweet. And it happens when you sear salmon, remove the fish, and add balsamic vinegar and garlic, or soy sauce and ginger, to the pan, let it cook in the skillet's heat, and then pour over the fish.

A famous example of caramelization is the classic Old-Fashioned Delta Caramel Icing (page 263). You caramelize sugar in the iron skillet, then use another pan to heat the rest of the ingredients. The two mixtures are combined and stirred with love until thick and smooth enough to frost a cake.

9. Grill: Take the Skillet Outdoors

Anything you cook on top of the stove in cast iron can be taken outside to the charcoal or gas grill and cooked in cast iron there. And if you are cooking foods with strong flavors, with a lot of smoke and heat, it just might be best to head outdoors anyhow so your smoke alarm doesn't go off! Trout, salmon, and all kinds of fish, especially fried fish, are best cooked outdoors. It becomes the perfect activity for entertaining, and just as guests tend to gather in the kitchen, they will gather outside when the cooking takes place there.

One of my favorite recipes to prepare in a skillet outside is burgers. They are so much moister and tastier than burgers cooked directly on a grill. You can really press down on the patties to get crispy edges and not worry about grease spattering all over your clean stove.

10. Cook with Residual Heat: Perfect for Sauces

As I have mentioned in these suggestions and will repeat throughout the recipes, you should take advantage of the residual heat that has built up in your skillet. Don't waste it! Toss something into that pan—off heat.

It might be slices of garlic bread, or a dash of vermouth and a pat of butter to sizzle and pour over your roasted trout, salmon, or red snapper. Or it might be pouring off the grease from frying chicken, and then mixing up a quick cream or tomato gravy to pour over the chicken and mashed potatoes.

After cooking steaks, chicken, chops, mushrooms, or fish, you can whip up a quick and easy sauce to pour over. Simply add a tablespoon or two of butter to the hot skillet, stir it around to scrape up bits of cooking juices, and then pour in about ⅓ cup of your choice of liquid and flavorings:

- Vermouth and 1 tablespoon chopped fresh tarragon
- Dry sherry and 1 tablespoon sorghum or molasses
- Cabernet and ¼ cup sautéed shallot
- Champagne and 1 tablespoon Dijon mustard
- Bourbon and 1 tablespoon bacon jam

I've even used the leftover heat in the pan to make ice cream. After toasting pecans in butter in the skillet, I remove the pecans and stir together a custard. It cooks to perfect thickness without heat. Then I pour the custard into a stainless steel bowl and chill it. An hour later, I'm churning homemade Butter Pecan Skillet Ice Cream (page 246). Delicious!

A HISTORY OF THE CAST-IRON SKILLET

Two hundred years ago, when Brittany fishermen brought fresh mussels back into port, their wives would toss some of the mussels on sheets of cast iron, under which they had built small fires. In this old French recipe called *moules brûles-doigts*—or burn-your-fingers mussels—the still-briny bivalves opened and provided instant satiation to the hungry fishermen. It was a far cry from the skillet we use in our kitchens today, but it is part of the intriguing use of cast iron in cooking.

Iron oxide—a compound of iron and oxygen—exists naturally in Earth's crust. Iron artifacts date back to 3000 BC, and the Chinese are credited with making the first cast-iron tools in the sixth century BC. When cast iron made its way to Europe in the fifteenth century, it was mostly used for artillery and in fashioning parts for bridges.

Cast iron is so named because the hot liquid iron is cast (poured) into molds, where it takes shape. Foundries today begin making a skillet by using what is called "pig iron," or a poured and hardened iron, along with scraps of steel. In the United States, foundries monitor the ingredients in the iron and added steel with a spectrometer so as not to include too many so-called tramp elements, such as titanium, tin, and chromium, in the process. In too large a concentration, these tramp elements can cause cracking in the cast iron. In addition, there is up to 4 percent carbon naturally found in cast iron, and carbon is important because it forms graphite flakes inside the iron that provide better heat retention and transfer when you cook.

One of the first cast-iron cooking pots was a three-footed round-bottomed iron pot designed to cook over a fire. These pots and pans became known as "spiders" because of their long legs. When indoor kitchen stoves arrived in the late eighteenth to mid-nineteenth centuries, the shape of the round-bottomed pots changed to flat-bottomed pans and skillets that fit snugly on stoves. The derivation of the word *skillet* is unclear—it's likely either Old Norse for "bucket" or Middle French for "a little dish."

Cast Iron Manufacturing in America

The first iron works in the United States was along the James River in Virginia, established in 1608. Named Falling Creek, it produced iron from bog ore, found in the Tidewater marshes and streambeds. But it was short-lived, and depleted thousands of acres of hardwood trees burned to make charcoal, which fueled the foundry. Later, Saugus Iron Works in Massachusetts, now a National Historic Site, was the scene of another colonial foundry, where cast-iron cookware and tools were produced from 1646 to 1670. But most of our country's cast iron production coincided with the Industrial Revolution of the late 1800s and early 1900s. Cast iron was the first important structural metal in building America because of its load-bearing strength. It was used to build railways and bridges and some of our first skyscrapers until stronger steel replaced it in the twentieth century.

Cast iron manufacturing took up shop in the coal- and iron-rich belts of America. That mostly meant the Appalachian Mountain states of Pennsylvania and Ohio, as well as a part of Tennessee on the Cumberland Plateau that so resembled a locale to the north, it was named South Pittsburg. Coke—made by heating coal in the absence of oxygen—was the new fuel that fed the industry. And in spite of the automation that came with America's growth, the first cast-iron skillets were made by hand. Sand molds for the skillets were formed, and the hot iron was hand-poured into the molds. After cooling, the skillets were sanded until smooth, creating a lighter, thinner, and smoother pan than what you can buy new today.

Iron skillet connoisseurs know the names of these early companies: Griswold in Erie, Pennsylvania (1865); Wagner in Sidney, Ohio (1881); Atlanta Stove Works in Atlanta, Georgia (1889); Lodge in South Pittsburg, Tennessee (1896). There were others, too, such as Birmingham Stove & Range, Favorite Stove & Range, Martin Stove & Range, Sidney Hollow Ware, Vollrath Manufacturing, and Wapak Hollow Ware. Lodge is the oldest continuously operating cookware manufacturer in the country and is still run by family members today.

Before electric ovens, before gas, when food was cooked over hot coals and in wood-fired chambers, cast iron helped feed families. When the heat from the burning wood was gone, cast-iron pans held that heat and allowed dinner to stay warm. And cast iron was essential to America's westward expansion. Pioneers could pack skillets and Dutch ovens and thus cook on the trail, at camp, over an open flame. The iron was durable, tough, and resilient, just like the people who forged the new territories.

Skillet Love in the Twentieth and Twenty-First Centuries

Americans never lost our love for cast iron—we just forgot about it. With all the new inventions in cookware in the twentieth century—aluminum, stainless steel, and nonstick pans—cast iron was replaced, and usage declined. A few vocal cooks and authors extolled its benefits in the 1970s, namely Lydie Marshall and Mollie Katzen. And in the early 1980s, at San Francisco's Zuni Café, the late Judy Rodgers roasted her legendary chicken and bread salad in cast iron. She preferred the way a cast-iron skillet cooked hamburgers, too. I like to think that Rodgers, Marshall, and Katzen were more ahead-of-the-game than old-school.

Today, cast iron is experiencing a revival. Pastry chefs as well as home cooks choose cast iron for baking cakes and pies, in addition to the much-loved cornbread. Serious cooks and chefs pick cast iron to sear steaks and oven-roast fish. Classic cast iron recipes like Dutch Baby (page 74) have moved out of the home and onto restaurant brunch menus. Social media loves food photographed in cast iron not only because it looks gorgeous in the black pan, but also because it evokes authenticity and comfort. And cooks concerned about sustainability and health gravitate to iron.

New skillet manufacturers such as Finex, Stargazer, Field, Smithey Ironware, and Butter Pat bring fresh designs plus hand-casting and sanding—and higher price tags. Iron is recycled, molds are made from sand that comes from nearby dunes, and the designs replicate old cherished family skillets. You might think the cast-iron skillet is back in style, but to some it never left.

CHOOSING A SKILLET

The 12-inch skillet was my choice for this book because it can fry a whole chicken, bake a dozen biscuits, fit a big loaf of bread or a whole pound cake, and have enough surface area to build a one-skillet meal. And, according to housewares and cast iron experts, the 12-inch is the most purchased skillet out there.

Focusing on one size allowed me a constant for testing recipes for this book. The 12-inch skillet measures 12 inches from rim to rim, but the inside bottom of the skillet is just 10 inches.

I found only one slight difference in the various 12-inch skillets, and that is an ever-so-slight height difference. For frying, you want the deepest skillet you own. However, for baking and browning, it helps if the skillet is shallow enough to let the bread or cake bake to golden. But rather than prejudice one pan with one particular type of cooking, I simply rotated the skillets with all the recipes. And in the end, all the skillets were beautifully seasoned when this book project concluded.

All the skillets were made in the United States, which was important to me. And I used two I already owned: the smooth-surfaced heirloom Griswold that inspired me to write this book and a Lodge I found on the seconds shelf at the factory store several years back. The others I purchased were a new Smithey, a Butter Pat, and a two-handled Lodge for those recipes that go from stove to table.

The Lodge "factory-seasoned" skillets worked great for all recipes. The finish of the new Lodge pans is more pebbly than the older pans and the new boutique brands. But food in the Lodge pans never stuck, and Lodge attests that the seasoning on the pan has a better chance to get into the crevices and form its own barrier against water if the surface isn't smooth as glass. Lodge was also the most affordable of the pans I purchased.

Did I have favorites? It depended on the day and the recipe. All the pans worked beautifully and are now cherished members of my family. In fact, when I see the Smithey, I think of how well it performed over the live fire and how I trusted it in frying and searing most anything. The Butter Pat developed the most beautiful sheen and deep patina after our photo shoot. Foods placed into it slid out without even asking. As for the old Griswold, well, I admit to being a little careful with it and not using it at temperatures of 450 degrees F and higher. She was the old girl, so I went easy on her.

Which leads me to this conclusion: You cannot compare brand-new skillets and your grandmother's. One might have been pre-seasoned and hand-sanded, and the other has been

How to ID Your Older Skillet

If you think you have a skillet produced by one of these old manufacturers, turn it over and look for a company name or identifying mark. If there is no name but a slash or line in the metal, this is called a "gate mark," and it signifies the oldest cookware, made before 1890. You can get help identifying the maker and the skillet's value online at thepan-handler.com. Older pans tend to be lighter and have thinner walls. Some older pans do not have helper handles, those short handles opposite the long handle that help you balance a heavy pan. And the length of the handle and size of the pouring spout may vary. If your pan says "made in the USA," it was made in the 1960s or after. That was when manufacturers were required to identify their country of origin. Both Griswold and Wagner have collectors clubs, and these members can be helpful as well.

cooked with for fifty years. That's why skillets find their way into family estates, as treasured an inheritance as stocks and bonds. If you buy one of the new skillets that are made in the heirloom fashion, you have a chance to begin a new tradition in your family. Look at it as an investment.

SHOW SOME LOVE:
HOW TO CARE FOR YOUR SKILLET

No skillet wants to be rusted and shoved into skillet hell in the back of a dark, humid kitchen cabinet. A happy skillet is sitting at the back of the stove right now, cared for, talked about, needed.

But don't get so obsessive about this process that you are fearful of using your skillet. There is a reason that iron skillets have survived the centuries. They withstand a little abuse but really appreciate being coddled, too.

If you have a new skillet that has been pre-seasoned, wash it with hot water and mild soap. Dry it well. Place it over the heat for a few minutes to further evaporate any moisture. (I do this every time I wash and dry my skillets.) Turn off the heat. Rub it with a little oil or shortening, wipe dry and store . . . or bake a pan of cornbread! There is nothing like baking cornbread or frying up some beignets to get that skillet seasoned.

If too much oil builds up on your skillet, the pan will get sticky. To clean up a sticky skillet, heat the oven to 400 degrees F and place a sheet of aluminum foil on the top rack. Place the skillet upside down on the foil (to catch the drips) and let the skillet "bake" for 1 hour. Wipe it dry and let it cool.

When cleaning your skillet after cooking, first let it cool off, since a hot skillet placed in a sink full of cold water could crack. And then remember that less is best. If you can wipe it out with a paper towel or rinse it in hot water and dry it well, do so. If you need to use some mild soap and scrub, that's OK, too, especially after frying bacon or cooking foods with strong flavors. Use the scrubber side of a kitchen sponge, or a "chain mail" scrubber, found where iron skillets are sold.

Some people never clean their skillets with soap. They advocate salt and scrubbing, for example. But I cooked so many different flavors in the skillets over the course of this book that I felt I had to clean them with mild soap, especially after roasting beef or fish. And when it comes to cooking acidic recipes like tomato sauce, I always use soap because I want to make sure to remove all food particles from the skillet. Do not let acidic foods sit in the skillet, because they can damage the seasoning on your pan as well as impart a slight metallic flavor to the leftovers. (A well-seasoned skillet, by the way, seems to be less affected by acidic recipes.)

Once dry, place the skillet over low heat,

Converting My 12-Inch Skillet Recipes to a 10-Inch Skillet

If you have a 10-inch skillet and need to convert my recipes to it, this shouldn't be difficult. Recipes that are griddled (pancakes, grilled cheese sandwiches, naan, English muffins, for example), and all things fried and roasted can go into the smaller skillet, but they need to be cooked in batches. You can sear one large steak or piece of fish instead of several. Reduce the Dutch Baby recipe by a quarter, and the same goes for the biscuits and cornbread. The crostata and clafoutis work well as is, but allow a little extra baking time. Forgo the big casseroles, cakes, breads, and skillet pizza. They are too much for a 10-inch pan.

and with paper towels carefully rub a little vegetable shortening or oil into the skillet as it heats for several minutes. Turn off the heat, wipe out any traces of oil, let cool, and then store at the back of the stove or on a rack or open shelf, and never, ever in a damp, dark cabinet.

HOW TO SEASON A SKILLET FROM SCRATCH OR SAVE A NEGLECTED SKILLET

Most new skillets today come pre-seasoned. However, if your skillet is not seasoned, follow the manufacturer's directions or the following guidelines.

The best oils to use for seasoning are the least saturated: canola, corn, soybean, sunflower, and flaxseed. Experts say you can also use lard if you want. Just make sure to wipe off any lard left on the surface of the skillet so it doesn't go rancid in storage.

Heat the oven to 500 degrees F and place a sheet of aluminum foil on the top rack. Rub about a tablespoon of oil onto all surfaces of the skillet, wipe off the excess oil with a dry cloth, and place the skillet upside down on the foil (to catch the drips). Let the skillet "bake" for 1 hour. Carefully remove the skillet from the oven and let it cool. Repeat this process five or six times, until the skillet is black and shiny.

For heavily rusted or badly neglected skillets, the process begins with cleanup. Try to scrub off as much food debris and rust from the pan as you can using steel wool. This will reduce the amount of smoke emitted during the oven-cleaning process. Remove the oven racks (or they will discolor). Place the pan on a brick in the bottom of the oven. Turn the oven on a self-cleaning cycle, and turn on your exhaust fan to reduce the smoke that accumulates in the kitchen. After the cycle is over and the skillet is cool enough to handle, remove it from the oven. (Wipe out your oven, and replace the oven racks.)

Scrub the skillet again with steel wool to remove any last bits of rust. Coat the skillet in flaxseed oil, rubbing it in well, and then rub it off with a dry cloth. Heat the oven to 500 degrees F, and proceed as described above to season a skillet, letting the skillet "bake" for 1 hour. Repeat this process five or six times, until your skillet has the shiny black patina you desire.

You can also soak the skillet in a solution of two parts water to one part white vinegar in the sink for at least an hour, then scrub. This works on skillets that are only mildly rusted. Once the skillet is free of rust, you can begin the seasoning process described above.

SECRETS BEHIND A SEASONED SKILLET

There is a difference between a "seasoned" skillet and the "seasoning" process you undertake with a new skillet.

A "seasoned" skillet has gone through a "seasoning" process. Repeating the process of seasoning creates a well-seasoned skillet. And that's why the more you cook with your iron skillet (the more you use this book!), the better your skillet will look—and the more nonstick its cooking surface will be.

When you sear and fry, over and over, the oils build up and create a hard, dry, protective barrier, which is impervious to moisture. This layer is not only on the surface of the pan, but it seeps into the pits of the iron and creates a naturally nonstick surface.

Iron has microscopic pores, and when you put oil on the surface and heat the skillet long enough and hot enough to bake off the free radicals in the oil, past the oil's smoke point, what is left on the surface of the skillet is a layer of hydrocarbons. These hydrocarbons are the protection for the seasoned skillet.

In contrast, if you don't rub the skillet with oil before you heat it to season it, the skillet will turn blue as the iron oxidizes. But if the skillet is rubbed with oil, and the skillet is sufficiently heated, over time it turns black.

Skillet seasoning experts have their own rogue methods of achieving a shiny, black pan. Some like the high heat of 500 degrees F and above in the home oven. Others place the oiled skillet in a well-heated outside grill, turn off the grill, and check on the skillet in the morning. And still others wipe a new skillet with lard and throw it into the campfire. Whatever works!

YOUR HEALTH AND THE SKILLET: BENEFITS OF THE NEW NONSTICK

Before you begin cooking, I thought you'd like to know that your skillet doesn't just make good food. It makes food that is good for you. And for several reasons.

First of all, a well-seasoned skillet doesn't need a lot of oil to sauté vegetables or proteins. Secondly, you can do a lot more than just fry in it. You can stir-fry, braise, and roast—all healthy ways to cook with less fat.

And finally, when heated, cast iron can release small amounts of iron into food. Yes, iron is best obtained from food sources like lean meat, leafy green vegetables, and whole grains and legumes. But new skillets, and acidic foods—such as tomato sauce or applesauce—as well as simmering and stirring food—bring a greater chance of getting a little iron in your diet.

Plus, because of its naturally nonstick properties, the cast-iron skillet does not contain perfluorooctanoic acid (PFOA), a toxic chemical that is used to make nonstick pans and that breaks down at high heat. While PFOA has been phased out, it is still present in older nonstick pans. Even new nonsticks without PFOA are not supposed to be heated above 500 degrees F. No wonder cooks today are returning to cast iron. You can cook hot, cook boldly, and not worry about it!

A NOTE ABOUT BLUEPRINT RECIPES

Much of what I cook day in and day out is a blueprint—that is, a way of cooking a certain type of dish. Whether it's chicken or fish or a berry pie, I adapt recipes to the season and to what's in my pantry. So, I decided to incorporate a few of these blueprint methods into the recipes. You will find Skillet Tartines (page 22) with the appetizers, Dutch Baby (page 74) in the brunch chapter, and Fried Rice (page 116) in the sides, plus several chicken recipes because chicken is just so easy to cook by blueprint. And I share my way of baking a crostata; it's up to you what berries to use. I could have included more, and this book is sprinkled with suggestions and loads of what-ifs in the hope that you will seize my suggestions and make these recipes yours.

1. **Cashews.** DRY-ROAST. Heat the oven to 375 degrees F. Scatter 1 pound cashews—without butter or oil—in a 12-inch skillet and bake until lightly golden, 8 to 10 minutes. Add 1 tablespoon butter and a pinch each of sugar, kosher salt, and cayenne pepper and toss to coat well. Remove the cashews from the skillet, let cool completely, and serve.

2. **Charred lemons.** CHAR. Heat a 12-inch skillet over medium-high heat until it smokes, about 4 minutes. Meanwhile, coat lemon slices in granulated sugar. When the skillet is very hot, add 1 tablespoon vegetable oil, then place the lemon slices in the skillet. Let the lemons char on both sides, getting as dark as you like, 4 to 5 minutes total. Serve with fried seafood.

3. **Whole Vidalia or other sweet onions.** BAKE. Heat the oven to 375 degrees F. Peel and cut off the tops of several onions. Place the onions in a 12-inch skillet, cut-side up. Season with sea salt and freshly ground black pepper and top each with a pat of butter. Bake until tender and caramelized, 35 to 40 minutes.

4. **Chopped onion.** CARAMELIZE. Heat 2 tablespoons olive oil in a 12-inch skillet over medium-high heat. Add 2½ cups finely minced sweet onions or shallots and season with kosher salt and freshly ground black pepper. Sauté, stirring constantly, until the onions are golden brown, softened, and a little crispy around the edges, about 15 minutes. For an easy dip, transfer the caramelized onions to a bowl and let cool, then fold in 1 tablespoon cider vinegar and 1½ cups plain low-fat Greek yogurt. Chill and serve with your favorite crackers or potato chips.

5. **Bacon.** FRY. Who needs a recipe, right? Believe it or not, there is a skill to cooking crispy bacon in a skillet. You need to lay no more than six or eight strips of bacon in a *cold* 12-inch skillet—do not crowd the pan! Bring the heat up to medium-low and regulate it, allowing the fat to render to lubricate the pan and prevent the bacon from sticking. Cook, flipping the bacon with a fork or tongs three or four times, until crispy, 4 to 5 minutes. Drain on paper towels.

6. **Sizzled mushroom caps with Madeira.** SAUTÉ AND CARAMELIZE. Trim the stems from cremini mushrooms and sauté the caps in butter in a 12-inch skillet over medium-high heat until they begin to exude liquid, 2 to 3 minutes. Add a splash of Madeira or dry sherry and continue to sauté until the juices have reduced to a glaze. Season with kosher salt and freshly ground black pepper, shower with chopped fresh chives or flat-leaf parsley, and serve with steak or cocktails.

7. **Garlic.** ROAST WITH OIL. Heat the oven to 350 degrees F. Slice ¼ inch off the top of a whole head of garlic. Place it, cut-side up, in a 12-inch skillet and drizzle with olive oil. Roast until soft, about 1 hour. Squeeze out the cloves and use in salad dressings or to spread on crusty bread.

8. **Frozen fish.** BAKE IN MILK WITH ONIONS. Heat the oven to 375 degrees F. Rub softened butter over the bottom of a 12-inch skillet and lay thawed frozen fish fillets in a single layer on top of the butter. Season generously with sea salt and freshly ground black pepper. Top with a thinly sliced onion. Pour in enough whole milk to cover the fish. Bake until the milk is bubbly and the fish is cooked through, about 30 minutes. Sprinkle grated Parmesan over the top during the last 10 minutes, if desired.

9. **Whole fish.** SEAR. Have the fishmonger clean a 1- to 1½-pound fish such as branzini. Stuff it with lemon slices and fresh herbs. Rub the whole fish with olive oil. Heat a 12-inch skillet over medium-high heat until it smokes, about 4 minutes. Place the fish in the skillet and let it cook, undisturbed, for 3 minutes. The skin should blister. Turn the fish with tongs and cook the other side until blistered, 3 minutes. Season with sea salt and freshly ground black pepper. Squeeze the juice of a whole lemon

over the fish. Add a tablespoon of butter to the pan and swirl around. Throw in a handful of drained capers. Test for doneness. If the fish hasn't cooked through, place it in a 400 degree F oven for up to 10 minutes. Serve with the pan juices poured over the top.

10. **Scallops.** SEAR. Choose dry scallops that have not been soaked in a phosphate solution to preserve them. Remove the small tendon on the side of the scallop. Pat them very dry with paper towels. Season with sea salt and freshly ground black pepper. Heat a 12-inch skillet over high heat until it smokes, about 4 minutes. Pour a teaspoon or two of vegetable oil in the skillet. Add the scallops, spacing them about 2 inches apart, and let them brown, undisturbed, for 1½ to 2 minutes. Add 1 tablespoon unsalted butter to the pan. Turn the scallops over and cook on the other side for 1 to 1½ minutes. Serve the scallops as is, or deglaze the pan with some soy sauce, lemon juice, and grated fresh ginger. Pour the sauce over the scallops.

11. **Steak.** SEAR. Let a 12-inch skillet get searing hot over medium-high heat, about 5 minutes. Add a teaspoon of oil, then sear dry-seasoned steaks for 3 to 4 minutes per side. Continue to cook until an instant-read thermometer inserted in the steak registers 130 to 135 degrees F.

12. **Peanuts in the shell.** DRY-ROAST. Heat the oven to 350 degrees F. Pile unshelled peanuts into a 12-inch skillet and roast for about 20 minutes. Taste for seasoning and add kosher salt, if desired. (Some raw peanuts in the shell are already salted.)

13. **Panini.** PRESS AND SEAR. Heat a 12-inch skillet and a 10-inch skillet over medium heat until very hot. Add a little oil to the larger skillet and brush oil on the bottom of the 10-inch skillet. Place your sandwich of meat and cheese or just cheese in the larger pan. Place the smaller skillet on top of the sandwich to press it down. Cook until the bread is golden brown on both sides and the cheese has melted, 2 to 3 minutes.

14. **Asparagus.** ROAST WITH OIL. Heat the oven to 450 degrees F. Lay 10 to 12 thick, meaty asparagus spears in a single layer in a 12-inch skillet. Drizzle with olive oil and season with a pinch of kosher salt. Roast for 5 minutes. Turn the asparagus over with tongs and let them continue to cook in the residual heat of the pan for 2 minutes. Sprinkle with freshly ground black pepper and shaved Parmesan cheese.

15. **Hoe cakes.** FRY. Bring 2 cups water and 1 teaspoon salt to a boil in a saucepan. Whisk in 1¼ cups white cornmeal until smooth and thick. Transfer the cornmeal mush to a bowl and chill for 30 minutes. Heat 1 inch vegetable oil in a 12-inch skillet over medium-high heat. Form the cornmeal mush into little flattened cakes and fry for about 2 minutes per side, until well browned. Serve hot with butter.

If you think the skillet is made just for roasting chicken, then you will be pleasantly surprised by all the nibbles and appetizers in this chapter that come to you courtesy of your cast-iron friend. What does the skillet do for apps? It griddles artichokes, blini, and grilled cheese sandwiches. It fries chicken wings, okra, latkes, pommes frites, and beer-battered sweet onions. It chars Brussels sprouts, green beans, and asparagus. It simmers queso fundido so you can serve it up stove to table with chips and salsa. It bakes pizza at a fierce, high heat that mimics a wood-fired oven. It roasts eggplant and cauliflower and toasts bread for elegant tartines. The question really becomes: What does the skillet *not* do for appetizers?

CHAPTER 1
SMALL PLATES & SNACKS

PAN-GRIDDLED ARTICHOKES
with Fresh Romesco Sauce

MAKES 8 SERVINGS / Prep: 40 minutes / Cook: 50 to 60 minutes

This bright, bold recipe was created by my friend David Patterson of Nashville who sears artichoke halves on the grill and spoons a vinaigrette for dipping into the hollow of each artichoke. I have adapted it for the cast-iron skillet for those times when you don't want to heat up the grill. The first step is to cook the artichokes in a big pot (this can be done a day ahead); then you sear the artichoke halves with the heat of the cast-iron pan. Instead of vinaigrette, I offer my version of the distinctive romesco sauce of Spain's Catalan region, which features tomato, pepper, almond, and paprika. The sauce can also be made a day ahead; chill it and then let it come to room temperature before spooning into the artichoke hollows. This is beautiful as a starter or part of a large vegetable buffet, or alongside grilled chicken or fish.

4 large artichokes

2 tablespoons olive oil, divided use

FRESH ROMESCO SAUCE

2 cloves garlic, peeled

½ cup jarred roasted red peppers, cut into pieces

1 cup chopped fresh tomatoes (about 2 medium tomatoes)

¼ cup chopped toasted almonds

2 tablespoons sherry vinegar

1 teaspoon sweet paprika (see Note)

¼ teaspoon cayenne pepper

½ cup olive oil

Kosher salt and freshly ground black pepper

NOTE: Most recipes for romesco call for smoked paprika, but I prefer sweet paprika because it allows the subtle flavor of the artichokes to come through.

1. Bring a kettle of water to a boil. Meanwhile, trim the outer leaves of the artichokes. Cut off the thorny tips of each leaf. Cut the stem level at the base so that it rests flat. Stand the artichokes up, side by side, in a large pot. Add enough boiling water to come about a third of the way up the artichokes. Cover the pot and let the artichokes simmer over low heat until a leaf pulls out easily, 40 to 45 minutes.

2. Drain the artichokes and let them rest until cool to the touch, about 20 minutes. Slice them in half lengthwise, through the stem, and with a small spoon, scoop out the choke from the center of each half. (At this point, you can put the artichoke halves in a container, cover, and refrigerate for up to 1 day.) Brush the cut sides of the artichoke halves with 1 tablespoon of the olive oil. Set aside.

3. Next, make the romesco sauce. With the food processor running, drop the garlic through the feed tube and let it process. Stop the machine and add the peppers, tomatoes, almonds, sherry vinegar, paprika, and cayenne pepper. Pulse 10 to 15 times, until the ingredients are nearly smooth. With the motor running, pour in the olive oil through the feed tube and process until thickened, about 15 seconds. Turn off the machine and season the sauce with salt and black pepper, if desired. Set the sauce aside.

4. Heat a 12-inch skillet over medium-high heat until quite hot, about 3 minutes. Dribble in the remaining 1 tablespoon olive oil. Working in batches of two or three at a time, place the artichoke halves, cut-side down, in the hot skillet. Let them sear for 2 minutes, undisturbed, then run a spatula underneath them and take a peek. If they are well browned, transfer them from the skillet to a platter. If not, leave them in the pan for another minute.

5. To serve, spoon a bit of romesco sauce into the hollow of each artichoke. Serve more sauce to the side. To eat, pull off the leaves and dip them into the sauce; then using a knife and fork, cut the artichoke bottom into pieces.

FRIED GREEN TOMATOES
with Roasted Garlic Ranch

MAKES ABOUT 4 SERVINGS
Prep: 50 minutes / Soak: 2 hours / Cook: 4 minutes per batch

When I see green tomatoes, I am reminded about the fried green tomatoes cooked at the late Betty Talmadge's farm, Lovejoy, about 25 miles south of Atlanta. In the 1980s, Talmadge would stage these lavish Southern-themed dinner parties for friends and clients. And her cook, Cile, turned out the best fried green tomatoes. I once walked into the insanely busy kitchen in the middle of one of these parties, and there was Cile, pulling sliced green tomatoes from their bath of salted ice water. She would dredge them in a mixture of seasoned white cornmeal and flour, then fry them until crispy in a big, shiny cast-iron skillet. Something this simple and pristine needs little adornment. But I sometimes like to serve them with a spoonful of homemade roasted garlic ranch dressing. Or, you can smear the fried green tomato slices with soft goat cheese and pesto and layer with ripe red tomato slices to create eye-catching tomato stacks.

3 or 4 medium-size green tomatoes

2 teaspoons salt

ROASTED GARLIC RANCH

1 head garlic

1 tablespoon olive oil

½ cup mayonnaise

¼ cup buttermilk

¼ cup grated Parmesan cheese

1 tablespoon fresh lemon juice

½ teaspoon Worcestershire sauce

¼ teaspoon hot pepper sauce

Salt and freshly ground black pepper

FOR DREDGING AND
FRYING THE TOMATOES

⅓ cup all-purpose flour

⅓ cup white cornmeal

½ teaspoon salt

Freshly ground black pepper

About 2 cups peanut or vegetable oil

1. Peel the tomatoes, and slice each into about 4 nice slices. Set aside. Fill a large mixing bowl with cold tap water and stir in the salt. Add a couple cups of ice cubes. Add the tomato slices to the salted ice water and refrigerate overnight, or at least 2 hours.

2. For the dressing, preheat the oven to 400 degrees F. Cut ½ inch off the head of the garlic, exposing the cloves. Place the garlic head on a square of aluminum foil and drizzle the exposed cloves with the olive oil. Pull the sides of the foil up around the garlic to encase it. Place the foil-wrapped garlic on the oven rack and bake until tender, about 45 minutes.

3. Remove the garlic from the oven and carefully open the foil so the garlic can cool, about 20 minutes. Squeeze the garlic pulp into a medium-size bowl, then mash with a fork until smooth. Add the mayonnaise, buttermilk, Parmesan, lemon juice, Worcestershire sauce, and hot pepper sauce and whisk until smooth. Season with salt and pepper. Cover with plastic wrap and chill until time to serve.

4. When ready to fry, remove the bowl of tomatoes from the refrigerator. Pour off the water and drain the tomato slices. Pat them dry with paper towels. Combine the flour, cornmeal, salt, and a few grinds of pepper in a shallow dish or pie plate and stir. Dredge the tomatoes in the mixture, coating well on both sides as well as on the outside peeled edges. Place the coated tomato slices on a rimmed baking sheet and chill in the fridge or freezer while you heat the oil. Set the oven at 200 degrees F.

5. Pour 1 inch of oil into a 12-inch skillet and heat over medium-high heat until the oil reaches 350 degrees F, or until a pinch of the cornmeal mixture sizzles when dropped in. Remove the tomato slices from the fridge and carefully drop three or four slices at a time into the hot oil. Fry until golden brown on both sides, about 2 minutes per side. Transfer the slices to a wire rack set over a baking sheet to drain. Once drained, transfer to another baking sheet and keep warm in the oven. Repeat with the remaining tomato slices.

6. To serve, arrange the warm tomato sauces on a platter or serving plates and spoon the garlic ranch dressing over them.

How to Crisp Up Leftover Fried Green Tomatoes

Place the green tomatoes on a baking rack set on a rimmed baking sheet. Heat the oven to 400 degrees F. Place the pan in the oven, and bake until the tomatoes begin to sizzle and the cornmeal coating starts to brown, about 5 to 7 minutes.

GILD THE LILY

Make a Fried Green Tomato BLT (shown below).

POTATO-ONION LATKES
with Cucumber Raita

MAKES ABOUT 16 (3-INCH) LATKES (6 TO 8 SERVINGS)
Prep: 40 minutes / Cook: 4 to 6 minutes per batch

Until I tried Joan Nathan's method of preparing latkes—the fried pancakes of grated potatoes traditional at Hanukkah—my attempts were just so-so. But once I did as Joan instructed—grated the russet potatoes along with the onions so the onion juice keeps the potatoes from darkening—I became more proficient. And the iron skillet can be credited for my success, too, because it is made for shallow-frying latkes, allowing them to fry up crisp and light. Go ahead and serve latkes with applesauce if you're feeling traditional. But when it's not Hanukkah and you want to prepare these for a party, try slathering them with this Indian-inspired sauce. Why raita? Latkes remind me so much of the crispy Indian bhajis.

CUCUMBER RAITA

1 cup plain full-fat or reduced-fat Greek yogurt

½ teaspoon ground cumin (see Note)

¼ teaspoon salt

Freshly ground black pepper

¼ teaspoon cayenne pepper

½ cup diced fresh tomato (about 1 medium tomato)

½ cup diced, peeled cucumber (about 1 small cucumber)

1 to 2 tablespoons minced fresh cilantro, chives, or mint

POTATO-ONION LATKES

2 pounds russet potatoes, peeled

1 medium onion

2 large eggs, lightly beaten

½ cup panko bread crumbs or matzoh meal

Kosher salt and freshly ground black pepper

About 2 cups vegetable oil

1. For the raita, combine the yogurt, cumin, salt, a few grinds of black pepper, and cayenne in a small bowl and stir. Fold in the tomato, cucumbers, and herbs. Cover the bowl and chill until time to serve. (The raita can be made a day in advance.)

2. For the latkes, grate the potatoes and onions together so that the onion keeps the potato from darkening. You need about 3 to 4 cups grated potatoes and 1 cup grated onion. Wrap all this up in a thin kitchen towel and squeeze out the liquid over a large bowl. Let the potatoes and onions stay in the towel while the liquid in the bowl settles. The potato starch will filter to the bottom of the bowl, while the liquid rises to the top. After 10 to 15 minutes, pour off the watery liquid, but leave that chalky potato starch in the bottom of the bowl. Add the potato and onion mixture to the starch, along with the eggs and panko, season with salt and pepper, and stir to combine.

3. Pour the oil into a 12-inch skillet and heat to 350 degrees F. Line a baking sheet with brown paper. When the oil is hot, measure ¼-cup spoonfuls of the latke batter and slide into the oil, working with three or four at a time. Press down on the mounds of batter slightly to flatten them. Cook until well browned on the bottom, 2 to 3 minutes, then turn and fry until brown on the other side, 2 to 3 minutes. Transfer to the brown paper to drain, and sprinkle with kosher salt. Repeat with the remaining latke mixture. You can keep the latkes warm between batches by placing the baking sheet in a low oven—about 250 degrees F.

NOTE: To make your own ground cumin, put 4 to 5 tablespoons whole cumin seeds in an iron skillet. Toast over medium heat, stirring, until the seeds turn darker in color, 3 to 4 minutes. Cool. Transfer the cumin seeds to a spice grinder and grind into a powder.

HOW TO FRY OKRA
Like a Southerner

MAKES 4 TO 6 SERVINGS / Prep: 20 minutes / Cook: 3 minutes per batch

Fried okra is one of summer's passions in the South, where the sturdy, drought-resistant okra plant soars and spits out a steady supply of pods. Those small, freshly clipped okra pods are the best to cook—either roasted in the skillet with a drizzle of olive oil, or dredged in white cornmeal and fried. Southerners keep it simple, and they rely on okra's inherent moisture to help the breading adhere. We fry okra until golden, drain it on brown paper, sprinkle with salt, then eat. While the cornmeal breading contains a good bit of black pepper, feel free to jazz it up further with a little cayenne pepper and garlic powder if you like. You can slice the okra pods crosswise or lengthwise right through the cap—the cap gives you something to hold onto when you pick up the okra.

12 ounces fresh okra
(about 32 small to medium-size pods)

1 cup white cornmeal (see Note)

½ cup self-rising flour

1 teaspoon freshly ground black pepper

About 2 cups peanut oil

Kosher salt, for sprinkling

1. Put the okra pods in a large bowl and pour in enough ice water to cover. Let the okra rest in the ice water while you prepare for frying.

2. Combine the cornmeal, self-rising flour, and black pepper in a large bowl and stir; set aside. Drain the okra. Cut the pods crosswise into ⅓- to ½-inch-thick slices, discarding the caps, or lengthwise right through the caps. Add the okra to the bowl with the cornmeal mixture and toss to coat.

3. Line a baking sheet with brown paper or paper towels. Pour 1 inch of oil into a 12-inch skillet and heat over medium-high heat until the oil reaches 365 degrees F. Grab a handful of okra, letting the excess cornmeal slip through your fingers. Carefully drop the okra into the hot oil and fry until golden brown, about 3 minutes. Use a slotted spoon to transfer the okra to the paper-lined pan, and sprinkle with salt. Repeat with the remaining okra. Serve warm. You can keep the okra warm between batches by placing the baking sheet in a low oven—about 250 degrees F.

NOTE: Southerners prefer white cornmeal over yellow for frying okra. And stone-ground is always best because it has a fresher flavor and more texture. If you live in an area where you can buy white self-rising cornmeal, use 1½ cups of it and omit the self-rising flour.

SORGHUM-GLAZED
Cauliflower Bites

MAKES 6 TO 8 SERVINGS / Prep: 15 minutes / Cook: 15 to 20 minutes

I remember the time a head of gorgeous purple cauliflower appeared in my CSA share. I was too intimidated by this beauty to steam it, so I cut the florets off the stem, tossed them with garlic and olive oil, then roasted them. The cauliflower that emerged from the oven was sweet and crunchy and actually had flavor. I was hooked. I would often drizzle on a little something extra after it roasted, which led me to this recipe for cauliflower roasted in the iron skillet. Not only does the skillet let the veggies cook to sweet, browned doneness, but when you pour over a syrupy vinaigrette, the retained heat of the pan sizzles that sauce, reduces it, and makes it even more wonderful. The sauce I make contains sorghum, that delightfully earthy sweetener popular in the Midwest and South. But you could just as easily use pomegranate molasses or honey. Serve warm from the skillet with toothpicks. You can also make this with a head of broccoli, and it's just as delicious.

1 small head white or purple cauliflower

4 cloves garlic

3 tablespoons olive oil

¼ teaspoon salt

GLAZE

3 tablespoons sorghum, pomegranate molasses, or honey

2 tablespoons balsamic vinegar

1 teaspoon Dijon mustard

½ teaspoon grated lemon zest

GARNISH

2 tablespoons chopped fresh cilantro or green onions

1. Preheat the oven to 425 degrees F.

2. Cut the florets from the head of cauliflower and separate them into small pieces. You will have 4 to 5 cups. If you have more than this, do not use more than 5 cups because it will crowd the skillet and the florets will steam instead of roast. Peel and slice the garlic into ¼-inch pieces. Toss the cauliflower and garlic with the olive oil and season with salt. Pile everything into a 12-inch skillet and place in the oven.

3. Roast the cauliflower until it is lightly browned, 15 to 20 minutes.

4. Meanwhile, prepare the glaze. In a small bowl, whisk together the sorghum, vinegar, mustard, and lemon zest.

5. Remove the skillet from the oven and pour the glaze over the top. Toss to distribute the glaze and let the glaze bubble up. Garnish with chopped fresh cilantro or green onions and serve right from the skillet with toothpicks. Or, pour the contents of the skillet into a serving bowl, garnish, and serve.

CHARRED BRUSSELS SPROUTS
and Sweet Raisins

MAKES 3 TO 4 SERVINGS / Prep: 20 minutes / Cook: 8 to 10 minutes

There is a reason that roasting Brussels sprouts is such a popular method. When you add cruciferous veggies to a hot pan, it caramelizes them and makes them taste sweet. That sweetness, combined with a crispy, charred exterior, provides the yin and the yang. Add yellow raisins, soy sauce, and onions and you get even more natural sweetness, and then balance with salt and pepper at the end. How a recipe with so few ingredients develops such complexity is a tribute to roasting in cast iron. Don't try to cook more than 4 cups of Brussels sprout halves in the pan at once or they will steam instead of sear.

2 tablespoons olive oil, divided use

1 pound Brussels sprouts, trimmed and halved (about 4 cups)

½ cup thinly sliced onion

1 tablespoon low-sodium soy sauce

¼ cup yellow raisins

Kosher salt and freshly ground black pepper

1. Preheat the oven to 400 degrees F.

2. Heat a 12-inch skillet over medium-high heat until smoking. Add 1 tablespoon of the oil and spread it out in the pan with a metal spatula. Dump the Brussels sprouts into the pan and let them sit, untouched until they begin to char, about 1 minute. Turn them with the spatula and let them begin to char on the other side, about 1 minute. Toss with the remaining 1 tablespoon oil and the onion slices.

3. Place the skillet in the oven and roast until the Brussels sprouts are browned and cooked through, 8 to 10 minutes, depending on their size. Remove the skillet from the oven, add the soy sauce and the raisins, and toss with the spatula to combine. Add more olive oil to coat if you like. Season with salt and pepper.

4. Transfer the mixture to a platter and serve warm or at room temperature.

> ### GILD THE LILY WITH CHERRIES
>
> Add dried cherries or other dried fruits instead of or along with the raisins. Scatter chopped fresh chives or cilantro over the top before serving.

ROASTED BABA GHANOUSH

MAKES 2 TO 3 SERVINGS / Prep: 10 minutes / Cook: 32 to 35 minutes

There are as many variations of this Middle Eastern eggplant spread as there are cooks making it. In my opinion, all of them are delicious! The cast-iron skillet is a perfect vehicle for roasting the eggplant so that all the water inside the eggplant is pulled out. When you split open the roasted eggplant with a sharp knife, that water is pooled inside the crisp skin and ready to be poured off. You still need to spin the eggplant pulp in a salad spinner to free it of any extra water. And once you do, then you can add the flavorings that appeal to you. Although tahini—sesame seed paste—is classic in this recipe, I prefer it without. I like the true roasted eggplant flavor to come through in concert with garlic, lemon, and parsley. Warm up some pita, roast some lamb, slice a ripe tomato, and you have the makings of a very fine meal or starter.

2 medium eggplants (1¾ pounds total)

¼ cup plus 1 tablespoon olive oil, divided use, plus more for serving

1 large clove garlic, peeled and minced

1 to 2 tablespoons lemon juice

Kosher salt and freshly ground black pepper

2 tablespoons minced fresh flat-leaf parsley

Warm pita bread, for serving

1. Preheat the oven to 450 degrees F.

2. Rinse the eggplants and pat dry. Rub them all over with 1 tablespoon of the olive oil. Put the eggplants in a 12-inch skillet and roast in the oven until the skin blisters, about 20 minutes. Use tongs to turn the eggplants over and continue to roast until tender, 12 to 15 minutes more. Set the eggplants aside until cool enough to handle.

3. Cut a slit in the top of each eggplant. Carefully spoon the pulp into a salad spinner. Spin a few times to get rid of the excess moisture. (Alternatively, put the eggplant pulp in a fine-mesh sieve and press down on it with a spoon to extract the moisture.) Transfer the drained eggplant to a bowl. Discard the drained water.

4. Add the garlic and lemon juice to the eggplant. Whisk in the ¼ cup olive oil until the texture is creamy. Season with salt and pepper. Fold in the parsley. Serve with warm pita bread and more olive oil, if desired.

NOTE: For a deeper flavor, add 1 tablespoon tahini—sesame seed paste—along with the olive oil.

Karen's Blistered
GREEN BEANS

MAKES 4 TO 8 SERVINGS / Prep: 25 minutes / Cook: 18 to 20 minutes

Nashville chef Karen Vanarsdel is an expert at Chinese cooking, and at one potluck a while back she brought the most delicious and unexpected green bean side dish. I know, you expect green beans at a potluck to be smothered in cream soup and covered with canned fried onions. But Karen created a medley of pork, green beans, ginger, garlic, chiles, and vinegar that had big, bold flavors. The secret, she said, was blistering the beans first in a cast-iron skillet, what she called "dry-frying." The recipe is adapted from one created by Grace Young, author of *The Breath of a Wok*.

¼ cup chicken broth or water

1 tablespoon sugar

1 teaspoon salt

2 to 3 tablespoons canola oil, divided use

1 pound Chinese long beans or green beans, washed, dried, and trimmed to 3 to 4 inches

4 ounces ground pork

2 tablespoons grated fresh ginger

4 cloves garlic, peeled and minced

1 or 2 Thai chiles, thinly sliced

1 tablespoon Chinkiang black vinegar or balsamic vinegar

2 teaspoons toasted sesame oil

2 green onions, thinly sliced on the bias, plus more for garnish

⅓ cup thinly sliced red bell pepper, plus more for garnish

1. In a small bowl, whisk together the broth, sugar, and salt. Set the bowl aside.

2. Heat a 12-inch cast-iron skillet over medium-high heat. When it is smoking, add 2 tablespoons of the canola oil. Working in batches, pan-fry the beans in a single layer, turning them frequently, until they have brown spots and start to wrinkle, 4 to 5 minutes. Transfer to paper towels to drain. Add a few more drops of oil as needed and continue to pan-fry the beans. Set aside the beans.

3. Add the ground pork to the skillet and stir-fry, breaking up the clumps, for 2 to 3 minutes. Toss in the ginger, garlic, and chiles and continue to cook until the pork has started to brown, 3 to 4 minutes. Add the broth mixture and cook until most of the liquid has been absorbed, 2 to 3 minutes more. Stir in the vinegar, sesame oil, green onions, and red pepper and stir-fry until the red peppers are tender but still have bite to them, 1 to 2 minutes more.

4. Return the beans to the skillet and toss to coat with the pork and sauce. Transfer to a serving dish and garnish with additional green onion and red bell pepper. Serve warm or at room temperature.

QUESTO FUNDIDO

MAKES 8 TO 10 SERVINGS / Prep: 20 minutes / Cook: 8 to 10 minutes

One of our favorite orders at Mexican restaurants is this molten cheese dip, and it's so easy to make at home in your skillet. First, start with the right cheese, which is called queso blanco or white American cheese. It melts smooth and creamy. To add more flavor, toss in a bit of shredded sharp Cheddar or crumbled cotija at the end. Don't use too much of these powerful cheeses lest this dip turn grainy. The best part of this recipe is that the skillet becomes the serving dish in true stove-to-table form. Arrange your choice of goodies on the top— crumbled chorizo sausage, chopped tomatoes or pico de gallo, cilantro leaves, radishes, you name it!

1 tablespoon vegetable oil or
light olive oil

3 jalapeño or serrano chiles,
seeded and diced

½ cup chopped onion

2 cloves garlic, peeled and minced

1 cup whole milk

½ cup heavy cream

½ teaspoon ground cumin
or chili powder (optional)

1 pound queso blanco, cut into cubes

1 cup (4 ounces) shredded
sharp white Cheddar cheese

1 cup (4 ounces) shredded pepper
Jack cheese

GARNISH (OPTIONAL)

Chopped fresh tomatoes
or pico de gallo

Sautéed crumbled chorizo

Fresh cilantro

Shaved radishes

FOR SERVING

Tortilla chips

Hot pepper sauce

1. Heat the oil in a 12-inch skillet over medium heat. Add the chiles, onion, and garlic and cook until they soften and begin to brown, 3 to 4 minutes. Add the milk, cream, and cumin and stir until the mixture is hot and comes nearly to a boil. Turn off the heat and stir in the queso blanco. Keep stirring until the cheese melts, turning the heat back to low if needed to melt all the cheese. Stir in the Cheddar and pepper Jack cheeses until smooth.

2. Top the queso with your choice of garnishes and serve with a basket of tortilla chips and hot sauce.

MESSY MEATBALLS
and Sauce

MAKES 8 SERVINGS / Prep: 35 minutes / Cook: 27 to 30 minutes

Not having been raised in an Italian family, I had to learn to make meatballs on my own. And I experimented with a number of versions until I hit on the perfect combination of flavors. I prefer to cook meatballs in an iron skillet because they brown better and develop more flavor. And this is the secret of really good meatballs: flavor from the browning process and a soft, pillowy interior. You can use a good-quality sauce from a jar, or make your own. And feel free to jazz this up by subbing pepper Jack cheese for the mozzarella, or by adding a minced jalapeño to the meatball mixture. This is a perfect dish to serve along with red wine and good bread to a group of friends gathered at your kitchen table on a winter evening.

4 slices bread

½ cup milk

1 pound lean ground pork

1 pound lean ground beef

2 ounces finely chopped prosciutto

2 large eggs, beaten

1 cup (4 ounces) grated Parmesan cheese, divided use

3 cloves garlic, peeled and finely chopped

⅓ cup chopped fresh flat-leaf parsley

½ teaspoon dried oregano

½ teaspoon dried basil

Salt and freshly ground black pepper

Olive oil, for frying

2 (24- to 26-ounce) jars tomato-based pasta sauce

1 cup shredded mozzarella cheese

1. Toast the bread, then let it cool. Break the bread into crumbs. Put the crumbs in a small bowl and stir in the milk. Let the bread soak up the milk, 8 to 10 minutes.

2. Meanwhile, in a large bowl, combine the ground pork and beef, prosciutto, eggs, ½ cup of the Parmesan, garlic, parsley, oregano, basil, 1 teaspoon salt, and a few generous grinds of black pepper. Use your hands to gently combine the mixture. Add the soaked bread crumbs and work them into the mixture only enough to incorporate. Use a ¼-cup measure to portion out 16 to 20 meatballs.

3. Heat 2 tablespoons olive oil in a 12-inch skillet over medium heat. When the oil shimmers, add half of the meatballs and let them brown on all sides, using a large spoon to turn them as they brown. This will take 7 to 8 minutes. Transfer the browned meatballs to paper towels to drain. Cook the second batch the same way.

4. Pour off the fat from the skillet. Add the pasta sauce to the skillet and let it come to a simmer over low heat. Return the meatballs to the skillet and let them simmer until cooked through, about 20 minutes.

5. Scatter the mozzarella cheese over the top of the hot meatballs. The cheese will melt from the heat of the skillet, or you can run it under the broiler for 15 seconds to melt, if desired. Serve the meatballs from the skillet at the table, with the remaining ½ cup Parmesan to spoon on top.

Best-Ever
SKILLET PIZZA

MAKES 4 TO 6 SERVINGS AS AN APPETIZER; 2 TO 3 SERVINGS AS A MEAL
Prep: 10 minutes / Cook: 15 to 20 minutes

This recipe freed me from overpriced, lukewarm pizza delivered to my door. Now when my family craves pizza, I simply pull out the iron skillet. With pre-made pizza dough, sauce, and cheese, I can bake an amazing deep-dish pizza in less time than it takes for mediocre pizza to be delivered. The skillet is key, and so is baking at a searing 450 degrees F. In the end, you get a hot pizza with a crisp crust, cheesy interior, and whatever toppings you like—all at an affordable price. Truly amazing!

1 recipe Easy Homemade Pizza Crust (page 21) or 1 pound store-bought pizza dough (see Note)

1 to 2 teaspoons cornmeal

1 to 2 tablespoons olive oil

2 cloves garlic, peeled and minced

½ to ¾ cup tomato-based pasta sauce

2 cups (8 ounces) shredded mozzarella cheese

Honey, for brushing

Red pepper flakes (optional)

1. Preheat the oven to 450 degrees F.

2. Heat a 12-inch skillet over medium heat until quite hot, 3 to 4 minutes. While the skillet is heating, stretch out the dough to get it as thin as possible, about 12 inches in diameter. You can do this in the air or by pressing it out with your hands on a cornmeal-dusted work surface.

3. Sprinkle cornmeal in the hot skillet.

4. Taking care not to burn your fingers, place the dough in the pan on top of the cornmeal, and press the dough halfway up the sides of the pan (it will shrink back, but this is OK). Whisk together the olive oil and garlic and brush this mixture over the dough. Spoon on the pasta sauce. (Note: If you like pepperoni on your pizza, this is where you would add it.) Scatter the cheese all over. Brush honey on the crust edges and sprinkle red pepper flakes on top of the honey, if you like. Turn off the stove, and place the skillet in the oven.

5. Bake until the cheese has melted and just starts to brown, and the crust edges are browned, 15 to 20 minutes. Carefully run a knife around the edges and slide the pizza out onto a board to slice and serve.

NOTE: You can purchase pizza dough at most supermarkets in the deli department. It's a good ingredient to keep in your freezer for pizza cravings. Let the dough rest on the counter for an hour to thaw. This dough takes slightly less time to cook (15 minutes) than the homemade crust takes (15 to 20 minutes).

EASY HOMEMADE PIZZA CRUST

**ENOUGH FOR 1 (12-INCH) SKILLET PIZZA,
ABOUT 1 POUND DOUGH**
Prep: 10 minutes / Rise: 1½ hours

¾ cup warm water (100 to 110 degrees F)

1 teaspoon active dry yeast

2 cups unbleached all-purpose flour

1½ teaspoons kosher or sea salt

Olive oil, for the bowl

1. In the bowl of a standing mixer fitted with the paddle attachment, whisk together the water and yeast to dissolve. Add the flour and salt and blend on low speed. Increase the speed to medium and beat until a soft dough forms. Remove the paddle, carefully pulling off all the bits of dough and putting those back in the bowl. Secure the dough hook attachment and beat on medium speed until the dough comes together into a ball and is springy, about 5 minutes. (If you don't have a dough hook, continue on with the paddle and then knead the dough with floured hands on a floured work surface until it is springy.)

2. You can use the dough right away, but your pizza will have a better texture if you let the dough rise. Dribble a little olive oil into a large glass or ceramic bowl and transfer the dough to the bowl. Turn the dough upside down so that the greased side is up. Cover the bowl with a thin kitchen towel and place the bowl in a warm spot in the kitchen until it has doubled in volume, 1 to 1½ hours. Punch down the dough with your fist, and use in the pizza recipe.

3. Alternatively, let the dough rise in a warm spot for 30 minutes, then cover the bowl with plastic wrap and refrigerate overnight to slowly rise. When ready to bake, remove the plastic, drape a kitchen towel over the bowl, and let the dough come to room temperature, about 2 hours.

SKILLET TARTINES
Blueprint

MAKES 12 TO 15 TARTINES (6 TO 8 SERVINGS)
Prep: 20 minutes / Cook: 6 to 8 minutes per batch

Tartines are fashionable open-faced sandwiches. They don't resemble soft white bread smeared with mayo and topped with cucumber any more than silk lingerie resembles Hanes. Which means that they wouldn't work at Southern receptions or funerals, but their crunchy, French-inspired deliciousness would be a hit at your next cocktail party. Be sure to begin with good baguettes, sliced on the diagonal and brushed with olive oil. Griddle in your skillet until crispy, and use the slices as the platform for colorful, flavorful toppings. Go over the top with smoked salmon or caviar, or just clean out your fridge. As a first attempt—to really get your tartine game going—try the Pan con Tomate variation.

1 (18-inch) baguette, about 3 inches wide at the center

¼ cup olive oil

Kosher salt, for sprinkling

Toppings (at right)

1. Cut off the rounded ends from the baguette. Cut the baguette into 6-inch sections, then cut each section on an extreme diagonal into ⅓- to ½-inch slices. You will get four or five long slices from each section. Brush both sides of each slice with olive oil.

2. Heat a 12-inch skillet over medium heat. When it is hot, work in batches to toast the baguette slices for 3 to 4 minutes, until golden brown on the bottom. Flip and repeat on the other side. Transfer to a platter and sprinkle with kosher salt. Repeat with the remaining bread slices.

3. Top each toasted baguette slice with your choice of toppings. Serve the tartines at room temperature.

TOPPINGS:

Pan con Tomate. Spread the tartines with herbed cream cheese or Boursin. Top with Roasted Cherry Tomatoes (page 264), along with some of the garlic and herbs.

Zucchini and Mint. Spread the tartines with soft goat cheese. Slice a medium zucchini into thin ribbons, toss with olive oil, salt, pepper, and chopped fresh mint. Arrange the ribbons on top of the goat cheese and garnish with more mint.

Fig and Honey. Spread the tartines with whole-milk ricotta. Top with quartered fresh figs. Sprinkle on red pepper flakes and a drizzle of wildflower honey.

GRILLED CHEESE
a Dozen Ways

MAKES 1 SANDWICH / Prep: 5 minutes / Cook: 4 to 5 minutes

I've never met a grilled cheese sandwich I didn't like. But I have met a few that were uninteresting, and thankfully I could dunk them in warm tomato soup. Recipes with just a handful of ingredients rely heavily on method and choice of ingredients to be successful. So, when making a grilled cheese, you've got to get the bread right, ditto the cheese, and be able to cook it to perfection. Armed with your trusty skillet, you'll be up to the task! I found that sourdough bread, without sugar and not too heavy in texture, is the perfect bread for grilled cheese sandwiches. It cooks up crispy around the edges and lets the cheese shine. As for the cheese, I prefer something melty but not greasy, such as a mild Cheddar, Colby, Monterey Jack, Havarti, or provolone. And instead of butter or olive oil for cooking? I like a little mayo. Yes, that's the secret.

3 slices (about 2 ounces) mild Cheddar, Colby, or Monterey Jack cheese, sliced

2 slices sourdough bread, crusts trimmed, if desired

2 teaspoons mayonnaise

1. Place the cheese on one slice of bread. Top with the other slice of bread. Spread each side of the sandwich with 1 teaspoon mayonnaise.

2. Heat a 12-inch skillet over medium heat until hot. Place the sandwich in the skillet and cook. After about a minute, pick up the sandwich and peek at the bottom slice of bread. If it is browning too quickly, reduce the heat slightly. Cook until it is golden brown on the bottom, 2 to 2½ minutes. Turn the sandwich over and brown on the second side until golden, about 2 minutes. Turn off the heat and let the sandwich rest in the pan for 1 minute. Transfer the sandwich to a board, slice, and serve.

GILD THE LILY A DOZEN WAYS

You can change up the filling of your grilled cheese with any of these suggestions. If you're adding meat to the sandwich, you will need to leave the sandwich in the skillet for 2 to 3 minutes after cooking to make sure the meat is warmed through.

- Pulled pork barbecue and pepper Jack cheese, plus a few pickled onion slices or jalapeños if you like
- Goat cheese and Roasted Cherry Tomatoes (page 264)
- Havarti and pepper jelly
- Fresh mozzarella and basil pesto
- Swiss or Comte and sautéed cremini mushrooms
- White Cheddar and caramelized onions
- Grilled eggplant and provolone, plus a sprinkling of dried Italian herb blend
- Apricot jam, crumbled blue cheese, and soft cream cheese
- Boursin and pear slices, sprinkled with fresh rosemary leaves
- Tuna melt, with ½ cup tuna salad and shredded mild Cheddar
- Roasted Butternut Slices with Lavender Honey (page 113; skins removed) and Monterey Jack
- Brie and Mindy's Roasted Cranberries and Jalapeños (page 253)

LITTLE CORN AND BUCKWHEAT BLINI
with Toppings

MAKES 36 TO 48 (1½- TO 2-INCH) BLINI (12 SERVINGS)
Prep: 35 minutes / Cook: 2 to 3 minutes per batch

Buckwheat is a nitrogen-rich cover crop and food to honeybees. It technically is a fruit, not a grain, and its kernels are ground into a nutritious, nutty-flavored flour. This recipe plays off that flavor but is streamlined with a buckwheat pancake mix from your supermarket or natural foods store. These small pancakes, called "blini," are griddled in your skillet and topped with smoked salmon, trout, or your favorite topping. Serve them on New Year's or any other festive occasion when you want to toast friends, family, and good times.

1 cup buckwheat pancake mix

1 cup buttermilk

1 large egg

2 tablespoons vegetable oil,
plus more for skillet

1 ear fresh corn, grated (see Note)

1 tablespoon chopped fresh dill

1 tablespoon minced onion

Freshly ground black pepper

TOPPING OPTIONS

Smoked salmon, sour cream or raita,
and chopped fresh herbs

Pulled pork or smoked turkey,
Lemon-Fig Barbecue Sauce (page 261),
and sliced pineapple

Avocado slices, tomato slices, and chutney

1. Combine the buckwheat pancake mix, buttermilk, egg, and oil in a large mixing bowl and stir for 1 minute. Fold in the grated corn, dill, onion, and a few grinds of pepper.

2. Lightly oil and heat a 12-inch skillet until a drop of water sizzles. Working in batches, ladle a teaspoon of batter for 1½-inch blini or 1 tablespoon of batter for 2-inch blini, onto the hot skillet. Cook until bubbles start to appear on the surface and the bottom is well browned, about 1 minute. Flip the blini and cook the other side until well browned, 1 to 2 minutes.

3. Transfer the cooked blini to a serving platter. Top with your chosen toppings.

NOTE: To grate an ear of corn, stand a shucked ear of corn in a bowl and hold on to the top end. With the other hand, run a sharp paring knife halfway down the corn kernels, so that you only cut off the most tender part of the corn and also get the milk from the inside of the kernel. You can rub your paring knife up and down the cob to get more milk out of the kernels. You should get about ½ cup.

Buckwheat Blini for Breakfast

You can turn these blini into pancakes that will suit even the pickiest child. Omit the corn, dill, onion, and pepper. Omit the toppings. Spoon ¼ cup batter into a hot skillet, cook for 2 minutes per side, and serve with melted butter and maple syrup. Makes 8 to 10 (4-inch) pancakes.

FRIED CHICKEN WINGS
with Dipping Sauces

MAKES 6 TO 8 SERVINGS / Prep: 25 minutes / Cook: 23 to 25 minutes per batch

The cast-iron skillet is ideal for frying chicken wings, which will make plenty of people happy come Super Bowl night or any Sunday afternoon during football season. To begin, you need peanut oil, which has a high smoke point, so it stays clean and fries evenly. If you can't find peanut oil, then any neutral vegetable oil will do. And you need a deep-fry or candy thermometer to gauge temperature, because really great chicken wings are fried twice—first at a lower temperature and again at a higher one to crisp them. Finally, to keep your kitchen and stove clean, it's nice to have a splatter screen that fits over the skillet. Serve the wings warm with your favorite sauces.

4 pounds chicken wings

Creole seasoning or seasoning salt,
for sprinkling

About 3 cups peanut oil

SAUCES
Roasted Garlic Ranch (page 4),

Korean Barbecue (at right),

Blue Cheese Ranch (at right)

1. Wipe the wings dry with paper towels. Leave them whole, with the drumette and flat part attached. Season with Creole seasoning. Place uncovered on a rimmed baking sheet in the fridge while you prepare the sauces.

2. Prepare the sauces. Or just one sauce, your pick. Set the sauces aside or chill.

3. Pour the peanut oil into a 12-inch skillet to a depth of 1¼ to 1½ inches. Heat the oil to 250 degrees F. Add half of the chicken wings and fry until the skin is glossy, 18 to 20 minutes. Remove with tongs and transfer to a rack set over a rimmed baking sheet. Repeat with the remaining wings.

4. Increase the heat so the temperature of the oil rises to 365 degrees F. Return half of the wings to the skillet and fry for 3 to 4 minutes, until well browned on all sides. Remove with tongs and transfer to the rack. Repeat with the remaining wings. You can speed up the process with two skillets going at once.

5. Pile onto a serving plate and serve with bowls of one or more sauces.

SAUCES:

Korean Barbecue. Whisk together ½ cup mayonnaise, 3 to 4 tablespoons gochujang (Korean hot and sweet sauce), and 2 teaspoons lemon juice.

Blue Cheese Ranch. Fold crumbled blue cheese into your favorite bottled ranch dressing.

POMMES FRITES

MAKES 8 SERVINGS AS AN APPETIZER; 3 TO 4 SERVINGS AS A SIDE DISH
Prep: 30 minutes / Cook: 5 to 7 minutes per batch

One Friday night, I made French fries and tossed them hot onto brown paper lining my kitchen table. Then we showered them with kosher salt, minced garlic, black pepper, and loads of chopped fresh parsley. We lined up little bowls of ketchup, garlicky aioli, and barbecue sauce for dipping. It was heaven. My husband brought in steaks cooked on the grill, and I had a salad already prepped in the fridge. Bliss, whimsy, recklessness, decadence, impulsiveness—I can think of dozens of nouns that fit that kitchen scene. But it was fun. And that type of foodscape can be staged when you have the iron skillet. Just allow enough time for two fryings—the first at a lower temp to cook the potatoes, and the second at a hotter temp to crisp and brown them.

2 pounds russet potatoes, scrubbed

4 cups peanut oil

FOR GARNISH

Kosher salt

Minced fresh garlic

Freshly ground black pepper

Minced fresh flat-leaf parsley

1. Cut the potatoes in half lengthwise, then cut each half into ⅓-inch-thick strips. Cut each strip into 4 pieces to yield 16 to 20 fries per potato. Put the fries in a large bowl and cover with cold water. Let rest for 15 to 20 minutes to draw off the starch from the potatoes. Drain the potatoes and pat dry with paper towels.

2. Heat the oil in a 12-inch skillet over medium-high heat to 275 degrees F. Add about a third of the potatoes and fry for 4 to 5 minutes, until the fries come to the surface and are translucent and soft. Transfer to a rack set over a rimmed baking sheet to drain. Repeat with the remaining potatoes, in two more batches.

3. Just before serving, increase the heat so the temperature of the oil rises to 375 degrees F. Add a third of the potatoes and fry until golden brown, 1 to 2 minutes, then transfer to brown paper to drain. Repeat with the remaining potatoes. Sprinkle with salt, garlic, black pepper, and parsley and serve hot.

Beer-Battered
ONION RINGS

MAKES 8 SERVINGS

Prep: 30 minutes / Chill: 2 hours / Cook: 4 to 6 minutes per batch

Not only do beer-battered onion rings sound good, they *are* good. And the reason just might be the beer, which tenderizes the batter and gives them great flavor. And another reason might be the sweet onions, especially Vidalia onions grown in southern Georgia and harvested each May. Keep those sweet onions in your fridge to keep them fresh for months to come. If you are looking for the prefect side to Sunday Night Cheeseburgers (page 185), look no further. For a fun twist, make the batter with a dark beer for even more flavor.

BEER BATTER

1⅓ cups all-purpose flour

¾ teaspoon salt

¼ teaspoon freshly ground black pepper

¾ cup (6 ounces) beer

1 tablespoon vegetable oil

2 large eggs, separated

4 medium sweet onions

4 cups (1 quart) peanut oil

1. For the batter, whisk together the flour, salt, and pepper in a large bowl. Add the beer, oil, and egg yolks and stir until smooth. Cover the bowl with plastic wrap and refrigerate for at least 2 hours, or as long as overnight. Refrigerate the egg whites in a separate covered bowl.

2. Peel the onions and cut them into ¼- to ⅓-inch slices. You will have about 4 packed cups of onions. Spread the slices out on a rimmed baking sheet so they dry out a bit while you prepare the oil and batter.

3. Heat the oil in a 12-inch skillet over medium-high heat until the oil comes to 350 degrees F.

4. While the oil is heating, beat the egg whites with an electric mixer on high speed until stiff peaks form, about 3 minutes. Fold the whites into the batter until just combined.

5. Dip 4 to 6 onion slices at a time into the batter and use tongs or your fingers to pull them from the batter and slide them into the hot oil, being careful not to crowd the pan. Fry until golden, 2 to 3 minutes per side. Remove with tongs and transfer to a wire rack set over a rimmed baking sheet. Repeat with the remaining onions and batter. You can place the rack and baking sheet in a low oven—250 degrees F— to keep warm between batches. Serve hot.

BEBE'S NUTS AND BOLTS

MAKES ABOUT 8 CUPS (16 SERVINGS) / Prep: 10 minutes / Bake: 1 hour 20 minutes

My mother, Bebe, slowly cooked this snack each Christmas in a big turkey roasting pan. The process went something like this: Open the oven door and stir, close the door, open the door and stir, close the door. For hours, it seemed, she went through this mundane process. All I knew is that it smelled so darned good that I couldn't wait for her to stop and hand me a bowlful for snacking. This was before Chex Mix was packaged and on the store shelf. Good cooks in the 1960s made their own mix, gave it to friends, and called it "nuts and bolts." I still make this before a long weekend of house guests, but I've scaled back the recipe to fit in an iron skillet.

½ cup (1 stick) unsalted butter

4 teaspoons Worcestershire sauce

1 teaspoon hot pepper sauce

1 teaspoon Creole seasoning

½ teaspoon garlic powder

½ teaspoon smoked paprika

3 cups rice Chex

2 cups Cheerios

1 cup Goldfish or pretzels

1 to 1½ cups pecan halves or shelled peanuts

1 cup potato sticks, broken pita chips, or Bugles

1 tablespoon fresh rosemary leaves (optional)

1. Preheat the oven to 250 degrees F.

2. Melt the butter in a 12-inch skillet over medium heat, about 2 minutes. Whisk in the Worcestershire sauce, hot pepper sauce, Creole seasoning, garlic powder, and smoked paprika.

3. Stir in the rice Chex, Cheerios, Goldfish, and pecans. Fold in the potato sticks and rosemary (if using). Bake, stirring every 20 minutes, until the cereal is golden brown and the pecans have toasted, about 1 hour 20 minutes.

4. Turn the mixture out onto a rimmed baking sheet to let it cool, about 1 hour. Store in a tightly covered container.

I had no idea how versatile the cast-iron skillet was until I started baking bread in it. Depending on the recipe and how the bread needs to be cooked, the nimble skillet can adapt. It can bake a yeast-risen potato bread, challah, or sticky buns one day and griddle Italian piadina or garlicky naan the next. It can cook buttermilk biscuits crispy around the edges, and without blinking, bake a moist and tender chocolate chip coffee cake. The fact that you can crank up the heat under the skillet before the batter is poured in is the secret behind crispy cornbread. And that hot skillet is the reason Yorkshire pudding puffs up like a golden balloon once in the oven. For all our fried guilty pleasures—fritters, hush puppies, doughnuts, and beignets—the trustworthy skillet heats oil and keeps it at an even temperature, which means less greasy frying and more enjoying.

CHAPTER 2

BREADS, BISCUITS & BUNS

My Grandmother's
SPOONBREAD

MAKES 8 SERVINGS / Prep: 20 minutes / Bake: 35 to 40 minutes

The index card sharing this recipe is one of the few I have in my grandmother's writing. She had been a teacher, and her penmanship was lovely, but she didn't write down many recipes. Spoonbread is that wonderful intersection between soufflé and cornbread—puffed and golden and quick to fall, so you must serve it at once! When you spoon inside you find the cornmeal texture, which must have been heaven to my father when he was a boy. Back in the 1930s, cooks would have beaten egg whites with rotary beaters, so this was a Sunday dinner kind of recipe, something special to serve alongside baked ham or fried chicken. Today, we are fortunate to have electric mixers do the work for us.

2 tablespoons butter, olive oil, or bacon grease

4 cups whole milk

2 teaspoons salt, plus a pinch

1¼ cups white stone-ground cornmeal

½ cup (1 stick) unsalted butter, cut into tablespoons

¼ teaspoon ground nutmeg

¼ teaspoon cayenne pepper

4 large eggs, separated (see Note)

1. Preheat the oven to 350 degrees F. Heat the butter, olive oil, or bacon drippings in a 12-inch skillet over medium heat to warm. Turn off the heat.

2. Combine the milk and 2 teaspoons salt in a large, heavy saucepan. Bring to a boil over medium-high heat, then slowly add the cornmeal, stirring to keep the mixture smooth. Reduce the heat to low and keep simmering and stirring the cornmeal until the mixture is very thick, about 5 minutes.

3. Remove the pan from the heat. Stir in the butter, nutmeg, and cayenne until the butter melts.

4. Put the egg yolks in a small bowl and stir in a spoonful of the cornmeal mixture to temper them (bring up their temperature). Add the egg yolk mixture to the pan of cornmeal and stir until smooth.

5. Put the egg whites in a large stainless steel or glass bowl and add a pinch of salt. Beat with an electric mixer on high speed until stiff but not dry, 2 to 3 minutes. Fold the beaten whites into the cornmeal mixture until nearly smooth. Pour the mixture into the skillet with the warm oil and smooth the top.

6. Bake until the spoonbread has puffed up and is golden brown, 35 to 40 minutes. Serve at once.

NOTE: If possible, take the eggs out of the fridge an hour before cooking because room-temperature egg whites beat up taller than cold whites.

BLACK SKILLET CORNBREAD

MAKES 8 SERVINGS / Prep: 5 minutes / Bake: 12 to 17 minutes

The best cornbread is made from white cornmeal, unsweetened, crusty on the outside, and creamy on the inside. Really, it's all about the crust. And to obtain this crust, you need a few things. First of all, a well-seasoned and, thus, black cast-iron skillet, in which you heat up some grease left from frying bacon or vegetable oil. Pour in your batter, which will sizzle if the pan and grease are hot enough. You also need enough full-fat buttermilk to achieve the consistency of pancake batter. But you don't need eggs, which make cornbread cakey in texture. The goal is to create a crisp, delicious crust on the top, bottom, and sides, so that when you slice this wheel into wedges, you will enjoy cornbread the way it was intended to be—back before Jiffy mixes, and before cheese, sour cream, and all the add-ins were piled into the batter. Back when crisp, white cornbread was a daily bread.

2 tablespoons bacon grease
or vegetable oil

1¾ cups self-rising white cornmeal

¼ cup all-purpose flour

¼ cup vegetable oil

1½ cups full-fat buttermilk

1 to 4 tablespoons water (optional)

1. Put the bacon grease or vegetable oil in a 12-inch skillet and place the pan in the oven. Preheat the oven to 450 degrees F.

2. In a large bowl, whisk together the cornmeal and flour. Stir in the oil and buttermilk until smooth. If the batter seems too thick, thin it with a little water.

3. When the oven comes to temperature, remove the skillet and pour in the batter. It should sizzle. Return the pan to the oven and bake until the cornbread is deeply browned, 12 to 17 minutes.

4. Run a knife around the edges of the pan and turn the cornbread out onto a cutting board, bottom-side up. Use a sharp knife or pizza cutter to cut it into wedges.

NOTE: If you can't find full-fat buttermilk, make your own by thinning full-fat plain yogurt with whole milk. This is a tip from my cornbread-guru friend, Mindy, who taught me the virtues of eating crisp cornbread.

NEW ENGLAND
Spider Cake

MAKES 8 TO 10 SERVINGS / Prep: 15 minutes / Bake: 40 to 45 minutes

This recipe might sound just right for Halloween, but it has nothing to do with arachnids and more to do with pots called "spiders" that the American colonists used for cooking. These cast-iron pots on legs raised them from the hearth, allowing air circulation and even space for coals underneath. They were the pan in which you baked breads and cakes. Today, this recipe is a reminder of times past and how far baking has come. Spider cake is a custardy New England version of cornbread and calls for yellow cornmeal (white is used traditionally in the South). It's a lovely cross between bread and cake, slightly sweet and traditionally served with maple syrup. And when you pour the cream into the batter in the skillet, you just might see a pattern of a spider bake into the top. So go ahead and bake it for Halloween!

2 cups whole milk

4 teaspoons white vinegar

1 cup all-purpose flour

¾ cup yellow cornmeal

½ cup lightly packed light brown sugar

½ teaspoon baking soda

½ teaspoon salt

2 large eggs

2 tablespoons unsalted butter
or vegetable oil

1 cup heavy cream

Maple syrup, for serving

1. Preheat the oven to 350 degrees F.

2. Combine the milk and vinegar in a medium glass bowl. Let the mixture rest until it curdles, 6 to 7 minutes. (You can skip this step and substitute full-fat buttermilk for the milk and vinegar if you have it.)

3. In another medium bowl, combine the flour, cornmeal, brown sugar, baking soda, and salt and stir to combine.

4. Whisk the eggs into the curdled milk mixture. Add the dry ingredients and stir until just combined, about 1 minute.

5. Melt the butter or heat the oil in a 12-inch skillet over medium heat, 2 to 4 minutes. Swirl the pan to coat the bottom with the butter or oil. Pour the batter into the hot pan. Pour the cream into the center of the batter, and place the skillet in the oven.

6. Bake the cake until it is lightly golden on top and firm to the touch, 40 to 45 minutes. Serve warm, spooned onto serving plates and topped with maple syrup.

SKILLET LOVE

ITALIAN PIADINA

MAKES 7 ROUNDS

Prep: 35 minutes / Rest: 40 minutes / Cook: 2 minutes per piadina

The first time I traveled to Italy, I was fortunate to visit the Emilia-Romagna region, home to Parmigiano-Reggiano and prosciutto di Parma, as well as the chewy flatbread called piadina, which is the simple, everyday bread of the farmers. It is griddled like fresh tortillas on the stove today, but originally it was cooked on a terra-cotta slab called a *testo*. The cooked piadina is wrapped around sautéed greens, cheese, and prosciutto, to make a sort of folded sandwich, and the flavor is phenomenal. So when planning this chapter, I put piadina on my "to cook" list very early on. I researched the key ingredients, and one was *strutto*, or lard—so it's no wonder piadina tastes so good! You can substitute olive oil for the lard. And the rest of the ingredients—flour, water, salt, and milk—are right at your fingertips. This recipe was shared by Carla Tomasi and Francesca Bruzzese (see box, opposite).

6 tablespoons olive oil

5 tablespoons whole milk

3¼ to 3½ cups unbleached all-purpose flour

2 teaspoons salt

½ cup plus 1 tablespoon lukewarm water

Fillings of your choice: soft cheese like stracciatella, prosciutto, arugula, sautéed spinach with garlic, fresh tomatoes, leftover roasted chicken

1. In a small saucepan, heat the olive oil and milk over low heat until warm, 2 to 3 minutes. Set aside.

2. In a large bowl, whisk together the flour and salt. Make a well in the center of the flour and pour in the olive oil–milk mixture and ½ cup water. Stir with a wooden spoon until the dough comes together. If needed, add another tablespoon of olive oil and another tablespoon water to pull the mixture together into a ball. (You may need to use your hands to get everything incorporated.) Cover the bowl and let the dough rest for 10 minutes.

3. Turn out the dough onto a work surface and knead it vigorously until it is shiny and smooth, about 5 minutes. Using a kitchen scale or just your eye, divide it into 7 equal portions. Roll each portion into a neat ball, cover the balls with a kitchen towel, and let rest for 30 minutes.

4. With a small rolling pin, roll the balls into thin circles, about 8 inches wide. Heat a 12-inch skillet over medium-high heat until very hot. Place one piadina at a time in the hot skillet and let it cook until the underside is bubbly, about 10 seconds. Turn the piadina over and prick it with a fork, then let it cook for another 10 seconds, or until the underside is bubbly and begins to brown. Turn again. Cook, turning every 10 seconds, until the piadina is opaque and the bubbly, rough surface has browned in little flecks, 1½ to 2 minutes in all. There shouldn't be any raw places showing, but the piadina should still be soft to the touch. Transfer to a platter and repeat with the remaining piadina.

5. Roll the warm piadina around the fillings of your choice to eat.

The Secret to Great Piadina

To find the secret to the best piadina, my contact was an American expat named Francesca Bruzzese, who lives in Rome and writes about Italian food. Francesca had been taking cooking classes from Carla Tomasi, who demystified piadina for her. And Francesca was kind enough to let me in on the secrets. First of all, I could griddle the piadina in the cast-iron skillet. The dough was simple, and I could substitute olive oil for the *strutto* (lard). But be sure, she said, to cover the dough at all times, because it easily dries out. Once I got to testing, I found it's important to take the time to let the dough rest between steps because the gluten—protein—in the dough relaxes and makes it easier to roll out. These puffy, tortilla-like rounds cook quickly in the hot skillet. I made mine with arugula, some good olive oil, a slice of fresh tomato from the garden, and a sprinkle of kosher salt. Yum! You can choose your fillings—stracciatella, a soft center of burrata, scrambled eggs and bacon, a sprinkling of cinnamon and sugar, a smear of peanut butter, or a soft wedge of ripe Brie.

STOVETOP NAAN
with Fresh Herbs and Garlic

MAKES 12 TO 15 NAAN

Prep: 25 minutes / Rise: 1½ hours / Cook: 2 to 3 minutes per batch

Living for a year in England gave me a love of Indian food that would last all my life. But I never thought I could create my own naan, the yeast-risen flatbread essential to Indian cuisine…that is, until I pulled out the iron skillet. It occurred to me that naan dough is only a simple flour mixture moistened by yogurt and needs a really hot surface to cook. It seemed natural to let the skillet mimic the floor of the tandoori oven, so I set to work. Naan is an old Indian bread, and some people believe it originally came from Persia (Iran). Because it contained yeast and required a good bit of technique to pull off, it was considered a bread of the wealthy and royal households, thus you see all the elaborate naan fillings on the menu at Indian restaurants. Fruit, coconut, meat, anything can be added to naan when your budget allows it. Today, we can make a much simpler version in our own kitchens. This recipe makes about a dozen, so save this for parties where Indian or grilled foods with nice sauces are served.

¼ cup (2 ounces) warm water

1 (0.25-ounce) package active dry yeast (2¼ teaspoons)

1 tablespoon sugar

4 cups unbleached all-purpose flour, plus more for dusting

1 teaspoon baking powder

1 teaspoon baking soda

¾ cup (6 ounces) whole milk, at room temperature

½ cup (4 ounces) plain full-fat yogurt

Vegetable oil, for greasing

4 tablespoons unsalted butter, melted, or olive oil

4 cloves garlic, peeled and thinly sliced

2 tablespoons roughly chopped fresh herbs (such as rosemary, thyme, and/or oregano)

Kosher salt, for sprinkling

1. In a small cup or glass measure, stir together the water, yeast, and sugar until dissolved. Set aside the yeast mixture to bubble up, 6 to 8 minutes.

2. In a large bowl, whisk together the flour, baking powder, and baking soda. Make a well in the center of the flour mixture and add the yeast mixture, milk, and yogurt. Stir with a wooden spoon until the mixture comes together. With oiled hands, knead the dough until it becomes a smooth ball, 3 to 4 minutes. Oil a large bowl and put the dough in it. Cover the bowl with plastic wrap and place it in a warm spot until the dough has doubled in size, about 1½ hours.

3. Punch down the dough with your fist and turn the dough out onto a lightly floured work surface. Knead it lightly and divide into 12 to 15 equal pieces. Roll each piece with a small rolling pin dusted with flour until it is about ¼ inch thick and 6 to 7 inches across.

4. Heat a 12-inch skillet over medium-high heat until it begins to smoke.

5. Brush both sides of each dough round with melted butter or olive oil. Press some garlic slices into the dough. Reduce the heat to medium and place two or three naan in the skillet. Cook until the naan puffs up on top and is lightly browned on the bottom, about 1 minute. Turn the naan and sprinkle with some herbs. Cover the skillet and cook for 1 to 2 minutes more. Transfer the naan to a platter and drizzle with more melted butter or olive oil, if desired. Sprinkle with kosher salt. Repeat with the remaining naan.

BUTTERMILK SKILLET
Biscuits

MAKES 12 (2½-INCH) BISCUITS / Prep: 10 minutes / Bake: 12 to 15 minutes

In my childhood home, we had hot biscuits on the dinner table five nights of the week. My father loved them and, thus, my mother learned to make them. She was an accomplished, self-taught cook, highly creative, and she loved working with her hands. Biscuits were an easy medium—you lightly mix the ingredients, cut, and bake in a hot oven. In an instant they are risen…and in another instant they are inhaled. So, the bar I set for biscuits was high. Not just any biscuit recipe would do. I wanted a soft and light interior, and a crispy top with a nice buttery flavor. This meant using a mix of butter for flavor and vegetable shortening for tenderness, plus self-rising flour, with the leavening all perfectly mixed into the flour. The skillet assures that the bottoms, sides, and tops have that nice tender, buttery crunch, a nod to my childhood. Serve them warm, with butter or honey.

½ cup (1 stick) unsalted butter, chilled and cut into 16 cubes, plus 1 teaspoon unsalted butter, melted

3 cups unbleached self-rising flour, plus more for dusting

1 tablespoon sugar

¼ cup vegetable shortening

1 cup low-fat or full-fat buttermilk

Tips on the Right Flour and How to Cut Biscuits

I bake with unbleached self-rising flour, so if you are using bleached self-rising flour, add ¼ cup more flour so the dough will pull together to the right consistency. Cut into rounds with a sharp cutter, and press down quickly into the dough—don't tug the cutter. That keeps the sides of the biscuits nice and straight. Patch the scraps together for the last few biscuits, and tuck them in the pan—no one will notice. Or pat the dough into a rectangle and cut the biscuits into squares for no scraps.

1. Preheat the oven to 450 degrees F. Brush a 12-inch skillet with the melted butter and set aside away from the stove so the pan stays as cool as possible. (You don't want to refrigerate it, but you want the pan to be at the same temperature as the biscuit dough so the biscuits don't spread too much before they bake.)

2. Combine the flour and sugar in the bowl of a food processor fitted with a steel blade. Pulse 5 times to incorporate. Distribute the cold butter cubes on top of the flour. Dollop the shortening in pieces on top of the butter. Pulse 12 to 15 times, until the butter is incorporated and forms clumps slightly larger than the size of peas. Pour in the buttermilk and pulse 5 times, or until the dough just pulls together.

3. Turn out the dough onto a floured work surface. With floured hands, pat the dough out to a 1-inch thickness. Fold it in half and again pat it gently to a 1-inch thickness. Dunk a 2½-inch biscuit cutter in flour and stamp out 12 rounds, pressing down firmly and then releasing the dough. Take care not to twist the cutter as you're cutting. With floured hands, transfer the biscuits to the prepared skillet. The biscuits will just touch in the pan. Bake until they are golden brown, 12 to 15 minutes. Serve warm.

NOTE: If desired, brush the tops of the biscuits with a little extra buttermilk, beaten egg, or melted butter before baking. This gives the biscuits a glossy top.

POTATO-RAISIN
Bread Spiral

MAKES 12 TO 16 SERVINGS / Prep: 35 minutes / Rise: 2 hours / Bake: 40 to 47 minutes

Potatoes have been used in bread baking for as long as iron pots and pans have been used to bake bread. Potatoes not only provide substance, but they keep the bread moist and flavorful for days—as do raisins and other dried fruit, often added to old-world breads to make them taste sweeter, stay moist, and look festive. This recipe is a nod to the old Irish fruit pan breads, but made in today's skillet. If you like, you can dump the dough right into the skillet rather than roll it into a rope to create the spiral pattern. But taking the time to create the spiral makes a visually interesting bread that is lovely for brunches, holidays, and special occasions. And you can glaze it with a beaten egg before it goes into the oven, if you prefer a glossy appearance.

1 medium baking potato, peeled and cubed

1½ cups water

1 (0.25-ounce) package active dry yeast (2¼ teaspoons)

⅓ cup sugar, divided use

4½ to 5 cups all-purpose flour, divided use

2 large eggs, lightly beaten

½ cup (1 stick) unsalted butter, melted

1 cup raisins

1 teaspoon salt

Vegetable oil, for greasing

1. Put the cubed potato in a small saucepan and cover with the water. Bring the water to a boil over medium-high heat, then reduce the heat to low, cover, and let simmer until the potatoes are tender, 15 to 20 minutes. Drain the potatoes, reserving the cooking water. Mash the potatoes in a small bowl and set aside.

2. Transfer 1 cup of the potato water to a large bowl. Whisk in the yeast and 1 tablespoon of the sugar until dissolved. Add 2 tablespoons of the mashed potatoes to the yeast mixture. Add 1 cup of the flour. Beat with a wooden spoon or an electric mixer on medium speed until the ingredients are combined. Let the mixture rest until it bubbles up slightly, about 20 minutes.

3. Add the remaining sugar, 3 cups flour, eggs, melted butter, raisins, and salt. Beat with the electric mixer on medium speed until the dough is soft and combined. Add ½ to 1 cup more flour as needed so that the dough comes together and away from the sides of the bowl. With the mixer fitted with a dough hook, beat the dough until it comes into a ball, 3 to 4 minutes. (Alternatively, you can knead by hand until it comes into a ball, about 5 minutes.) Lightly grease a large mixing bowl with vegetable oil and put the dough in the bowl. Cover the bowl with a kitchen towel and place in a warm spot until the dough doubles in size, about 1 hour.

4. With oiled or floured hands, punch down the dough. Turn it out onto a floured surface and roll with your hands into a rope that is about 18 inches long. Lightly grease the bottom and sides of a 12-inch skillet with vegetable oil. Pick up the dough rope and lay it in the skillet, starting at the edge and letting it coil like a snake, ending in the center. Cover the skillet with a kitchen towel and let rise in a warm spot until doubled, about 40 minutes.

5. When ready to bake, preheat the oven to 350 degrees F. Bake until the top of the bread is golden brown, 20 to 22 minutes. Tent the skillet with aluminum foil and continue to bake until the bread sounds hollow when tapped, 20 to 25 minutes more.

6. Remove the skillet from the oven and cool for 10 minutes. Run a knife around the edge of the skillet. Lift up the potato bread and place it on a wire rack to cool completely before slicing, about 30 minutes.

Skillet
YORKSHIRE PUDDING

MAKES 8 SERVINGS / Prep: 10 minutes / Bake: 25 to 30 minutes

Back before fat was taboo, drippings left in the beef roasting pan were put to good use. They formed the bed for the classic Yorkshire pudding, which baked right in the pan where the meat once stood. Even before that, Yorkshire pudding would be baked in a pan underneath meat roasting on a spit. Drippings from the meat dribbled onto the pudding and flavored it while it baked. You most likely don't have that sort of oven setup today, but you can still re-create the flavors of old, and here is how: Pour the beef drippings (or butter) into an iron skillet and get that skillet good and hot, then pour in the batter and place the skillet in the hot oven. The Yorkshire pudding will puff up gloriously, and you will have just a moment to spoon in before it deflates—but rest assured that even if your timing is off, the pudding stays delicious. It's that cross between custard and bread that marries perfectly with roasted meats or even just a green salad.

6 tablespoons beef drippings
or lightly salted butter

2 large eggs

1 cup whole milk

1 cup sifted all-purpose flour (see Note)

½ teaspoon salt

1. Preheat the oven to 450 degrees F.

2. Heat the meat drippings or butter in a 12-inch skillet over medium heat until the drippings are quite hot, or the butter has melted but not burned, about 3 minutes.

3. Meanwhile, working quickly, whisk together the eggs and milk in a large bowl. Whisk in the flour and salt. (You can also do this quickly by pulsing the four ingredients in a food processor or blender.) When the skillet is hot, pour in the batter and place the skillet in the oven.

4. Bake for 15 minutes, then reduce the temperature to 350 degrees F and continue to bake until puffed and golden brown, 10 to 15 minutes more. Serve immediately.

NOTE: It's important to get the right amount of flour. If you do not sift the flour before measuring, use only ⅞ cup flour.

EASY GARLIC
Skillet Knots

MAKES 16 (6 TO 8 SERVINGS) / Prep: 10 minutes / Bake: 20 to 25 minutes

This little recipe is proof that there is more you can create from pizza dough than just pizza. The dough is a canvas for all sorts of fun and interesting breads, especially these garlic knots. It's really more technique than recipe—you divide the dough into pieces and roll each piece into a rope, which you tie into a knot and dredge through a slurry of oil and garlic, then top with a cheese and spice mix before baking. These are perfect to serve alongside fall soups, winter chili, spring salads, and even alongside a platter of your best summer tomatoes.

1 recipe Easy Homemade Pizza Crust (page 21) or 1 pound store-bought pizza dough (see Note)

3 tablespoons olive oil

4 cloves garlic, peeled, 2 thinly sliced and 2 minced

¼ teaspoon kosher salt, plus a pinch

⅛ teaspoon freshly ground black pepper, plus a pinch, or cayenne pepper or harissa seasoning

¼ cup grated Parmesan cheese

½ teaspoon dried oregano

1. Preheat the oven to 425 degrees F.

2. With a heavy knife, cut the dough into four equal pieces. Divide each piece into four equal pieces. Roll each piece into a rope 5 to 6 inches long. Set the ropes aside.

3. Heat the olive oil in a 12-inch skillet over medium heat. Add the sliced garlic and sauté until golden, 3 to 4 minutes. With a slotted spoon, remove the sliced garlic from the skillet and set aside on paper towels. Remove the skillet from the heat.

4. Add the minced garlic to the skillet, along with a pinch each of salt and black pepper.

5. Roll one dough rope in the garlicky oil in the skillet, then tie it into a loose knot. Tuck it at the side of the pan. Continue with the remaining dough ropes, coating in oil, tying, and then placing in the skillet until it is filled with 16 garlicky knots, in a single layer.

6. In a small bowl, combine the Parmesan cheese, oregano, ¼ teaspoon salt, and ⅛ teaspoon black pepper. Top each knot with a generous teaspoon of the cheese mixture.

7. Bake until the garlic knots are deeply golden brown, 20 to 25 minutes. Scatter the reserved golden brown garlic slices on top. Serve warm.

NOTE: You can buy fresh pizza dough at many supermarkets, usually in the bakery section. You might even be able to buy from your favorite pizzeria and keep in the freezer.

CAST IRON STICKY BUNS
with Caramel Sauce

MAKES 12 SERVINGS / Prep: 1 hour / Rise: 2½ hours / Bake: 40 to 50 minutes

Sticky buns have been a Pennsylvania Dutch specialty for so long we could possibly say they own them. And without a doubt, the most delicious, authentic sticky buns are found in Philadelphia's Reading Terminal Market. But if you study the recipes—as I did after several visits—and figure out the important parts, then you can bake these successfully at home. Your cast-iron skillet will allow the caramel sauce to get nice and sticky! First you need a yeast dough that is easy to work with and stays moist after baking. I settled on challah dough. Then, you need a sauce to simmer up, and it must contain butter and molasses. The filling is really up to you, but my choice is cinnamon, brown sugar, butter, and a little nutmeg. Get crazy if you like and add grated orange zest or cardamom.

DOUGH

¾ cup warm water

1 (0.25-ounce) package active dry yeast (2¼ teaspoons)

¼ cup granulated sugar

2 large eggs, lightly beaten

½ cup vegetable oil

3¾ cups bread flour

1½ teaspoons salt

CARAMEL SAUCE

1½ cups coarsely chopped pecans

½ cup (1 stick) unsalted butter

¾ cup packed light brown sugar

¾ cup heavy cream

⅓ cup molasses (not blackstrap)

¼ teaspoon salt

FILLING

½ cup (1 stick) unsalted butter, at room temperature

½ cup packed light brown sugar

¾ teaspoon ground cinnamon

½ teaspoon ground nutmeg (optional)

Pinch salt

ASSEMBLY

All-purpose flour, for dusting

½ cup soft raisins (optional)

1 large egg

1 teaspoon water

1. For the dough, in a large bowl, whisk together the water and yeast to dissolve. Whisk in the sugar. Add the eggs and oil and whisk to combine. Add the flour and salt and stir with a wooden spoon until smooth. Cover the bowl with a kitchen towel and place it in a warm spot to rise until doubled, about 1 hour.

2. Punch down the dough in the bowl, knead it a little with floured hands, and cover the bowl with the towel while you prepare the sauce and filling.

3. For the caramel sauce, scatter the pecans in a 12-inch skillet. Preheat the oven to 350 degrees F and place the skillet in the oven while it preheats. Let the pecans roast until they begin to turn golden brown, 8 to 10 minutes. Remove the skillet from the oven and turn off the oven. Transfer the pecans to a bowl and set aside. Reserve the skillet.

4. In a small saucepan, heat the butter over medium heat until it begins to melt, 30 seconds to 1 minute. Stir in the brown sugar, cream, molasses, and salt and bring the mixture to a boil. Reduce the heat to medium-low and let the sauce simmer until it is glossy, about 4 minutes. Pour 1 cup of the sauce into the skillet, turning the pan to coat the bottom. Set aside the saucepan with the remaining sauce. Sprinkle ½ cup of the toasted pecans on top of the sauce in the skillet. Let this cool.

5. For the filling, combine the butter, brown sugar, cinnamon, nutmeg (if using), and salt in a medium bowl and beat with an electric mixer on medium-low speed until fluffy, 2 minutes. Set aside.

Continued

6. On a floured work surface, roll the dough into a rectangle about 12 by 16 inches. It will be about ⅓ inch thick. Spread the filling evenly over the dough. Sprinkle ¾ cup of the toasted pecans on top of the filling. Add raisins if you like. Beginning with the long edge of the dough, and with floured hands, roll the dough into a log, taking care to keep it about the same thickness. Pinch the edges of the dough to seal. Roll the log so it is seam-side down.

7. With a sharp, floured knife, cut the dough into 12 slices, flouring the knife between cuts to make slicing easier. Place two slices in the center of the skillet, cut-side up, touching each other. Arrange the other 10 slices around the edges, overlapping them as necessary so all the slices fit. Cover the skillet with a kitchen towel and place it in a warm spot so the buns can double in size, about 1½ hours.

8. When ready to bake, preheat the oven to 350 degrees F. Whisk together the egg and water in a small bowl. Brush the buns with the egg wash and place the skillet in the oven. Bake until the buns are golden brown on top, 20 to 25 minutes. Tent the skillet with aluminum foil and continue to bake until the buns test done (dough is cooked, not gooey), another 20 to 25 minutes. When they are done, remove the foil and spoon the remaining caramel sauce over the top. (Gently reheat the remaining caramel sauce over low heat if needed.) Scatter the remaining ¼ cup toasted pecans on top. Let cool for 20 minutes, then serve.

IRISH SODA BREAD
with Drunk Raisins

MAKES 8 TO 10 SERVINGS
Prep: 35 minutes / Bake: 55 to 60 minutes

Soda breads are an easy entree into bread making. They don't require yeast, and you probably have most of the ingredients right at your fingertips. This recipe is full of flavor, from the whiskey-soaked raisins to the caraway seeds or orange zest. It uses a mix of white and whole wheat flour, which results in a soft bread with texture. And as soda breads rely on buttermilk to keep them moist, there is a good deal of buttermilk in this recipe. That makes for a sticky dough, but you can use a wooden spoon to help push the dough into the skillet. And if you don't want to discard the whiskey, you can brush it on top of the bread once it cools—or sip it while the bread bakes.

½ cup (1 stick) plus 1 tablespoon unsalted butter, at room temperature, divided use

2 cups raisins, mix of dark and golden

½ cup Irish whiskey

3 cups all-purpose flour

2 cups whole wheat flour

½ cup sugar (see Note)

1 tablespoon baking powder

1 teaspoon baking soda

1 teaspoon salt

2 tablespoons caraway seeds or 2 teaspoons grated orange zest

3 cups full-fat buttermilk

1 large egg, lightly beaten

1. Preheat the oven to 350 degrees F.

2. Grease the bottom and sides of a 12-inch skillet with 1 tablespoon of the soft butter. Set aside.

3. Put the raisins in a small bowl. Warm the whiskey in a small saucepan or in the microwave, and pour the whiskey over the raisins. Toss to coat the raisins well, and set aside to soak while you prepare the dough.

4. In a large bowl, whisk together both flours, the sugar, baking powder, baking soda, and salt. Cut the remaining ½ cup soft butter into pieces and scatter them on top of the flour mixture. Use your hands or a pastry blender to rub the butter into the flour mixture. Add the caraway seeds or orange zest. Drain the raisins and add them to the dough. Add the buttermilk and beaten egg and stir with a wooden spoon until well combined. The dough will be very sticky.

5. With the help of the wooden spoon, transfer the dough to the prepared skillet. If desired, dust a sharp knife with flour and cut an X in the top of the dough. Bake until the bread is golden brown and makes a hollow sound when you tap the top with your fingers, 55 to 60 minutes. Remove the skillet from the oven and let the bread rest in the skillet for 10 to 15 minutes. Run a knife around the edges of the skillet to release the bread and let it cool on the rack for about 1 hour. Slice and serve or cover in aluminum foil and store at room temperature for several days.

NOTE: For a darker soda bread, use half sugar and half molasses.

No-Knead
SKILLET SOURDOUGH

MAKES 1 LOAF (ABOUT 8 SERVINGS)
Prep: 20 minutes / Rise: 12 to 18 hours / Bake: 45 to 50 minutes

This slow-risen bread is a popular way to bake yeast bread at home because it's hands-off. You do need to plan ahead, though, because it requires a long, slow rise—from 12 to 18 hours. That creates bread with good yeasty flavor and a texture reminiscent of sourdough. And baking it in a covered cast-iron skillet mimics a wood-fired oven, so the bread develops a crisp and crunchy crust. It is the most sophisticated bread you can bake in your home oven.

3 cups unbleached all-purpose flour

1¾ teaspoons salt

½ teaspoon active dry yeast

1½ cups warm water (100 to 110 degrees F)

2 teaspoons yellow or white cornmeal

1 tablespoon olive oil

Kosher salt and freshly ground
black pepper to taste

1 teaspoon fresh rosemary leaves

1. In a large bowl, whisk together the flour, 1¾ teaspoons salt, and yeast. Add the water and stir with a wooden spoon until well combined. Cover the bowl with plastic wrap and let it rest at room temperature for at least 12 hours or up to 18 hours.

2. Preheat the oven to 450 degrees F. Place a 12-inch cast-iron skillet and lid in the oven. Remove both when the oven has preheated.

3. Sprinkle the cornmeal in the bottom of the skillet. Run a silicone spatula around the edges of the dough in the mixing bowl, and dump the dough into the hot skillet. Carefully place the lid on the skillet, and place the skillet in the oven.

4. Bake for 30 minutes. Remove the lid. Drizzle the top of the bread with olive oil, season with salt and pepper, and sprinkle the rosemary on top. Continue to bake, uncovered, until the bread is golden brown, 15 to 20 minutes. Turn the bread out onto a board to cool for 30 minutes, then slice and serve.

CHALLAH WREATH

MAKES 2 LOAVES OR 1 WREATH
Prep: 30 minutes / Rise: 1 hour 30 to 45 minutes / Bake: 35 to 40 minutes

Baking yeast bread in an iron skillet seems quite natural, as the skillet allows the bread to bake evenly and enhances its golden crust. You might think you are limited to round breads, what with the shape of the skillet. But in the case of this recipe, you can bake challah in two braids, which join and form a circular wreath. For a festive party presentation, place a small bowl of mustard or chutney in the center and surround the wreath with sliced meats and cheeses. Or, if you choose, break the two halves of the wreath apart and slice one for serving and freeze the other. This challah, a recipe from my Atlanta friend Sara Franco, is beautifully textured and moist.

1 tablespoon unsalted butter,
at room temperature

¾ cup warm water (100 to 110 degrees F)

1 (0.25-ounce) package active
dry yeast (2¼ teaspoons)

¼ cup sugar

2 large eggs, lightly beaten

½ cup vegetable oil

3¾ cups bread flour

1½ teaspoons salt

GLAZE

1 large egg

Poppy or sesame seeds (optional)

1. Rub the bottom and sides of a 12-inch skillet with the soft butter and set aside.

2. In a large bowl, whisk together the water and yeast to dissolve. Whisk in the sugar. Add the eggs and oil and whisk to combine. Add the flour and salt and stir with a wooden spoon until smooth. Cover the bowl with a kitchen towel and place it in a warm spot to rise until doubled, about 1 hour.

3. Punch down the dough in the bowl and knead it until the dough is smooth, 3 to 4 minutes. Divide the dough in half. Divide each half into three pieces.

4. Working with one set of three pieces of dough at a time, roll each piece of dough between your palms or on the work surface into a rope 12 to 15 inches long. Lay the 3 ropes side by side. Beginning at the center, braid them, left over right, right over left, until you reach the ends, and tuck them under. Turn the braid 180 degrees (so the braided part at the top is now at the bottom) and braid the other half in the same fashion. Place this braided loaf in one half of the reserved skillet. Repeat the process with the remaining set of three pieces of dough, rolling and braiding, then place this braided loaf in the other half of the pan. Attach the loaves at their ends by pressing them together slightly to form a ring around the skillet. Cover the skillet with a kitchen towel, and let rise in a warm spot until nearly doubled, 30 to 45 minutes.

5. Preheat the oven to 350 degrees F. In a small bowl, lightly beat the egg for the glaze. Brush the braided wreath with the beaten egg, then sprinkle with poppy or sesame seeds, if desired.

6. Bake the challah until it is golden brown, about 20 minutes, then tent the skillet with aluminum foil. Continue baking for 15 to 20 minutes more, until it tests done (golden brown and firm to the touch). Transfer the challah to a rack to cool completely, about 1 hour, then slice and serve. Wrap leftovers in foil and store at room temperature for up to 5 days or in the freezer for up to 6 months.

GILD THE LILY

Sprinkle the top with poppy and sesame seeds before baking. When ready to serve, nestle a small round of Camembert in the center of the wreath.

Homemade
ENGLISH MUFFINS

MAKES 11 OR 12 ENGLISH MUFFINS
Prep: 35 minutes / Chill: 12 to 24 hours / Rise: 1 hour / Cook: 13 to 16 minutes

If there's a bread recipe that is made for skillet baking, it's the English muffin. First you griddle it until crispy, then you bake it until done. And if you have never tasted homemade English muffins, then you need to put this on your bucket list. The taste is so delicious and unexpected—and the secret could very well be letting the dough rise slowly in the refrigerator so it develops flavor and texture. These are good untoasted, unbuttered, and unadorned, but let me tell you, they are out of this world when toasted and spread with butter. And they turn Sunday Night Cheeseburgers (page 185) into restaurant-quality fare. If you have two skillets for this recipe, all the better, but if you have just one, you can bake half of the muffins on a sheet pan.

1 cup warm water (100 to 110 degrees F)

1 (0.25-ounce) package active dry yeast (2¼ teaspoons)

1 tablespoon sugar

1 cup buttermilk, at room temperature

4 tablespoons unsalted butter, at room temperature

2 tablespoons vegetable oil, plus more for greasing

2 teaspoons kosher salt

3½ cups bread flour

Yellow cornmeal, for dusting

1. In a large bowl, whisk together the warm water, yeast, and sugar to dissolve. Let rest until foamy, about 5 minutes. Add the buttermilk, butter, oil, and salt and beat with an electric mixer on low speed just to combine. Add the flour and beat on low speed until a loose dough forms. Increase the mixer speed to medium and beat until the dough pulls away from the sides of the bowl, 4 to 5 minutes. Grease a large bowl with vegetable oil and put the dough in the bowl. Cover with plastic wrap and refrigerate overnight, or up to 24 hours.

2. When ready to bake, dust two rimmed baking sheets with cornmeal. Lightly oil your hands and punch down the dough with your fist. Divide the dough into 11 or 12 equal portions. (If you make 11, the English muffins will be about 3 ounces each, which is a good size for burgers. If 12, they will be smaller.) Working with one piece of dough at a time, fold and tuck the edges underneath to form a slightly domed, nearly flat bun. Place it on the cornmeal-dusted sheet. Repeat with the remaining dough, placing 5 or 6 on one sheet and 6 on the other. Sprinkle the tops of the muffins with cornmeal. Drape both pans with a light kitchen towel to cover. Let them rise in a warm spot until doubled in size, about 1 hour.

3. When ready to bake, preheat the oven to 350 degrees F and heat two 12-inch skillets over medium heat. Carefully transfer each muffin to the hot skillet using two small metal spatulas, one on each side of the muffin. Do not allow the muffins to touch. Let them griddle until they are golden brown on the bottom, 3 to 4 minutes, then turn and cook the other side until golden, 3 to 4 minutes. Place the skillets in the oven. (If you do not have two skillets, you can brown the muffins in the skillet in batches, then transfer half of them back to one of the baking sheets.) Bake until the muffins spring back and are firm when lightly touched with your finger and are cooked through, 7 to 8 minutes. Transfer the muffins to a wire rack to cool for 30 minutes, then split with a fork, toast, and serve. Store leftovers in a zipper-lock bag at room temperature for up to 3 days or in the freezer for up to 6 months.

BUTTERMILK SPICE DROP DOUGHNUTS
Blueprint

MAKES 2 DOZEN DOUGHNUTS / Prep: 15 minutes / Cook: 2 minutes per batch

Homemade doughnuts are not something you are going to prepare every day, but when you do, you want to wow everyone. And that's what's great about this recipe: It will wow. If you like, add some grated lemon zest to the dough in addition to or in lieu of the spices for lemony buttermilk doughnuts. Or add a little ground ginger. And you can dust the hot doughnuts with powdered sugar instead of granulated sugar. It's a blueprint recipe just waiting to be customized.

4 cups peanut oil

1 cup unbleached all-purpose flour

1 cup cake flour (see Note)

½ cup sugar

1 teaspoon baking powder

½ teaspoon baking soda

½ teaspoon kosher salt

½ teaspoon ground cinnamon

¼ teaspoon ground nutmeg

1 cup buttermilk

1 large egg, lightly beaten

1 tablespoon unsalted butter, melted

1 teaspoon vanilla extract

SPICED SUGAR COATING

¼ cup sugar

½ teaspoon ground cinnamon

¼ teaspoon ground nutmeg

1. Heat the oil in a 12-inch skillet over medium-high heat until the oil reaches 375 degrees F.

2. While the oil is coming to temperature, whisk together both flours, the sugar, baking powder, baking soda, salt, cinnamon, and nutmeg in a large bowl. Add the buttermilk, egg, melted butter, and vanilla and stir with a fork until just combined.

3. For the sugar coating, whisk together the sugar, cinnamon, and nutmeg in a small bowl and set aside.

4. When the oil is hot, scoop 1-tablespoon portions of the batter into the hot oil. Cook 7 or 8 at a time so as not to crowd the pan. The doughnuts will float in the oil and some may turn over on their own. Let them cook until deeply browned, turning them in the oil so they cook on all sides, 2 to 2½ minutes.

5. Using a slotted spoon, transfer the doughnuts to brown paper to drain. Toss the hot doughnuts in the sugar coating and serve warm.

NOTE: Cake flour has lower gluten—protein—than all-purpose. If you do not have cake flour, use additional all-purpose flour, but less of it—about ⅞ cup.

FRESH CORN HUSH PUPPIES
Blueprint

MAKES 12 HUSH PUPPIES / Prep: 5 minutes / Cook: 3 minutes per batch

I could eat these hush puppies with any meal. They are a rendition of the traditional hush puppies served across the country at fish fries and seafood restaurants, but these are softer and more fritter-like. They melt in your mouth. Feel free to use this recipe as a blueprint, adding the peppers of your choice, or perhaps a small handful of peeled tiny shrimp or ground country ham. You can even fold in a couple tablespoons of cooked black-eyed peas. And for gatherings, you can easily double the recipe and let your trusty iron skillet do the work while you get all the credit.

1 cup white or yellow self-rising cornmeal

1 large egg

½ cup buttermilk

3 tablespoons fresh corn kernels

1 tablespoon finely chopped jalapeño or bell pepper

1 tablespoon finely chopped onion

3 cups vegetable oil

1. In a large bowl, combine the self-rising cornmeal, egg, and buttermilk and stir with a fork just to combine. Fold in the corn, pepper, and onion.

2. Heat the oil in a 12-inch skillet over medium-high until the oil reaches 365 degrees F. Working in batches so as not to crowd the pan, scoop or spoon generous tablespoons of the hush puppy batter into the hot oil. Cook, turning once, until golden brown, about 3 minutes. Using a slotted spoon, transfer to brown paper to drain. Serve hot.

NOTE: After frying the hush puppies, you can let the oil cool down, then skim the top with a slotted spoon to remove any fried bits. Strain the oil through a fine-mesh strainer into a container with a lid. Store in a cool, dark place for up to 1 week or in the refrigerator for up to 2 weeks to reuse for frying.

CHOCOLATE CHIP SOUR CREAM
Coffee Cake

MAKES 12 SERVINGS / Prep: 25 minutes / Bake: 40 to 45 minutes

The iron skillet is a great vessel for baking coffee cake. Any favorite recipe that fits into a Bundt-size pan can be baked in a 12-inch skillet. This recipe is for a sour cream coffee cake loaded with chocolate chips and flavored with cinnamon and orange. It is more cake than bread, but it falls into that wonderful gray area we know as "coffee cake," which allows us to eat cake before noon! If you're not a fan of the orange and chocolate combination, then simply grease the skillet and pour in the chocolate chip batter, omitting the sugar and orange slices. But if you love the orange and chocolate marriage and like drama, you will adore this coffee cake and want to run it under the broiler after baking to darken the top and caramelize the oranges even more. You can also dust the top of the coffee cake with confectioners' sugar, if desired.

½ cup (1 stick) plus 1 tablespoon unsalted butter, melted, divided use

1½ cups plus 2 tablespoons sugar, divided use

12 to 16 thin orange slices (see Note)

2 cups all-purpose flour

2 teaspoons baking powder

1 teaspoon baking soda

¼ teaspoon ground cinnamon

¼ teaspoon salt

½ cup vegetable oil

1 cup sour cream

1 tablespoon vanilla extract

2 cups (12 ounces) miniature semisweet chocolate chips

1. Preheat the oven to 350 degrees F.

2. Melt 1 tablespoon of the butter in a 12-inch skillet over medium heat, swirling the skillet to distribute the butter evenly, about 2 minutes. Sprinkle 2 tablespoons of the sugar evenly over the melted butter. Place the orange slices on top of the sugar, creating a decorative pattern, either overlapping them in circles or creating concentric circles of slices. Heat the skillet for another 2 to 3 minutes to allow the sugar to dissolve. Remove the skillet from the heat.

3. In a large bowl, whisk together the flour, the 1½ cups sugar, baking powder, soda, cinnamon, and salt. Add the remaining ½ cup melted butter, oil, sour cream, and vanilla and mix with an electric mixer on medium speed (or by hand) until just combined, 1 minute. Fold in the chocolate chips.

4. Dump the batter into the skillet on top of the oranges. Bake until the top of the coffee cake has lightly browned and is firm to the touch, 40 to 45 minutes.

5. Run a knife around the edges of the skillet to loosen the coffee cake. Invert the skillet onto a wooden board lined with parchment paper. If any of the oranges stick to the bottom of the skillet, slide under them with a small metal spatula and place them on top of the cake. If you want a more dramatic look, slide the parchment onto a baking sheet and run it under the broiler until the oranges and sugar are caramelized.

NOTE: If possible, choose thin-skinned, seedless oranges.

NEW ORLEANS BEIGNETS

MAKES ABOUT 3 DOZEN BEIGNETS

Prep: 45 minutes / Rise: 1 hour 20 minutes / Cook: 3 minutes per batch

If you've never experienced the thrill of dunking a beignet in warm coffee at Café du Monde in the French Quarter of New Orleans, don't feel left out: I've figured out how to make luscious beignets at home. I pulled out my iron skillet, filled it with oil, and assembled a simple yeast dough of flour, sugar, egg, and milk. I cut the dough into little rectangles, and when they rose up to the top of the hot oil, they browned like little golden pillows. Then I shook those hot beignets in a brown paper sack with powdered sugar until they were coated . . . and pulled one out of the sack, still warm, and took a bite. And at that moment, I knew this was the best beignet I'd had in my life. But I'm still giving NOLA credit because they—and the French—came up with the idea!

1 (0.25-ounce) package active
dry yeast (2¼ teaspoons)

¼ cup warm water (100 to 110 degrees F)

¼ cup granulated sugar

½ teaspoon salt

1 large egg, beaten

¾ cup evaporated milk

2 tablespoons unsalted butter,
melted and cooled, or vegetable oil

3 to 3½ cups all-purpose flour,
plus more for dusting

4 cups peanut oil

½ cup confectioners' sugar

1. In a large bowl, combine the yeast and warm water and stir with a fork to dissolve. Stir in the sugar and salt. Add the beaten egg, evaporated milk, and melted butter or oil and beat with a wooden spoon until smooth. Add 3 cups of the flour and beat until well incorporated. Add another ½ cup of the flour as needed to pull the dough together. It should no longer be sticky. Cover the bowl with plastic wrap and place it in a warm spot to rise until doubled, about 1 hour.

2. Punch down the dough and turn it out onto a lightly floured surface. Knead it with your hands a few times and roll it into a rectangle 18 by 12 inches. It will be about ⅛ inch thick. Cut the dough into rectangles measuring about 2 by 3 inches, cover them with waxed paper or plastic wrap, and let rise again for about 20 minutes.

3. Heat the oil in a 12-inch skillet over medium-high heat until it reaches 365 degrees F. Drop two or three rectangles into the oil and fry until they are golden brown on one side, about 1½ minutes, then turn them over to cook on the other side about 1½ minutes more. Use a slotted spoon to transfer the beignets to a rack set over brown paper to drain. Repeat with the remaining dough.

4. Put the confectioners' sugar in a paper bag and add the warm beignets, a few at a time. Toss until well coated. Serve immediately.

Throughout history the skillet has been synonymous with breakfast. Look at it and try to say you don't immediately think bacon and pancakes. And I don't want to mess with a good thing that has satisfied generations. I just want to open your eyes to the infinite brunch possibilities that can spring from this pan—like Dutch baby, a restaurant staple that soars in a hot skillet at home. I'll share a way of making French toast—in the oven—that allows you to mix and mingle with brunch guests. And while fried eggs are fine, why not poach them in a bed of simmered tomatoes and peppers for shakshuka? Or turn them into south-of-the-border chilaquiles, whisk them into a classic quiche, or pour atop asparagus spears for an easy frittata? You even can fry green tomatoes and stack them into BLTs. Or bake croque monsieur sandwiches until golden. Best of all, the skillet goes right to the table, keeping brunch food warm and festive.

CHAPTER 3

BRUNCH AT HOME

Fresh
BLUEBERRY PANCAKES

MAKES ABOUT 12 (3- TO 4-INCH) PANCAKES (4 SERVINGS)
Prep: 20 minutes / Cook: 2 to 4 minutes per batch

Cottage cheese has long been used as a lighter alternative to ricotta when making pancakes and blini. When griddling pancakes like these in an iron skillet, it's important to add only as much oil to your seasoned pan as you need to keep the pancakes from sticking. Then the skillet remains greased, and some of the best pancakes in the batch will be the ones cooked last. I start with 2 teaspoons oil and spread it out, and that's all that's needed. Some people like to add a little butter to the pan as the pancakes cook, but I'd rather put the butter right on my pancakes once cooked! Fold in the smallest blueberries you can find so they don't exude so much moisture into the batter. Fresh wild blueberries or huckleberries are the best if you can find them.

4 large eggs, separated

1⅓ cups small-curd cottage cheese

2 tablespoons sugar

1 teaspoon grated lemon zest

½ cup all-purpose flour

¼ teaspoon salt

1 cup fresh blueberries, rinsed and patted dry

2 teaspoons vegetable oil

Butter and maple syrup, for serving

1. In a large bowl, whisk together the egg yolks, cottage cheese, sugar, and lemon zest. Whisk in the flour and salt until just combined. Set aside.

2. In another large bowl, beat the egg whites with an electric mixer on high speed until stiff peaks form, about 2 minutes. Using a silicone spatula, fold about a third of the whites into the egg yolk mixture to lighten it, then fold in the remaining whites. Fold in the blueberries.

3. Heat a 12-inch skillet over medium heat. When it is hot, add the oil and tilt the pan to spread it out over the bottom. When a few drops of water dance on the skillet, you are ready to cook. Measure out ¼ cup batter per pancake and cook three pancakes at a time. Cook until deeply golden, 1 to 2 minutes; lift the corner of a pancake and peek under to see how quickly it is cooking. Turn and cook on the other side until deeply golden, 1 to 2 minutes. Transfer to a warm platter or baking sheet to keep the pancakes warm, and repeat with the remaining batter. Serve warm with butter and maple syrup.

How to Make Silver Dollar Pancakes

A diner favorite, these tiny pancakes are fun to make. Use a tablespoon to portion out the pancakes into the hot skillet and cook for 1 to 2 minutes per side, or until deeply golden brown and they test done.

THE ONLY PANCAKE RECIPE
You'll Ever Need

MAKES 18 TO 24 (3-INCH) PANCAKES (6 SERVINGS)
Prep: 20 minutes / Cook: 4 to 5 minutes per batch

This reliable, memorable pancake recipe is like other good cooking basics—indispensable. This is your go-to when you're frying bacon and scrambling eggs for weekend guests, or serving someone a special breakfast in bed. And while it takes a little time to assemble the batter from scratch, your rewards will be hugs and high-fives. Separating the eggs and using cake flour both contribute to the light-as-air texture. Buttermilk is key, but you probably already knew that!

½ cup (1 stick) unsalted butter

2 large eggs, separated

2½ cups buttermilk

2 tablespoons sugar

1 teaspoon vanilla extract

2½ cups cake flour or all-purpose flour

1 teaspoon baking powder

1 teaspoon baking soda

½ teaspoon salt

2 teaspoons vegetable oil

Sliced fresh fruit, melted butter, maple syrup, and/or honey, for serving

1. Preheat the oven to 275 degrees F.

2. Melt the butter in a small saucepan over low heat, then let it cool to room temperature.

3. In a large bowl, whisk together the egg yolks, buttermilk, sugar, and vanilla until well combined.

4. In another large bowl, whisk together the flour, baking powder, soda, and salt. Pour the buttermilk mixture into the flour mixture and stir just to combine. Pour in the cooled melted butter and stir until smooth.

5. In a medium bowl, beat the egg whites with an electric mixer on high speed until soft peaks form, 1 to 2 minutes. Fold the egg whites into the batter until just incorporated.

6. Heat a 12-inch skillet over medium heat. When it is hot, add the oil and tilt the pan to spread it out over the bottom. When a few drops of water dance on the skillet, you are ready to cook. Measure out ¼ cup batter per pancake and cook three pancakes at a time. Cook until bubbles form on top, 2 to 2½ minutes. Turn the pancakes and let them cook on the other side until bubbles form and the underside is lightly browned, 2 to 2½ minutes. Transfer to an oven-safe platter or baking sheet and place in the warm oven while you make the remaining pancakes. Serve warm with your favorite toppings.

DUTCH BABY
Blueprint

MAKES 3 TO 4 SERVINGS / Prep: 15 minutes / Bake: 20 to 25 minutes

What's a cross between a pancake and a popover? A Dutch baby, the German skillet pancake popularized by the Pennsylvania Dutch in America. It's important that the skillet is hot when the batter goes in and that the Dutch baby is baked at high heat to give it the best rise. Some recipes call for baking powder, but I find this makes the mixture heavy and prefer the simplicity and lightness of this recipe. It's just a blueprint, a blank canvas: If you want to jazz up the baby, look at my ideas below. And make sure the rest of the meal—and your guests—are ready when the Dutch baby goes into the oven. It will rise and then abruptly fall, and you don't want anyone to miss the drama!

2 tablespoons unsalted butter

4 large eggs

1 cup whole milk

3 tablespoons granulated sugar, divided use

1 teaspoon vanilla extract

½ teaspoon grated lemon zest

1 cup unbleached all-purpose flour

Pinch salt

Fresh berries, confectioners' sugar, and maple syrup, for serving

1. Preheat the oven to 425 degrees F. Place a 12-inch skillet in the oven while the oven preheats.

2. When the oven comes to temperature, remove the skillet and add the butter. Set aside.

3. In a large mixing bowl, whisk the eggs to break up the yolks. Whisk in the milk to combine. Sprinkle in 2 tablespoons of the sugar and the vanilla and lemon zest. Whisk to combine. Add half of the flour and whisk until smooth, then whisk in the other half and the salt. (Alternatively, you can make the batter in a blender.)

4. Place the skillet over medium-high heat until the butter foams but does not burn. Pour in the batter. Sprinkle the remaining 1 tablespoon sugar around the edges of the Dutch baby. Place the pan in the oven and bake until the sides are browned and puffed up and the center begins to lightly brown, 20 to 25 minutes. Remove the pan from the oven and garnish with fresh berries, a dusting of confectioners' sugar, and maple syrup, if desired.

VARIATIONS

Cremini Mushroom and Spinach Dutch Baby

Sauté 1 cup sliced cremini mushrooms in 2 tablespoons butter in the skillet until soft, 2 to 3 minutes. Add 3 cups fresh spinach leaves and stir to wilt. Turn off the heat.

Make the batter as the recipe directs, with these changes: Replace the sugar with grated Parmesan cheese. Omit the vanilla and lemon zest. Add 1 teaspoon fresh thyme or basil leaves, if desired. Add a sprinkling of cracked black pepper.

When the batter is ready, reheat the skillet until the mushrooms and spinach are hot. Pour in the batter and sprinkle the top with the reserved 1 tablespoon Parmesan. Place the pan in the oven and bake as directed.

Bananas Foster or Apple-Cinnamon Dutch Baby

Peel and slice 1 large or 2 small bananas lengthwise into ¼-inch pieces. Or, peel 3 medium Granny Smith apples, quarter, and slice into ¼-inch pieces to yield about 3 cups apples.

Sauté the bananas or apples in 2 tablespoons butter in the skillet until soft, 3 to 4 minutes. Sprinkle with ⅓ to ½ cup sugar and ¼ teaspoon ground cinnamon. Do not stir. Turn off the heat.

Make the batter as the recipe directs, with these changes: Omit the sugar. Replace the vanilla with dark rum, if desired.

When the batter is ready, reheat the skillet until the fruit is hot. Pour in the batter and sprinkle the top with 2 teaspoons sugar. Place the pan in the oven and bake as directed.

Here are two other ideas…

Add ricotta and prosciutto, and garnish with pea shoots, for a savory springtime Dutch baby. Replace the sugar with grated Parmesan cheese.

Sprinkle on miniature semisweet chocolate chips and marshmallows instead of the berries and confectioners' sugar in the basic recipe.

FRENCH TOAST
Challah Bake

MAKES 12 SERVINGS / Prep: 25 minutes / Bake: 28 to 30 minutes

This brunch main dish will remind you of your favorite bread pudding—minus the rum-soaked raisins and cream poured on top. But feel free to add those elements if you like, because this beauty deserves some attention. When you pull it out of the oven, you will see why cast iron has been loved for baking. The bread plumps up in the spiced custard and then puffs up like a soufflé. The little bit of topping adds the perfect amount of crunch. Serve with vanilla yogurt and fresh fruit or, to gild that lily, drizzle with maple syrup.

1 tablespoon unsalted butter, at room temperature

12 ounces challah bread, cut into 1-inch pieces (about 6 lightly packed cups)

8 large eggs

2 cups whole milk

½ cup heavy cream

½ cup packed light brown sugar

¼ cup granulated sugar

2 teaspoons vanilla extract

2 teaspoons ground cinnamon

¼ teaspoon ground nutmeg

¼ teaspoon ground cardamom

TOPPING

¼ cup all-purpose flour

¼ cup packed light brown sugar

¼ cup coarsely chopped pecans

Pinch salt

2 tablespoons unsalted butter, at room temperature

1. Preheat the oven to 400 degrees F.

2. Rub a 12-inch skillet with the soft butter. Add the challah pieces and place the skillet in the oven to let the bread cubes bake until they nearly brown, about 5 minutes. Remove the pan from the oven.

3. Combine the eggs, milk, cream, both sugars, vanilla, cinnamon, nutmeg, and cardamom in the bowl of a food processor fitted with a steel blade. Process until well combined. Pour the milk mixture over the bread cubes. Press down on the bread cubes with a small spatula to push the bread down into the liquid. Bake until the bread begins to puff up and brown, about 15 minutes.

4. Meanwhile, make the topping. Combine the flour, sugar, pecans, and salt in the food processor and process until just mixed. Add the soft butter and pulse 5 or 6 times, until the mixture comes together in moist crumbs, 5 to 6 pulses. Remove the pan from the oven after 15 minutes and crumble the topping over the top. Return the skillet to the oven, and bake until the topping browns, 13 to 15 minutes more.

5. Serve at once, or set it aside for up to 30 minutes before serving. It will stay warm, although it will deflate an inch or two.

VARIATION

How to Make Traditional Challah French Toast
In a shallow dish, beat 4 large eggs, 1 cup whole milk, ¼ cup cream, ¼ cup packed light brown sugar, 2 table-spoons granulated sugar, 1 teaspoon vanilla extract, 1 teaspoon ground cinnamon, and a pinch each of ground nutmeg and ground cardamom. Soak 6 to 8 slices of challah in this mixture. Heat 3 tablespoons butter or oil in a 12-inch skillet; when hot, add three slices at a time. Cook for 2 to 3 minutes per side, until deeply golden. Keep warm and repeat with the remaining slices.

CROQUE MONSIEUR

MAKES 8 SERVINGS / Prep: 20 to 25 minutes / Cook: 16 to 20 minutes

One of my favorite things to order at cafés in Paris—and even Seattle—is this golden, gooey sandwich of Gruyère and ham. Its name comes from the French verb *croquer*, which means "to bite," and *monsieur* tells us that this is the version designed to be eaten by men. There is also a croque madame, distinguished by a fried egg on top! If you have ever eaten one—monsieur or madame—you know it is something wonderful to bite into. And the skillet makes the preparation easy because not only does it toast the bread, but it also serves as the pan in which the sandwiches bake and broil to crispy doneness. You can even cook the béchamel sauce in the skillet, then wipe the skillet clean before assembling the sandwiches. Serve with a green salad and sliced ripe tomatoes. This recipe can be halved.

16 slices white sandwich bread

3 tablespoons unsalted butter, at room temperature, divided use

1½ cups whole milk

3 tablespoons all-purpose flour

½ teaspoon salt

¼ teaspoon freshly ground black pepper

¼ teaspoon ground nutmeg

12 ounces Gruyère cheese, shredded (about 3 cups), divided use

½ cup grated Parmesan cheese

2 tablespoons Dijon mustard

8 ounces ham, thinly sliced

1. Cut the bread into 4-inch rounds, using a cutter or a glass. Reserve the bread scraps for making croutons or bread crumbs. Lightly spread both sides of half of the rounds using 1 tablespoon of the butter. Set all 16 rounds aside.

2. Preheat the oven to 400 degrees F. To make the béchamel sauce, warm the milk in a small saucepan over low heat. In another small saucepan, melt the remaining 2 tablespoons butter over low heat. Whisk in the flour and stir until thickened, about 1 minute. Slowly whisk in the warm milk until the mixture has thickened into a sauce, about 3 minutes. Turn off the heat and whisk in the salt, pepper, nutmeg, ½ cup of the shredded Gruyère, and the Parmesan. Set aside.

3. Toast four of the buttered bread rounds in a 12-inch skillet over medium heat until browned, about 2 minutes. Turn and brown the other side, 1 to 2 minutes. Repeat with the remaining four buttered rounds. Toast the remaining eight unbuttered rounds in a toaster until lightly browned.

4. Spread four of the buttered toasted rounds with half of the mustard and place them in the skillet. Place 1 ounce of ham on each round, and top each with ¼ cup Gruyère cheese. Top with an unbuttered toasted round. Spoon a heaping tablespoon of the cheese sauce on top of the bread round. Top with 1 tablespoon grated Gruyère. Place the skillet in the oven.

5. Bake until the sandwiches are cooked through, about 5 minutes. Switch the oven to broil, and broil on high until the sandwiches are bubbly and golden brown, 4 to 5 minutes. Cover and keep warm. Repeat with the remaining ingredients to make four more sandwiches, baking and then broiling. Serve at once.

CHILAQUILES

MAKES 2 TO 3 SERVINGS / Prep: 25 minutes / Cook: 6 to 8 minutes

If you love chilaquiles at your favorite restaurant, you will love it even more at home made in your iron skillet. Sort of scrambled eggs meets Mexican stir-fry, chilaquiles is a delightful contrast of flavors and textures, just the sort of brunch dish that can be prepped ahead and finished off at the last minute. While some recipes call for packaged tortilla chips, it is much better to use freshly fried corn tortillas. They add a subtle crunch on top and creaminess within. This blank canvas of a recipe can be adapted to your tastes and tolerance for heat. Use jalapeños or serrano peppers if you like things hot; if not, opt for sweet bell, Anaheim, or banana peppers. And the cheese is up to you—use a blend of shredded Mexican cheeses for milder palates or crumbled queso fresco for a more authentic vibe. For crowds, you can double this recipe in one skillet, then can cook another double batch in a second skillet, feeding 8 to 12.

½ cup vegetable oil

4 (5- to 6-inch) corn tortillas, cut into ½-inch strips

Kosher salt and freshly ground black pepper

½ cup chopped green onion

1 tablespoon minced jalapeño or serrano pepper

½ cup fresh cilantro leaves, divided use

4 large eggs

1 tablespoon water

2 tablespoons salsa

¼ cup crumbled queso fresco or shredded Mexican cheese blend

1. Heat the oil in a 12-inch skillet over medium heat. When the oil is hot, add 1 tortilla strip; when it begins to sizzle, add the rest, stirring gently to separate them in the hot oil. Let them fry for 2 to 3 minutes. They will first wilt, then crisp up and turn lightly golden brown. Turn off the heat and use a slotted spoon to transfer the fried strips to paper towels to drain. Season with kosher salt and set aside.

2. Discard all but 1 tablespoon of the oil in the skillet. Add the green onion and pepper and cook over medium-low heat until they soften, 1 minute. Add ¼ cup of the cilantro leaves and stir to combine.

3. In a small bowl, whisk together the eggs and water. Add the eggs to the skillet and cook until they just begin to stick around the edges, about 1 minute, then use a silicone spatula to fold the edges of the eggs inward. Add the salsa and half of the fried tortilla strips. Fold over once more and turn off the heat.

4. Season with salt and pepper and sprinkle with the cheese. Top with the remaining tortillas and remaining ¼ cup cilantro leaves. Serve at once.

FRIED GREEN TOMATO BLTS

MAKES 6 BLT STACKS / Prep: 40 minutes

Fried green tomatoes are the "bread" in this sandwich recipe. In between are layers of sliced red tomato, basil, greens, bacon, and mayo, forming an easy do-ahead brunch or lunch stack. For parties, prep the layers ahead of time and assemble just before serving.

12 slices Fried Green Tomatoes
(page 4)

6 slices bacon

6 slices ripe red tomato

6 slices ripe yellow tomato

6 large fresh basil leaves

1 cup baby spinach leaves
or spring greens

Mayonnaise

Freshly ground black pepper

1. Prepare the Fried Green Tomatoes, or, if prepared ahead, reheat and crisp them up in a 400 degree F oven (see box, page 5). Once fried or re-crisped, you can set the oven at 200 degrees F to keep them warm while you prepare the bacon.

2. In a 12-inch skillet, fry the bacon over medium-low heat until crisp, then drain on paper towels. Let the tomato slices drain on paper towels. Pat dry the basil leaves and spinach.

3. Place one fried green tomato on a plate or platter. Spread generously with mayonnaise. Top with a slice of red tomato, followed by a basil leaf, a slice of ripe yellow tomato, a few spinach leaves, and a piece of bacon. Sprinkle with black pepper.

4. Spread a second fried green tomato with mayonnaise, and place it mayonnaise-side down on top of the bacon to form one "sandwich." Repeat to assemble the remaining BLTs.

SMOKED TURKEY AND
Potato Hash

MAKES 6 SERVINGS / Prep: 20 minutes / Cook: 23 to 25 minutes

This recipe is a take-off on a dish I remember from childhood. On Christmas morning at my aunt Elizabeth's home, turkey hash was spooned over rice and served alongside Tennessee ham and cheese grits—it was the ultimate "waste not, want not" recipe. Hash has been the great extender of meals through history, the economical way to stretch a little and serve many. You don't have to wait until the holidays to make hash—although it is a fabulous way to use up leftover turkey! You can find roasted or smoked turkey in the supermarket deli. This is wonderful served over rice, or at brunch with scrambled eggs, cheese grits, and hot sauce.

1 pound red-skinned potatoes,
peeled and cut into ½-inch dice

Salt and freshly ground black pepper

3 tablespoons olive oil

1 cup chopped onion

1 cup chopped bell pepper

6 ounces smoked turkey,
cut into 1-inch dice

1 tablespoon fresh thyme leaves

Pinch cayenne pepper

1 cup reduced-sodium chicken broth

1 cup shredded spinach or
baby kale (optional)

1. Put the potatoes in a 12-inch skillet, cover with water, and add ¼ teaspoon salt. Bring the water to a boil over medium heat, then cover the pan, reduce the heat to low, and simmer until the potatoes are nearly cooked through, 5 to 7 minutes. Drain the potatoes and set aside. Discard the cooking water and wipe the skillet dry.

2. Heat the skillet over medium heat, then add the oil, onion, and bell pepper. Cook, stirring, until the onion softens and browns around the edges, 5 to 6 minutes. Add the drained potatoes, turkey, thyme, and cayenne and season with salt and black pepper. Stir to combine. Add the broth and let the mixture simmer until the potatoes are tender and the liquid has nearly evaporated, about 10 minutes.

3. If desired, add the spinach or kale to the skillet and stir until the greens wilt, about 2 minutes. Serve hot.

BIG SKILLET SCRAMBLE

MAKES 4 TO 6 SERVINGS / Prep: 20 minutes / Cook: 10 minutes

Cast iron manufacturers will sell you on the ability to slide a fried egg off their skillet. That's achievable as long as the pan has been seasoned and there is sufficient butter or olive oil in the pan. The fat—and the polymer of coating that builds up on a well-seasoned skillet—acts as a barrier, preventing the proteins in the egg from sticking when heated. The same principle is at work for scrambling eggs, too, but the problem with scrambling in cast iron is there often isn't sufficient fat in the pan, so the eggs stick and are easily overcooked because they stay too long in the skillet. The solution is to have a nice sauté of veggies in the pan—just as this recipe suggests. Serve with grilled slices of sourdough bread.

3 tablespoons olive oil

1 cup chopped purple or white onion

2 cups sliced cremini mushrooms

1 cup chopped fresh tomato

½ teaspoon dried oregano

Kosher salt and freshly ground black pepper

6 large eggs

1 tablespoon water

3 packed cups fresh spinach leaves (see Note)

¼ cup crumbled feta cheese

Oil-cured or Kalamata olives, pitted and halved for garnish (optional)

1. Heat the olive oil in a 12-inch skillet over medium heat. Add the onion and sauté until softened, about 2 minutes. Add the mushrooms and sauté until softened, 3 to 4 minutes. Add the tomato and oregano and season with salt and pepper. Stir and cook until the tomato loses some of its moisture, about 2 minutes.

2. In a medium bowl, whisk together the eggs and water. Turn the heat under the skillet to medium and add the eggs. Let them cook, without stirring, until they begin to cling to the sides of the pan, about 1 minute. Fold in the spinach leaves, then toss the mixture just until the eggs are nearly set, 1 minute more. They will continue to set even off the heat, so do not overcook them in the skillet.

3. Transfer the scrambled eggs and veggies to a platter and scatter the feta cheese over the top. Garnish with olives, if desired.

NOTE: If you have time before assembling this scramble, remove the stems from the spinach leaves for a nicer presentation.

> ### GILD THE LILY
>
> Serve with Fresh Romesco Sauce (page 3) and grilled bread.

SHAKSHUKA

MAKES 4 SERVINGS / Prep: 20 minutes / Cook: 41 to 46 minutes

This spicy Tunisian tomato-pepper medley (sometimes spelled "chakchouka") is popular throughout the Mediterranean and Middle East. It's the perfect brunch dish, because burrowed into the thick, peppery tomato stew are eggs, allowed to poach to soft doneness. The big flavor here is harissa, the North African blend of chili, garlic, cumin, and caraway that you can make or buy in paste or powder form. And the iron skillet does it all—from simmering down the sauce to evenly and slowly poaching those eggs. Serve with plenty of crusty bread for dunking, and add a green salad to round out the meal.

3 tablespoons olive oil

3 cups thinly sliced onions
(2 large onions)

1 (28-ounce) can whole Italian plum tomatoes

2 teaspoons harissa seasoning or paste

2 cups diced bell or Anaheim peppers
(a mix of green, yellow, and red)

6 to 8 cloves garlic, peeled and minced

4 medium eggs (see Note)

Salt and freshly ground black pepper

Crumbled feta cheese, for garnish (optional)

Crusty bread, for serving

1. Heat the oil in a 12-inch skillet over medium heat. When it is hot, add the onions and sauté until they are soft and just beginning to turn golden brown, 12 to 15 minutes.

2. Meanwhile, drain the tomatoes and reserve the tomato liquid. Cut the tomatoes into three or four pieces each and add them to the pan. Stir in the harissa. Reduce the heat to medium-low and cook, stirring occasionally, until the tomatoes lose half of their liquid and cook down, about 10 minutes. Add the peppers and garlic. Cover the skillet, reduce the heat to low, and let the mixture simmer until the peppers are soft, about 15 minutes. Add some of the reserved tomato liquid if necessary to keep the mixture from sticking to the pan.

3. Make four depressions in the sauce with the back of a big soup spoon. Crack one egg into each depression. Cover the pan and cook until the egg whites are nearly set but the yolks are still soft, 4 to 5 minutes. Remove the pan from the heat (the eggs will continue to cook from the residual heat of the pan). Season the eggs with salt and pepper and garnish the top with feta, if desired. Spoon onto plates and serve with crusty bread.

NOTE: When cooking eggs in sauce, choose medium eggs instead of large because they don't take up so much room in the skillet.

Substituting Shrimp for Eggs

This stew is also delicious with shrimp. Instead of adding the eggs, burrow 12 extra-large peeled and deveined shrimp into the sauce, cover the pan, and let them cook to doneness, 4 to 5 minutes.

QUICHE LORRAINE
in a Skillet

MAKES 6 SERVINGS / Prep: 20 minutes / Bake: 30 to 35 minutes

This classic quiche is where it all began. Before goat cheese and roasted red peppers, before pesto and tomatoes, the true French quiche contained just Gruyère cheese, some ham, and a bit of onion. It is the perfect combo, really, and when deciding which quiche to include in this chapter, I decided to go classic. I like prosciutto, but you can use any ham you have on hand, as well as crumbled, fried bacon. This was the recipe my mother baked in the 1960s and, in turn, I started baking. And speaking of baking, you really need to make your own pie crust, which is so much better tasting than the premade and is a snap to pulse together in a food processor.

1 recipe Food Processor Pie Crust (page 247)

8 ounces Gruyère cheese, shredded (about 2 cups)

1 tablespoon all-purpose flour

2 ounces prosciutto or thinly sliced country ham, torn into pieces

10 to 12 thin onion rings (see Note)

Freshly ground black pepper

5 large eggs

1⅔ cups half-and-half

Freshly grated nutmeg

Cayenne pepper

1. Preheat the oven to 425 degrees F.

2. Press the pie crust dough into the bottom and halfway up the sides of a 12-inch skillet. Prick the crust with a fork along the sides and bottom.

3. In a small bowl, toss the shredded Gruyère with the flour. Scatter half of the cheese over the bottom of the pie crust. Scatter the prosciutto over the cheese, then sprinkle on the remaining cheese. Arrange the onion slices on top. Sprinkle with pepper.

4. In a medium mixing bowl, whisk together the eggs and half-and-half. Pour the egg mixture over the cheese and ham in the skillet. Sprinkle a bit of nutmeg and cayenne pepper on top. Place the skillet in the oven.

5. Bake until the crust begins to brown, about 15 minutes, then reduce the heat to 350 degrees F and bake until the top has set and is golden, 15 to 20 minutes more. Remove the quiche from the oven and let it rest for 20 minutes before slicing.

NOTE: Thinly slice an onion and pull the slices apart to form individual rings. You need just 10 to 12 of these rings.

FRESH ASPARAGUS FRITTATA
Blueprint

MAKES 6 SERVINGS / Prep: 20 minutes / Cook: 19 to 23 minutes

I had tried my hand at frittatas but, to be honest, they often disappointed. But once I started making frittatas in a cast-iron skillet, I could not stop. The frittata loves high heat, and in fact, it cooks best when the skillet is searing-hot. Here is the result of my many dozens of eggs cracked. Use it as a blueprint for a frittata, dictated by the seasons. I love small zucchini and yellow squash in the summertime. Add oregano in the wintertime if you can't find fresh basil. Add a handful of chopped ham or crumbled drained sausage for the meat-eaters. Do your thing! But don't change the ratios of 8 eggs to ¼ cup cream, which is just the right amount for this size skillet, allowing the eggs to cook up lofty and beautiful. I find that about 3 cups veggies is the right amount, but feel free to add more if you like.

8 large eggs

¼ cup heavy cream

3 tablespoons grated Parmesan cheese, divided use

3 tablespoons olive oil

1 cup finely chopped onion

½ cup thinly sliced mushrooms (optional)

1½ cups thin asparagus spears, trimmed and cut into 2- to 3-inch-long pieces (see Note)

2 tablespoons chopped fresh basil

Salt and freshly ground black pepper

GARNISH

Small salad greens

Basil pesto

Quartered cherry tomatoes

Good olive oil

1. Preheat the oven to 450 degrees F.

2. In a medium bowl, whisk together the eggs, cream, and 2 tablespoons of the Parmesan. Set aside.

3. Heat the oil in a 12-inch skillet over medium-low heat. Add the onion and sauté until soft and translucent, 4 to 5 minutes. Add the mushrooms (if using) and sauté until soft, 2 to 3 minutes. Stir in the asparagus and fresh basil and season with salt and pepper.

4. Pour the egg mixture on top of the veggies. Let the mixture cook until it begins to puff up around the edges, 8 to 10 minutes. Turn off the heat, sprinkle the top with the remaining 1 tablespoon Parmesan, and place the skillet in the oven.

5. Bake the frittata until it puffs up across the entire surface and is lightly browned, about 5 minutes. If desired, switch the oven to broil and place the skillet under the broiler for less than a minute, just until slightly deeper brown.

6. Run a knife around the sides of the skillet to loosen it. Shake the pan and slide the frittata onto a serving board or plate. You may need to slide a large metal spatula under the frittata to get it moving.

7. Slice into wedges and garnish each slice with greens, pesto, tomatoes, and a drizzle of olive oil. Or, present the frittata unsliced and garnish the center of it.

NOTE: In the summertime, when zucchini and yellow squash come into the garden, substitute thinly sliced squash for asparagus.

The skillet skillfully roasts, bakes, and fries vegetables of all textures and colors. The natural sweetness in crucifers—broccoli, cauliflower, and Brussels sprouts—caramelizes in the heat of the iron pan. Roots like potatoes and sweet potatoes take on an irresistible crispiness from the heat the skillet provides. They also transform into elegant pommes Anna or sweet potato soufflé and go straight from oven to table. Then there is the Persian tahdig, with its exotic layer of crispy rice created by the low, constant heat of the skillet. Butternut squash, summer squash, and eggplant are all perfect for roasting and serving with a drizzle of good olive oil or turning into your favorite salad. In fact, it's a wide world of salad possibilities when you have the skillet: It fries bacon and croutons, roasts nuts and chickpeas, amplifies the flavor of spices, and creates hot vinaigrettes to make salads suitable even for cold winter nights.

CHAPTER 4

SALADS & VEGGIE SIDES

HOT BACON AND ROMAINE SALAD
with Basil Buttermilk Dressing

MAKES 6 SERVINGS / Prep: 45 minutes

This is the perfect salad to go with steaks and burgers. It has that classic steakhouse look and taste, and while the skillet does not play a starring role in this recipe, it is an important supporting actor. It fries the bacon to go on top, and a little of that grease is poured over the romaine leaves to wilt them. This is an age-old technique, used throughout the Appalachian region of our country and known as "killed" or "kilt" salad. You can omit this step if you like, but know that while you fry the bacon, the grease is seasoning your iron skillet and building up the important nonstick layer, too!

BASIL BUTTERMILK DRESSING

1 packed cup fresh basil leaves

2 tablespoons chopped green onion

⅓ cup buttermilk

2 tablespoons mayonnaise

Salt and freshly ground black pepper

SALAD

2 heads romaine lettuce, chopped
or left whole

2 ripe tomatoes (see Note)

12 slices bacon

GARNISH

¼ cup shaved Parmesan cheese

Small fresh basil leaves

Homemade Croutons (page 257)

1. For the dressing, combine the basil, green onion, buttermilk, mayonnaise, and a little salt and pepper in the bowl of a food processor fitted with a steel blade. Process until the basil and onion are well minced and the mixture is smooth, about 30 seconds. Spoon into a glass bowl, cover with plastic wrap, and chill until time to serve.

2. For the salad, trim the ends from the romaine and discard the tough outer leaves. Slice each head lengthwise into thirds. Rinse with cool water and pat dry on paper towels. Peel and core the tomatoes. Cut into quarters, then slice the quarters into thirds to yield 24 pieces of tomato. Set aside.

3. Cook the bacon in a 12-inch skillet over medium-low heat for a few minutes to render some fat, then increase the heat to medium. Cook the bacon until browned on one side, then turn and brown the other side, 10 to 12 minutes total cooking time. Transfer the bacon to paper towels to drain. Pour off all but 1 tablespoon bacon fat from the skillet. Keep warm.

4. To serve, place a slab of romaine on each plate. Top each with some tomatoes, then lay the bacon slices on top. Drizzle a little of the warm bacon grease on top of the bacon, tomato, and romaine. Spoon over the dressing, and garnish with shavings of Parmesan, fresh basil leaves, and croutons. Serve at once.

NOTE: This salad is even more beautiful if you use one yellow tomato and one red tomato.

GILD THE LILY : HOT BACON AND SALMON SALAD

Add a piece of seared salmon to the top for
a main-course salad.

WARM BABY KALE SALAD
with Skillet-Roasted Chickpeas

MAKES 6 SERVINGS / Prep: 20 minutes

I love the contrast of flavors and textures in this salad: the crisp kale leaves, the crunchy chickpeas, and the tangy dressing. This is a great do-ahead for parties and potlucks because the kale keeps so well when prepped in advance. And the dressing is easy to warm and pour over the greens just before serving. The chickpeas become the unexpected "croutons," and you may find it difficult to stop nibbling them off the top!

GREENS

5 ounces baby kale or arugula

Olive oil

Salt and freshly ground black pepper

WARM DRESSING

3 tablespoons olive oil

2 cloves garlic, peeled and minced

2 tablespoons lemon juice

¼ cup grated Parmesan cheese

Salt and freshly ground black pepper

GARNISH

1 cup Skillet-Roasted Chickpeas
(page 251), warm

1. Put the kale in a large salad bowl. Drizzle with a little olive oil and season with salt and pepper. Set aside.

2. For the dressing, heat the olive oil in a 12-inch skillet over medium heat. Add the garlic and sauté until it just begins to color, 1 to 2 minutes. Pull the pan off the heat and add the lemon juice. Stir in the grated Parmesan cheese and season with salt and pepper.

3. Spoon the dressing over the kale. Top with the warm roasted chickpeas and serve.

ARUGULA SALAD
with Orange, Avocado, and Sweet Pan Drizzle

MAKES 6 SERVINGS / Prep: 30 minutes

This is one of my favorite salads, a perfect combo of greens, citrus, avocado, and crunchy almonds. When the warm olive oil, onion, brown sugar, and red wine vinegar dressing is poured over, the greens wilt and the flavors combine. The skillet is a handy way to toast nuts quickly and bring out their rich flavors. As the skillet is already in use, make the dressing in it, and you've got only one pan to wash.

¼ cup sliced almonds

6 cups fresh arugula or
baby spinach leaves

1 large navel orange

1 ripe avocado, peeled, pitted,
and cut into ½-inch cubes

2 tablespoons olive oil, plus
more if needed

½ cup thinly sliced Vidalia or
other sweet onion

2 tablespoons red wine vinegar

1 tablespoon light brown sugar

¼ teaspoon dried oregano

Salt and freshly ground black pepper

1. In a 12-inch skillet, toast the almonds over medium heat, stirring, until they just begin to brown, 4 to 5 minutes. Transfer to a plate and set aside.

2. Put the arugula in a large bowl. Cut the orange in half; set one half aside for the dressing. Peel the other half and separate into sections. Cut each section into three pieces. Put the orange pieces on top of the arugula, then add the avocado cubes. Set the bowl aside.

3. Heat the olive oil in the skillet over medium heat. Add the onion and sauté until it begins to brown and turn translucent, 6 to 7 minutes. Squeeze the juice from the reserved orange half into the pan. Add the vinegar and stir. Reduce the heat to low and stir in the brown sugar and oregano. Season with salt and pepper.

4. Pour the hot pan dressing over the arugula, orange, and avocado. Toss to combine, adding more olive oil if needed. Season with salt and pepper and garnish the top with the toasted almonds. Serve at once.

PAN-ROASTED BEETS
with Spinach, Cherries, and Candied Pecans

MAKES 6 TO 8 SERVINGS / Prep: 50 minutes

The color of this salad cries summer, but you can easily turn it into a fall recipe by substituting diced crisp apple for the cherries and using shaved fennel instead of the onion. Beets not only meld into this color palette, but the flavor profiles are complementary, too. For color, look for a mix of golden and red beets.

ROASTED BEETS

2 large or 3 medium beets

1 tablespoon olive oil

Kosher salt

BALSAMIC VINAIGRETTE

¼ cup balsamic vinegar

2 tablespoons honey

1 tablespoon Dijon mustard

1 clove garlic, peeled and minced

⅛ teaspoon salt

⅛ teaspoon freshly ground black pepper

½ cup light olive oil or safflower oil

SALAD

6 to 8 cups baby spinach leaves

1 cup fresh sweet cherries, stemmed, pitted, and sliced

2 tablespoons shaved purple onion

2 tablespoons crumbled blue cheese (optional)

½ cup Candied Pecans (recipe follows)

1. Preheat the oven to 450 degrees F.

2. To prep the beets, peel them and cut them in half lengthwise. Place each half cut-side down and cut into five to eight slices, depending how large you like the beets in the salad. You need 3 to 4 cups sliced beets. (They will shrink when roasting.) Put the beets in a 12-inch skillet and toss with the olive oil to coat. Roast the beets until tender and crispy around the edges, 28 to 32 minutes. Remove the skillet from the oven, season with kosher salt, and set aside.

3. Meanwhile, make the dressing. In a large bowl, whisk together the vinegar, honey, mustard, garlic, salt, and pepper. Whisk in the oil until thickened. Set the dressing aside.

4. Run a metal spatula underneath the beets to release them from the skillet. You can either serve the salad right in the skillet or transfer the beets to a platter. Cover the beets with the spinach, then scatter the cherry slices and onion across the top. Scatter the blue cheese (if using) and pecans on top.

5. When ready to serve, spoon a couple of table-spoons of the vinaigrette on top of the salad, toss the salad, and add more vinaigrette as needed.

CANDIED PECANS

Preheat the oven to 250 degrees F. Scatter ½ cup pecan halves in a 12-inch skillet. Sprinkle 1 tablespoon brown sugar over the top. Drizzle with 1 tablespoon melted butter. Season with a pinch each of kosher salt and cayenne pepper. Toss to combine. Roast the pecans, stirring every 10 minutes, until they are glazed and crunchy, about 30 minutes. Transfer to a plate and let cool.

If you don't have time to make Candied Pecans, toss ½ cup pecan halves with 2 teaspoons olive oil and roast in a skillet at 350 degrees F for 8 to 10 minutes. Season with a sprinkling of kosher salt.

Our Favorite
TACO SALAD

MAKES 4 TO 6 SERVINGS / Prep: 30 minutes / Cook: 14 to 17 minutes

Taco salad is a lifesaver. It cleans out the fridge and quickly becomes a meal that everyone loves. Here is a basic skeleton of what goes into a taco salad and how your skillet can get you there. Take the detours you need to suit your timetable and please picky palates. I choose ground turkey, but you can go with beef, or make it vegetarian with pinto or black beans cooked in the garlic, onion, pepper, and seasonings. The skillet not only simmers the meat (or bean) mixture to perfection, but it fries the yummy tortilla strips. (In a pinch, you can use chips from a bag.)

TORTILLA STRIPS

½ cup vegetable oil

6 (5- to 6-inch) corn tortillas, cut into ½-inch strips

Kosher salt

MEAT SAUCE

1 tablespoon olive oil

1 cup chopped onion

1 cup chopped bell pepper

1 pound ground turkey

2 cloves garlic, peeled and minced

1 tablespoon ground cumin

2 teaspoons chili powder

1 teaspoon dried oregano

¾ teaspoon Creole seasoning

½ teaspoon cayenne pepper

½ cup water

SALAD

8 to 12 cups mixed salad greens or chopped romaine

2 cups (8 ounces) shredded Mexican blend cheese

1 cup salsa

1 cup sour cream

1 ripe avocado, peeled, pitted, and thinly sliced

1 cup fresh cilantro leaves

Favorite salad dressing (see Note)

1. For the tortilla strips, heat the oil in a 12-inch skillet over medium heat. When the oil is hot, add one strip; when it begins to sizzle, add half of the remaining strips, stirring gently to separate them in the hot oil. Let them fry for 2 to 3 minutes. They will first wilt, then crisp up and turn lightly golden brown. Turn off the heat and use a slotted spoon to transfer the fried strips to paper towels to drain. Season with kosher salt. Repeat with the remaining strips. Set aside. Let the oil in the skillet cool, then pour it off into a heat-safe container and save for another use. Wipe out the skillet.

2. To make the meat sauce, add the olive oil to the skillet. Add the onion and pepper and sauté over medium heat until they soften and begin to brown around the edges, about 4 minutes. Transfer the onion and pepper to a bowl.

3. Crumble the turkey into the skillet and add the minced garlic. Sauté over medium heat until the turkey is cooked through, 3 to 4 minutes. Add the cumin, chili powder, oregano, Creole seasoning, and cayenne and toss to coat. Return the onion and pepper to the skillet and add the water. Let the mixture simmer until most of the liquid evaporates but the mixture is still moist, 3 to 4 minutes.

4. To assemble, put the greens in a large, wide bowl. Pour the meat mixture on top. Sprinkle on the cheese. Add the salsa, sour cream, and avocado. Pile the fried tortilla strips on top. Garnish with cilantro and serve with your favorite dressing.

NOTE: We use a basic bottled oil and vinegar salad dressing on taco salad—pretty boring, right? But you can use ranch or Trader Joe's Cilantro Salad Dressing.

ROASTED TOMATO, BASIL,
and Orzo Salad

MAKES 8 SERVINGS / Prep: 40 minutes

Roasted Cherry Tomatoes (page 264) not only make a quick hors d'oeuvre slathered on toasted French bread, but they can be folded into warm orzo with a few other roasted vegetables and voilà, you've got an unbelievable main dish salad for buffets and picnics. The recipe originally came from my friend Evelyn, who made this salad to use up what was growing in her summer garden. I also found the beauty in this salad, not only in summer when zucchini grows like weeds, but also in the winter when you crave a blast of summer flavor. When you think about it, most any vegetable can be chopped, tossed with olive oil, and roasted to go into orzo salad. And with the already roasted cherry tomatoes and garlic medley, you have a head start. Feel free to substitute farro for the orzo.

VEGETABLES

1 medium zucchini, trimmed and cut into ¾-inch cubes

1 small eggplant, peeled and cut into ¾-inch cubes

1 red or yellow bell pepper, seeded and cut into ½-inch dice

1 small red onion, peeled and cut into ½-inch dice

¼ cup olive oil

½ teaspoon salt

Freshly ground black pepper

DRESSING

5 tablespoons olive oil

3 tablespoons fresh lemon juice

Freshly ground black pepper

1 clove garlic, peeled and minced

2 tablespoons chopped Kalamata olives

ORZO SALAD

½ teaspoon salt

8 ounces orzo

1 tablespoon olive oil

2 cups Roasted Cherry Tomatoes (page 264)

½ cup fresh basil leaves, for garnish

½ cup crumbled feta cheese, for garnish

1. Preheat the oven to 400 degrees F.

2. For the roasted vegetables, toss the zucchini, eggplant, bell pepper, and onion in a large mixing bowl with the olive oil and season with salt and pepper. Transfer the mixture to a 12-inch skillet and roast until the veggies cook through and are browned around the edges, 25 to 30 minutes, turning once with a metal spatula. Set the skillet aside to cool.

3. For the dressing, whisk together the olive oil and lemon juice in a small bowl. Season with black pepper, then fold in the garlic and olives. Set the dressing aside.

4. For the orzo, bring a large saucepan of water to a boil over high heat. Add the salt and stir in the orzo. Bring the water back to a boil, then reduce to medium heat and cook the orzo for 7 to 8 minutes, until al dente. Drain the orzo, transfer to a large serving bowl, and toss with the olive oil.

5. Top the orzo with the roasted vegetables and cherry tomatoes, and garnish with basil leaves and crumbled feta. Just before serving, pour over as much dressing as desired. Toss, then serve.

MIKE'S SWEET POTATO
Soufflé

MAKES 8 SERVINGS / Prep: 25 minutes / Cook: 18 to 22 minutes

For many years our family traveled to Chattanooga for Thanksgiving dinner, and I always looked forward to my husband's cousin Mike Patten's sweet potato casserole. It was different from the usual in that it was less sweet and contained orange juice, sherry, and raisins. Flashforward to working on this book, and I had to create a nostalgic rendition of Mike's sweet potatoes. The yolks of the egg went into the mashed sweet potato mixture, and the whites were beaten into a meringue to spread on top. This turned out to be the easiest and most delicious sweet potato casserole I've ever made—it tastes of sweet potatoes, and the meringue really tops it in grand style.

2¼ pounds fresh sweet potatoes, peeled and cut in quarters

½ teaspoon salt

3 tablespoons unsalted butter

⅓ to ½ cup lightly packed light brown sugar

2 tablespoons orange juice

1 tablespoon dry sherry or rum

1 teaspoon salt

½ teaspoon ground cinnamon

¼ cup golden raisins

2 large eggs, separated

2 teaspoons granulated sugar

1. Put the sweet potatoes in a large saucepan, cover with water, and add the salt. Bring the water to a boil over medium-high heat, then reduce the heat to low, cover, and let simmer until the potatoes are tender, about 20 minutes. Drain the potatoes and dump them into a 12-inch skillet.

2. Preheat the oven to 350 degrees F.

3. Add the butter and brown sugar to the skillet with the sweet potatoes and set the pan over medium heat. Mash the potatoes into the butter and sugar until smooth. Remove the pan from the heat. Fold in the orange juice, sherry, salt, cinnamon, and raisins.

4. In a small bowl, beat the egg yolks with a fork. Add a tablespoon of the sweet potato mixture and mix well. Add another tablespoon and mix well. Add a third tablespoon and mix until the egg yolks have warmed. Transfer the yolk mixture to the sweet potatoes in the skillet and stir to combine. Set aside.

5. In a medium bowl, beat the egg whites and granulated sugar with an electric mixer on high speed until stiff peaks form, 1½ to 2 minutes. Spread the egg whites on top of the sweet potatoes, leaving a 2-inch border of sweet potatoes uncovered around the edges.

6. Bake the soufflé until the meringue on top is golden brown, 18 to 22 minutes. Remove from the oven and serve at once.

How to Roast Sweet Potatoes in a Skillet

One of the most delicious flavors in this world is a bite of roasted sweet potato. Lightly salted, perhaps drizzled with balsamic, it is crispy on the edges and creamy within. Here is how to do it: Place a 12-inch skillet in the oven, and preheat the oven to 400 degrees F. Peel a sweet potato and cut it into 1-inch pieces. Toss these with olive oil. Remove the hot skillet from the oven, and transfer the potatoes into the skillet and roast until golden on the bottom, about 10 minutes. Using a metal spatula, flip the sweet potato pieces over and let them brown on the other side for another 10 minutes. Remove from the oven and sprinkle with kosher salt and drizzle with fresh lime juice or balsamic glaze, if desired. Shower with chopped fresh flat-leaf parsley or cilantro, and enjoy!

BRITISH HOME FRIES

MAKES 4 SERVINGS / Prep: 25 minutes / Cook: 40 to 45 minutes

This recipe could be called "How to Roast Potatoes Like a Brit," or "What I Learned about Roasting Potatoes While Living in England." The year I spent in England didn't teach me how to drive on the other side of the road, but it did teach me how to roast a proper potato. And I've never forgotten. My new British friends tried to explain how to cook these potatoes—they are magically creamy inside and crispy outside—but when that failed, they suggested I consult with Delia Smith, the beloved British cookbook author. So I did, and with her guidance, I eventually perfected the most sublime roasted potato, which can also dub as a home fry. The type of potato matters—you want a potato that is fluffy and dry like a russet, not starchy like a red potato or Yukon gold. They go great with scrambled eggs, steaks, chops, roasted chicken, or lamb, or just serve them on their own, showered with chopped fresh parsley and with a glass of ale.

½ cup vegetable oil or beef
or chicken drippings

4 pounds russet potatoes,
peeled and cut into 1- to 1½-inch pieces

Kosher salt

1. Place a rack in the top third of the oven. Pour the oil into a 12-inch skillet and place it on the rack. Preheat the oven to 425 degrees F.

2. Bring a kettle of water to a boil. Put the potatoes in a medium saucepan and pour the boiling water over them just to cover. Add ½ teaspoon salt and bring the water back to a boil over medium-high heat. Reduce the heat to low, cover, and simmer for 6 to 7 minutes, until the outside edge of the potatoes begins to fluff up. Test one potato for doneness by running a skewer along the outside edge; if it fluffs up, it's done. If the surface stays smooth, cook for a minute or two longer.

3. Drain the water from the pan. Place the lid on the pan and, holding the lid firmly, shake the pan vigorously up and down. The shaking roughens the edges of the potatoes and makes them fluffy, which will result in crunchy potatoes.

4. Carefully remove the hot skillet of oil from the oven. Use a long-handled spoon to lower the fluffed potatoes into the hot oil. When all the potatoes are in the pan, tilt the pan and use the spoon to baste the potatoes with the oil. Return the skillet to the top rack of the oven and roast the potatoes until golden brown, 40 to 45 minutes. Spoon the potatoes into a serving dish, sprinkle with kosher salt, and serve at once.

Last-Minute
SCALLOPED POTATOES

MAKES 8 SERVINGS / Prep: 10 minutes / Cook: 46 to 51 minutes

For a decade or more, this has been my go-to potato for both summer barbecues and holiday dinners. It's not so much that this is a secret recipe, but more the fact that no one guesses it begins with frozen diced potatoes—hash browns. The addition of Parmesan cheese, garlic, and cream elevates them considerably! And letting them cook in the iron skillet creates a crusty, crispy, cheesy ring around the pan that is delicious, along with the warm, gooey interior. Top them with a little extra cheese and run the pan under the broiler, or finish with a layer of buttered bread crumbs.

1 (32-ounce) bag frozen diced
hash brown potatoes

½ cup plus 1 tablespoon grated
Parmesan cheese

3 cloves garlic, peeled and minced

2 cups heavy cream

Salt and freshly ground black pepper

¼ cup shredded Gruyère or
sharp white Cheddar cheese (optional)

½ cup soft bread crumbs tossed
with 1 tablespoon melted butter (optional)

1. Preheat the oven to 400 degrees F.

2. Empty the bag of hash browns into a 12-inch skillet. Stir in the ½ cup Parmesan, garlic, and cream and season with salt and pepper. Cover the skillet with a lid or aluminum foil and bake until the mixture is bubbly, 45 to 50 minutes. Remove the skillet from the oven.

3. Switch the oven to broil. Uncover the skillet and scatter the remaining 1 tablespoon Parmesan and the Gruyère on top, and broil until the cheese melts and turns golden, no more than 1 minute. Remove and serve at once. Alternatively, forgo the cheese topping and scatter the buttered bread crumbs on top about 10 minutes before the potatoes are done. Continue baking until golden brown.

NOTE: For a dressier presentation, finely chop green onion tops or fresh flat-leaf parsley and scatter on top.

POMMES ANNA

MAKES 6 TO 8 SERVINGS / Prep: 30 minutes / Cook: 42 to 45 minutes

When you see pommes Anna slide out of a cast-iron skillet, you have to look twice. This simple but elegant classic French recipe, constructed just of thinly sliced potatoes and butter, is stunning—crispy around the edges and soft within. It's a little finicky to assemble because you must slice those potatoes on a mandoline, and you should use clarified butter. You'll also need a second skillet—a 10-inch skillet—to rest on top of the 12-inch skillet full of potatoes while it cooks. Grill a steak and toss a salad, but know that the pommes Anna will steal the show.

3 pounds russet or golden potatoes, peeled

6 tablespoons clarified butter (see Note)

Salt and freshly ground black pepper

Chopped fresh flat-leaf parsley, for garnish

1. Preheat the oven to 425 degrees F.

2. Using a mandoline or very sharp knife, slice the potatoes into ⅛-inch-thick slices.

3. Heat 2 tablespoons of the clarified butter in a 12-inch skillet over medium heat. Arrange one-third of the potato slices in an overlapping spiral in the bottom. Sprinkle with salt and pepper and drizzle with 1 tablespoon more butter. Use half of the remaining potatoes to make a second layer, sprinkle with salt and pepper, and drizzle with another tablespoon of butter. Turn off the heat. Add the third and final layer of potatoes, add salt and pepper, and drizzle with another tablespoon of butter.

4. Brush the remaining 1 tablespoon butter on the bottom of a 10-inch cast-iron skillet. Place the 10-inch skillet on top of the potatoes in the 12-inch skillet, and place both in the oven. Bake until the potatoes are crispy on the bottom, 42 to 45 minutes. Remove the pans from the oven. Carefully remove the 10-inch skillet, replacing any potato slices that stick to it. Run a knife around the edges of the 12-inch pan, and let the skillet rest for 2 to 3 minutes.

5. Invert the 12-inch skillet onto a board or platter. Slice the potatoes into wedges and serve, garnished with chopped parsley.

NOTE: To clarify butter, melt ½ cup (1 stick) unsalted butter in a small saucepan over medium heat. Continue to cook until the white milk solids rise to the top. Remove the solids with a slotted spoon. You should have 5 to 6 tablespoons clarified butter remaining in the saucepan. You can also cook the butter further, until the water cooks out and it stops spattering, to make ghee, the clarified butter used in Indian cooking. The solids will turn dark brown and may start to burn, but you will strain the ghee through cheesecloth to collect those solids.

SWEET POTATO
Hasselback Bake

MAKES 6 TO 8 SERVINGS / Prep: 25 minutes / Bake: 45 to 53 minutes

Hasselback potatoes are a Swedish favorite in which a potato is thinly sliced crosswise, almost all the way down but left intact at the bottom. The idea is to speed the cooking time and infuse flavors between the slices. And with the extra surface area exposed to the oven's heat, the potato gets crispy and roasted on top. The skillet is a perfect pan in which to roast these sweet potatoes because the flavorings and maple syrup cook down and caramelize on the bottom of the potato. These are delicious with roasted turkey and cranberry sauce as well as roasted pork.

4 tablespoons unsalted butter or olive oil

6 to 8 (8-ounce) sweet potatoes, peeled

Salt and freshly ground black pepper

Chili powder or harissa seasoning

¼ cup maple syrup

Fresh lime wedges, for serving (optional)

Fresh thyme or rosemary sprigs, for garnish (optional)

1. Preheat the oven to 450 degrees F.

2. Melt the butter in a 12-inch skillet over medium heat. Turn off the heat. Pour out all of the butter except what clings to the skillet. Reserve the melted butter.

3. Slice each potato into ⅛-inch-thick slices, cutting most but not all the way down to leave the potato intact. Arrange the potatoes in a single layer in the skillet. Fit the potatoes in the skillet—6 will have space around them to brown and 8 will be tighter. Brush the potatoes liberally with the reserved melted butter. Sprinkle the tops of the potatoes with salt and pepper and a dusting of chili powder or harissa.

4. Roast until the potatoes are well browned, 40 to 45 minutes. Remove the skillet from the oven and drizzle each potato with a little maple syrup. Return the skillet to the oven and roast until the tops glaze, 5 to 8 minutes more.

5. Serve with wedges of lime for squeezing on top or garnish with fresh herb sprigs.

How to Clean This Pan after Roasting

The long roasting of sweet potatoes and added maple syrup can make for a sticky pan. The best way to clean your cast-iron skillet after making this recipe is to fill it with about ½ inch of water. Heat the pan over medium heat until the water nearly boils, and scrape up the sticky bits with a metal spatula. Dump out the water and wash the skillet clean as you normally would.

ROASTED BUTTERNUT SLICES
with Lavender Honey

MAKES 4 TO 6 SERVINGS / Prep: 15 minutes / Cook: 24 to 31 minutes

Less is more in this perfectly flavored vegetable side dish in which the distinct, seasonal flavor of roasted butternut squash shines. All you need is olive oil and kosher salt for seasoning, but that brushing of lavender honey is such a nice touch. Can't find lavender honey? Use wildflower honey instead.

1 (1¼- to 1½-pound) butternut squash

1 tablespoon olive oil

2 tablespoons lavender honey

Kosher salt

1. Preheat the oven to 425 degrees F.

2. Cut the squash in half lengthwise. Scoop out the seeds and fibrous interior from the hollow and discard. Cut each half lengthwise into three slices.

3. Heat a 12-inch skillet over medium heat for 2 minutes, or until it nearly smokes. Add the oil and tilt the skillet to spread the oil evenly on the bottom. Add the unpeeled squash slices, cut-side down, to the skillet. Let cook for 2 to 3 minutes on each cut side, until well browned. Turn off the heat. Turn the slices upright (peel-side down). Brush with the honey and sprinkle with salt.

4. Place the skillet in the oven and bake until the squash is fork-tender, 20 to 25 minutes. Serve hot.

How to Make Roasted Butternut Squash Soup from Leftovers

Make a double batch of roasted butternut squash and enjoy one batch as is. For the second batch, omit the lavender honey. Let the roasted squash cool, then scrape the cooked squash from the peel into a saucepan. Cover with chicken or vegetable broth. Heat until bubbling, then reduce the heat to a simmer and add a splash of cream. Use an immersion blender to purée the soup right in the pan. Taste for seasoning, adding salt, black pepper, a little grated nutmeg, or pinch of curry powder. Or, add sweetness with a little brown sugar, honey, or fig preserves. Add more broth if needed to thin out the soup. Serve warm with toasted bread.

CHARRED CORN
Salad

MAKES 6 SERVINGS / Prep: About 50 minutes

This festive salad features the flavors of Mexican street corn. From the corn to the tangy lime dressing to the toppings of chiles, cucumbers, radishes, and cilantro, this is a party in a bowl. It is perfect for potlucks when corn is coming into season. When you cut the corn off the cobs, try to keep the kernels together in slabs, which look beautiful in the bowl.

1 tablespoon vegetable oil, plus more if needed

8 ears white and/or yellow corn, husks and silk removed

¼ cup chopped green onions

DRESSING

3 tablespoons fresh lime juice (from 2 medium limes)

2 tablespoons olive oil, plus more if needed

¼ teaspoon ground ancho chile

Salt and freshly ground black pepper

TOPPINGS

1 cup chopped yellow and red cherry tomatoes

½ cup peeled and diced cucumber

¼ cup thinly sliced radishes

1 teaspoon minced fresh jalapeño pepper

½ cup crumbled cotija cheese

¼ cup fresh cilantro leaves

1. Heat a 12-inch skillet over medium-high heat until smoking, 3 to 4 minutes. Pour the oil into the pan. Add 4 ears of corn to the pan and cook, turning with tongs, until they are charred to your liking, 10 to 15 minutes. Remove the corn and repeat with the remaining 4 ears.

2. When cool enough to handle, stand each ear of corn in a bowl and slice the kernels off the cobs, keeping the corn together in a slab as much as possible. Fold in the green onions.

3. For the dressing, in a small bowl, whisk together the lime juice, olive oil, and ground ancho and season with salt and pepper. Pour over the corn mixture.

4. To serve, transfer the corn and green onions to a shallow bowl. Reserve any dressing remaining in the bottom of the bowl. Top the corn with the tomatoes, cucumbers, radishes, jalapeño, cotija, and cilantro. Pour any remaining dressing over the top; if there isn't any remaining dressing, drizzle the top with olive oil. Serve.

> GILD THE LILY: GRILLED SHRIMP
> AND CORN SALAD
>
> Top the salad with grilled or seared shrimp
> or fresh crabmeat.

FRIED RICE
Blueprint

MAKES 2 SERVINGS / Prep: 10 minutes / Cook: 8 to 10 minutes

I intentionally cook too much rice just so I can have the pleasure of eating fried rice the next day. I did this when my kids were younger, and they loved the haphazard combinations I would throw in that skillet. Now that they're gone, fried rice is just the right last-minute meal for two. The trick is to use a good bit of oil to keep the skillet greased so the egg doesn't stick. As this is a blueprint recipe, feel free to add whatever veggies you have on hand—preferably those that have crunch and color, such as carrots, bell peppers, okra, and green beans. You can turn this into a meal by sautéing chopped shrimp or chicken along with the onion.

2 tablespoons vegetable oil, plus more as needed

½ cup finely chopped onion

1 cup finely chopped fresh or frozen veggies

Soy sauce or teriyaki sauce

Hot pepper sauce (optional)

2 cups cooked rice

1 large egg

Freshly ground black pepper

Fresh cilantro leaves and/or sliced jalapeño peppers, for garnish (optional)

1. Heat the oil in a 12-inch skillet over medium heat. Add the onion and sauté until it turns translucent, 3 to 4 minutes. Add the veggies and cook for 3 to 4 minutes (or less if using frozen, just to warm through). Season with 1 teaspoon soy sauce and a dash of hot sauce, if you like.

2. Add the cooked rice and stir to combine, adding a little more oil if the rice sticks to the pan. Add another dash of soy sauce. In a small bowl, beat the egg with a fork to break up the yolk, then gradually pour the egg into the skillet, stirring to scramble the egg and blend it into the rice. Season again with soy sauce and a few grinds of black pepper. Garnish with cilantro and/or jalapeño, if desired. Serve at once.

GLAZED CARROTS
Like Mom Made

MAKES 6 SERVINGS / Prep: 15 minutes / Cook: 12 to 15 minutes

While roasted carrots are sweet and delicious, they often shrink so much that I don't get to enjoy the full carrot experience. So, I make them in my skillet the way my mom taught me. This is a brilliant method that you can use for other crisp vegetables, like okra, that benefit from braising to soften them. Use orange carrots or carrots of all colors. To turn this into a meal, serve the carrots on a generous spoonful of plain Greek yogurt or stracciatella, the soft fresh cheese at the center of burrata.

1 pound carrots

2 tablespoons unsalted butter, cut into cubes

1 tablespoon sugar

½ teaspoon kosher salt

Freshly ground black pepper

½ cup water

Grated zest and juice of 1 small lemon

Chopped fresh dill or flat-leaf parsley, for garnish

1. Peel the carrots, but leave the tops on for presentation, if you like. Leave the smaller ones whole, but slice the larger ones in half lengthwise.

2. Spread out the carrots in a single layer in a 12-inch skillet and top with the butter, sugar, salt, and a few grinds of pepper. Pour the water into the skillet. Bring the water to a boil over medium-high heat, then reduce the heat to low. Cover the skillet and let simmer until the carrots are fork-tender and the water has almost evaporated, 12 to 15 minutes. Turn off the heat.

3. Remove the lid from the skillet and add the lemon zest and 1 to 2 tablespoons lemon juice. Stir and let the juices bubble. Test the carrots for doneness. If the carrots are not done, add a little more water and turn the heat back on until they are done.

4. Garnish the carrots with chopped dill or parsley and serve at once.

SKILLET TAHDIG

MAKES 6 TO 8 SERVINGS

Prep: 10 minutes / Soak: 30 minutes / Cook: 53 to 58 minutes

Who doesn't like crispy pan scraps? This Iranian recipe is designed to provide you with not only golden, crispy rice at the bottom of the pot, but also steamed rice above it. *Tahdig*, which in Farsi means "bottom of the pot," is easily prepared in the iron skillet with a lid. You first parboil basmati rice, then you pack some of the rice in the bottom of the greased skillet and mound the rest on top. The domed cast-iron or tempered glass lid goes on and the heat under the skillet crisps the bottom. When the tahdig is done, you invert it onto a platter so that the cooked rice is covered with a disk of crispy browned rice. Flavor just with salt or with saffron or turmeric, if you like. Some variations call for adding bread or potatoes or yogurt to bind the bottom rice, but I have found if you follow the directions, you don't need all that.

2 cups white basmati rice

Kosher salt

5 tablespoons coconut oil or unsalted butter

1. Put the rice in a large bowl and cover with water. Let the rice soak for 30 minutes. Drain the rice through a sieve and run fresh cold water over it to rinse. Set aside.

2. Fill a large pot with 6 cups of water, add 1 tablespoon salt, and bring to a boil over medium-high heat. Stir in the rice, bring back to a boil, and cook uncovered until the rice is al dente, 4 to 5 minutes. Drain the rice and rinse under cold water.

3. Melt the coconut oil or butter in a 12-inch skillet over low heat. Measure out 2 cups of the rice and pack it into the bottom of the skillet, pressing it into place with the measuring cup. Sprinkle the rice with salt. Spoon the rest of the rice on top, forming it into a low pyramid (low enough for the skillet lid to fit over). Poke a few holes in the sides of the pyramid with the end of a spoon so that steam can escape. (The bottom rice layer will crisp, and this upper rice will steam.) Cover the skillet. Turn the heat to medium and cook for 10 minutes. Remove the lid. Fold a thin dish towel and place it on top of the rice. Replace the lid. Reduce the heat to the lowest setting and cook until the bottom is browned and crisp, 35 to 40 minutes.

4. To serve, remove the lid from the skillet swiftly so that the steam that collects inside the skillet is poured off and not back into the skillet. Scoop the steamed rice onto a platter. Run a knife around the edges of the skillet and under the crisp bottom. Flip the skillet upside down over the platter of rice so that the crispy layer is on top. Serve at once.

BAKED SKILLET APPLES
with Brown Sugar and Cinnamon

MAKES 6 SERVINGS / Prep: 15 minutes / Bake: 2 hours

One of the joys of fall is welcoming fresh, local apples, and apples and skillets go hand in hand. If you think back on our country's history and the wealth of apple recipes that the generations before us made in their skillets—apple butter and apple stack cake come to mind—you'll see the connection. Here is a very lazy method for baking apples in a skillet. Once you have the apples prepped, the oven does most of the work. You will need to check to make sure a little water stays in the bottom of the skillet to keep the apples from sticking and to protect the "sauce" that accumulates in the skillet as the apples, spices, butter, and sugar cook down and caramelize. Serve as a side dish to roasts or as dessert with a scoop of vanilla ice cream or yogurt.

6 medium Honeycrisp, Jonathan,
or Winesap apples, cored

3 tablespoons unsalted butter,
cut into 6 pieces

¾ cup lightly packed light brown sugar

1½ teaspoons salt

½ teaspoon ground cinnamon,
plus more as needed

1. Preheat the oven to 350 degrees F.

2. Stand the apples in a 12-inch skillet. If necessary, cut off a thin slice from the rounded bottom of the apples to keep them upright in the skillet. (Be careful not to cut into the cavity that will hold all the butter and sugar.)

3. Place a piece of butter in each apple cavity. Add 1 rounded tablespoon brown sugar and ¼ teaspoon salt to each. Sprinkle the tops of the apples generously with cinnamon.

4. Pour about ½ cup water into the bottom of the skillet to prevent the apples from sticking and to provide steam to keep the apples plump and moist as they bake.

5. Bake until the apples are browned and tender, about 2 hours. Check the skillet every 30 minutes to make sure there is a thin layer of water in the bottom, and add another ½ cup as needed.

6. Carefully remove the apples from the skillet, taking care not to tip over the butter and brown sugar juices inside the cavity. Pour the pan juices from the skillet over the apples before serving.

This chapter shows off all the ways the skillet can get dinner on the table. I begin with vegetarian recipes, move into chicken, follow with seafood, and end with the meats—beef, lamb, and pork. When you think about it, creating a main dish to feed your family or a group of friends is what the skillet has always done well. It has been the trusted pan to fry chicken, and now it is the pan in which you sear steak better than your favorite restaurant. It handles seafood with intensity but also care, cooking halibut, shrimp, salmon, or even freshly caught trout over the fire. It is the pan where you sear cauliflower, fry eggplant, and simmer a ragout of chickpeas. The possibilities for meatless meals are endless, from baked mac and cheese to a to-die-for eggplant parm. From stratas to pot pies to hearty casseroles like shepherd's pie, the skillet bakes as well as it fries cheeseburgers or roasts mussels with white wine and butter. There really isn't anything on your dinner list that the skillet can't accomplish. So let's get cooking.

CHAPTER 5
MAINS

Vegetarian Skillet Suppers

Chicken in the Skillet

Seafood in the Pan

Steaks, Chops, Roasts & More

Nancy's
VEGETARIAN PAELLA

MAKES 6 TO 8 SERVINGS / Prep: 25 minutes / Cook: 48 to 66 minutes

My friend Nancy made this most delicious one-dish supper for a recent potluck. She cooked the rice in vegetable broth with tomato paste, paprika, saffron, and wine. And for the topping, she cut a head of cauliflower into florets and roasted them with peppers until browned. This is a recipe made for the skillet, and it's adaptable to what's in your fridge, too.

ROASTED VEGGIES

1 small head cauliflower or broccoli, cut into florets

½ large red onion, peeled and diced

1 sweet red bell pepper, seeded and cut into ¼-inch strips

3 tablespoons olive oil

Salt and freshly ground black pepper

TOMATO-SAFFRON RICE

2 cups vegetable broth

¼ cup dry red wine

1 tablespoon tomato paste

1 tablespoon sweet paprika

Pinch saffron threads

1 tablespoon unsalted butter

1 tablespoon olive oil

½ medium onion, peeled and finely chopped

3 cloves garlic, peeled and minced

1¼ cups basmati rice

Salt and freshly ground black pepper

¼ cup chopped fresh flat-leaf parsley

1. Preheat the oven to 400 degrees F.

2. For the roasted veggies, toss the cauliflower, onion, and red pepper in a large bowl with the olive oil. Season with salt and pepper. Transfer the veggies to a 12-inch skillet and roast, tossing occasionally, until the cauliflower has browned, 20 to 25 minutes. Return the veggies to the same bowl. Set aside.

3. To make the rice, whisk together the broth, wine, tomato paste, paprika, and saffron in a large glass measuring cup or bowl. Set aside.

4. Heat the butter and olive oil in the skillet over medium heat. When the butter has melted, add the onion and garlic and sauté until soft, 3 to 4 minutes. Add the rice and stir to coat the grains with oil. Pour in the vegetable broth mixture and cook until the liquid comes to a boil, then reduce the heat to low, cover, and simmer until the rice is nearly done, 15 minutes.

5. Uncover the skillet and add the roasted veggies on top of the rice. Place the skillet in the oven to finish cooking the rice and heat through, 10 to 12 minutes. Season with salt and pepper, garnish with chopped parsley, and serve.

Skillet
EGGPLANT PARMESAN

MAKES 8 SERVINGS / Prep: 40 minutes / Cook: 40 to 45 minutes

You know the feeling when you've made a recipe so many times it is committed to memory? That's how I feel about this eggplant Parmesan. But the first time I made it was an eye-opener, as I had never fried eggplant slices dipped in egg first. Since then, I will forever extol the benefit of an egg batter when prepping eggplant, to help bind the eggplant with the other ingredients. And the skillet is a natural here, seamlessly moving from frying into baking.

2 (24- to 26-ounce) jars tomato-based pasta sauce

¼ cup dry red wine

4 cloves garlic, peeled and minced

½ cup torn fresh basil leaves

1 cup olive or vegetable oil, plus more if needed

4 large eggs

Salt and freshly ground black pepper

2 (1½-pound) eggplants, peeled and cut crosswise into ¼-inch slices

3 cups shredded mozzarella cheese

1 cup grated Parmesan cheese

1. Combine the pasta sauce, wine, garlic, and basil in a small saucepan and bring to a simmer over medium-low heat. Cook, stirring occasionally, for 10 to 15 minutes.

2. Meanwhile, heat ½ cup of the oil in a 12-inch skillet over medium-high heat until it reaches 350 degrees F. Crack the eggs into a shallow bowl, season with salt and pepper, and lightly beat with a fork. Arrange a double thickness of paper towels or a sheet of brown paper on the counter near the skillet.

3. Add two or three eggplant slices to the beaten eggs and turn them to coat. Using a fork, transfer the eggplant to the hot oil and fry until golden brown on both sides, about 1 minute per side. Drain on the paper towels and repeat with the remaining eggplant, wiping out the pan when the oil darkens, and adding more oil as needed.

4. Once all the eggplant slices have been fried, pour off all the oil from the pan. Wipe it dry with paper towels. Preheat the oven to 375 degrees F.

5. Arrange a third of the eggplant slices in the bottom of the skillet, overlapping them as needed. Pour a third of the sauce over the eggplant, spreading it out evenly with a spatula. Scatter 1 cup of the mozzarella and ⅓ cup of the Parmesan over the sauce. Repeat with the remaining eggplant, sauce, and cheeses, making two more layers. Lightly cover the skillet with aluminum foil and place the skillet in the oven.

6. Bake the mixture for 30 minutes. Remove the foil and continue baking until the sauce is bubbling and the cheese has melted, 10 to 15 minutes more. Let the eggplant rest for 5 minutes before serving.

MUSHROOM AND CHEDDAR
Dinner Strata

MAKES 8 SERVINGS / Prep: 20 minutes / Cook: 45 to 50 minutes

Strata may be one of my favorite recipes to prepare for brunch, but it makes a terrific one-dish vegetarian dinner, too. This skillet recipe is based on our family strata formula. (Yes, we love strata so much that we have our own formula!) If you aren't crazy about mushrooms, substitute sliced zucchini instead. And feel free to change up the cheeses, opting for Gruyère or Comte. Serve a green salad to the side.

1 tablespoon olive oil

1 tablespoon unsalted butter

1 cup minced green onions

2 cups sliced cremini mushrooms

2 cloves garlic, peeled and thinly sliced

Pinch dried or fresh thyme

Salt and freshly ground black pepper

10 slices sourdough or Italian-style bread, cut into 1-inch cubes (5 packed cups)

2 cups (8 ounces) shredded sharp white Cheddar cheese, divided use

½ cup grated Parmesan cheese, divided use

6 large eggs

3 cups whole milk

1 teaspoon Dijon mustard

1. Preheat the oven to 350 degrees F.

2. Heat the olive oil and butter in a 12-inch skillet over medium heat. Add the green onions, mushrooms, and garlic and cook until the mushrooms give off their liquid, about 4 minutes. Reduce the heat to low and continue to cook, without stirring, until they turn golden. Turn off the heat, add the thyme, and season with salt and pepper. Transfer the mushroom mixture to a medium bowl. Leave the oil that remains in the skillet.

3. Scatter half of the bread cubes in the skillet. Top with 1½ cups of the Cheddar and ¼ cup of the Parmesan. Top with the mushroom mixture. Add the remaining bread cubes.

4. In a medium bowl, whisk together the eggs, milk, and mustard. Pour the egg mixture over the bread cubes and press down on them to submerge them in the liquid. Scatter the remaining ½ cup Cheddar and ¼ cup Parmesan on top.

5. Bake until the strata is golden brown, 45 to 50 minutes. Serve at once.

How to Reheat the Leftovers

Transfer any leftover strata to a glass dish, cover with aluminum foil, and refrigerate overnight. When ready to reheat, preheat the oven to 350 degrees F. Add 2 or 3 tablespoons water to the dish and replace the foil. Reheat until warmed through, about 20 minutes.

FAMILY-STYLE MEXICAN
Lasagna

MAKES 6 TO 8 SERVINGS / Prep: 25 minutes / Cook: 30 to 35 minutes

We used to make this lasagna with ground beef, and then we switched to turkey. And now we've switched to beans, either pinto or black. It's such a flavorful and substantial main dish, and I love how the flavors and corn tortillas bake together into ooey-gooey cheesy goodness in the iron skillet! For added drama, arrange a fresh salad garnish of baby greens, sliced avocado, and sliced yellow tomatoes on top.

1 tablespoon olive oil

½ cup chopped onion

½ cup chopped red bell pepper

1 (15- to 16-ounce) can pinto or black beans, rinsed and drained

1 (15-ounce) can tomato sauce

1 cup salsa

1 tablespoon chili powder

2 teaspoons ground cumin

1 (16-ounce) container low-fat, small-curd cottage cheese

2 large eggs, lightly beaten

¼ cup grated Parmesan cheese

2 cloves garlic, peeled and minced

1 teaspoon dried oregano

12 (5- to 6-inch) corn tortillas, torn into quarters

1 cup shredded Cheddar or Monterey Jack cheese

1. Preheat the oven to 375 degrees F.

2. Heat the olive oil in a 12-inch skillet over medium heat. Add the onion and bell pepper and sauté until soft, 2 to 3 minutes. Add the beans, tomato sauce, salsa, chili powder, and cumin and stir to combine. Reduce the heat to low and let the mixture simmer until the flavors come together, 2 to 3 minutes. Turn off the heat and transfer the bean mixture to a large bowl. Wipe out the skillet.

3. In a medium bowl, combine the cottage cheese, eggs, Parmesan, garlic, and oregano. Set aside.

4. To assemble the lasagna, scatter half of the torn tortillas in the bottom of the skillet. Spoon on half of the bean mixture. Spoon all of the cottage cheese mixture over the top, and spread it out evenly. Scatter the remaining torn tortillas on top of the cottage cheese mixture. Top with the remaining bean mixture. Cover the skillet with a lid or with aluminum foil.

5. Bake the lasagna until it bubbles and is cooked through, 30 to 35 minutes. Remove the skillet from the oven. Remove the lid or foil and sprinkle the Cheddar cheese over the top. Replace the lid or foil and let the lasagna rest for 20 minutes before serving. Serve from the skillet at the table.

EASY TORTILLA
Espanola

MAKES 6 TO 8 SERVINGS / Prep: 25 minutes / Cook: 24 to 26 minutes

In Spain, this egg and potato omelet is served as a tapa with sherry. Regardless of where you live, this satisfying dish is ready when you are, ready to nourish, stave off hunger, and get you through to the next meal. And the simplicity of this recipe is largely to credit, because it just involves poaching onions and potatoes in olive oil, adding beaten eggs, and cooking as you might an omelet. Unlike some recipes where you flip the half-cooked tortilla onto a plate and slide it back in the skillet to cook on the other side, I suggest you just broil it to doneness on side two.

2 pounds russet potatoes

¾ cup olive oil

1 medium onion, peeled and thinly sliced

8 large eggs

Kosher salt and freshly ground black pepper

1. Peel the potatoes and cut into ⅛-inch-thick slices using a sharp knife or mandoline.

2. Heat the olive oil in a 12-inch skillet over medium heat. When the oil shimmers, add the potato and onion slices to the skillet. Sauté until soft, 18 to 20 minutes. Remove the skillet from the heat and drain off the oil from the pan (see Note).

3. Preheat the broiler with a rack about 6 inches away from the heat source.

4. In a large bowl, whisk the eggs with a pinch of salt. Add the eggs to the skillet and stir to combine. Return the skillet to medium heat and let the eggs cook until lightly browned on the underside, about 3 minutes.

5. Place the skillet under the broiler and broil until the top of the tortilla turns light brown, less than 2 minutes.

6. Season the tortilla with salt and pepper. Slide a spatula under the tortilla and slide it onto a serving plate, or cut the tortilla into wedges and serve it right from the pan.

NOTE: You can strain the leftover olive oil, refrigerate, and use to cook other recipes.

CURRIED CHICKPEA
Ragout

MAKES 6 TO 8 SERVINGS / Prep: 25 minutes / Cook: 39 to 45 minutes

Chickpeas are too often relegated just to hummus, yet they're fully worthy of making the meal. I like to stew them with onions and tomatoes and add bold, bright flavors—here I use a combination of cumin, za'atar, and cayenne pepper. The spices balance with the natural sweetness of the carrots, onions, and raisins. Serve this with couscous Moroccan-style, or with steamed rice. Add steamed spinach for a colorful and healthy accompaniment. And if you like, serve Cucumber Raita (page 7) on top.

3 tablespoons olive oil

1½ cups chopped onions

1 cup chopped carrots

½ cup chopped red bell pepper

2 cloves garlic, peeled and minced

2 teaspoons ground cumin

1 teaspoon za'atar

¼ teaspoon cayenne pepper

2 (15-ounce) cans chickpeas, rinsed and drained (or cook from dried, see Note)

2 cups vegetable broth

1 (14- to 15-ounce) can diced tomatoes, undrained

¼ cup yellow raisins

Salt and freshly ground black pepper

1. Heat the oil in a 12-inch skillet over medium heat. When it is hot, add the onions, carrots, bell pepper, and garlic. Cook, stirring often, until the onions soften, 4 to 5 minutes. Stir in the cumin, za'atar, and cayenne. Add the chickpeas, broth, tomatoes with their juices, and raisins, and season with salt and black pepper.

2. Bring the mixture to a boil, then reduce the heat to a simmer, cover, and cook until the vegetables are tender, the flavors have combined, and the pan juices have naturally thickened, 35 to 40 minutes. Serve.

NOTE: To cook chickpeas from scratch, put 8 ounces dried chickpeas in a large bowl and pour boiling water over to cover them by 1 inch. Let rest for 1 hour. Drain and rinse the chickpeas, drain again, and put them in a saucepan. Pour in cold water to cover by 1 inch. Add a quarter onion and a bay leaf. Bring to a boil, then reduce the heat to simmer, cover, and cook until tender, about 1½ hours. Drain and discard the bay leaf. You should have about 3½ cups.

CAROLINA SUCCOTASH
with Fried Okra Slices

MAKES 6 TO 8 SERVINGS / Prep and Cook: 45 to 50 minutes

Southerners may claim succotash as their own, but really it's an old East Coast recipe with Native American roots. The critical ingredients are beans (or anything in the pea family) and corn. Down in South Carolina and the Low Country, okra is added, either stewed along with the vegetables or fried and placed on top. You can also add chopped tomatoes, fresh herbs, and bacon. Seafood lovers know that succotash is a natural partner to crab cakes and shrimp. This rendition reflects the Low Country flavors and brings in the bright freshness of lime and cilantro in the dressing. Cubes of avocado added on top really make this a meal.

CILANTRO-LIME DRESSING

2 tablespoons fresh lime juice
(from 2 limes)

1 tablespoon honey

1 teaspoon hot pepper sauce

1 clove garlic, peeled and minced

Salt and freshly ground black pepper

⅓ cup olive oil

¼ cup chopped fresh cilantro

VEGETABLES

1 cup purple-hull peas, black-eyed peas,
or baby lima beans (fresh or frozen)

Salt and freshly ground black pepper

1 tablespoon olive oil

½ cup finely minced onion

2 cups fresh white corn kernels (from 3 ears)

1 cup halved cherry or grape tomatoes

GARNISH

1 large avocado, peeled, pitted, and cubed

2 tablespoons chopped fresh cilantro
or flat-leaf parsley (optional)

Fried okra slices (see How to Fry Okra
Like a Southerner, page 8)

1. For the dressing, in a small bowl, whisk together the lime juice, honey, hot sauce, and garlic. Season with salt and pepper. Whisk in the olive oil in a steady stream until the vinaigrette thickens. Fold in the cilantro and set aside.

2. For the vegetables, put the peas in a small saucepan, add a pinch of salt, and pour in cold water to cover by 1 inch. Bring the water to a boil over medium-high heat, then reduce the heat and simmer until the peas are cooked through, 25 to 30 minutes. Drain and transfer the peas to a large bowl.

3. Heat the olive oil in a 12-inch skillet over medium heat. Add the onion and sauté until soft, 2 to 3 minutes. Stir in the corn, reduce the heat to low, and cook until the corn is just cooked through, 3 to 4 minutes. Transfer the corn and onion mixture to the bowl with the peas. Add the tomatoes and stir gently to mix the ingredients. Season with salt and pepper.

4. Spoon the corn and pea mixture onto a long platter. Drizzle with the dressing, and garnish the top with avocado, fresh herbs (if desired), and fried okra.

NOTE: Keep frozen black-eyed peas and white corn in the freezer to make this main dish regardless of the season.

Skillet
MAC AND CHEESE

MAKES 8 SERVINGS / Prep: 45 minutes / Bake: 10 to 12 minutes

Children gladly offer their opinion—and disapproval—of food if it doesn't suit them. I learned this by trying to please my children with homemade mac and cheese. Whether saucy, baked, crispy on top, or doctored up from the box, I just never seemed able to make a mac and cheese that suited them all—until I created this recipe. And when sliced tomatoes are placed underneath the bread crumb topping, it's a beautiful sight to behold! I promise your kids will love it.

PASTA

8 ounces macaroni or whole wheat penne rigate

1 teaspoon salt

TOPPING

1 tablespoon unsalted butter

1 tablespoon olive oil

1 cup panko bread crumbs

¼ cup grated Parmesan cheese

Salt and freshly ground black pepper

SAUCE

4 tablespoons unsalted butter

3 tablespoons all-purpose flour

2 cups whole milk

½ cup heavy cream

¼ teaspoon ground nutmeg

¼ teaspoon cayenne pepper

¼ cup grated Parmesan cheese

1 cup shredded extra sharp Cheddar cheese

1 cup shredded mild Cheddar cheese

Salt and freshly ground black pepper

2 large ripe tomatoes, peeled and sliced (optional)

1. Bring a large pot of water to a boil over high heat. Add the pasta and salt and cook until al dente, 7 to 8 minutes. Drain the pasta and run cold water over it to stop the cooking process. Drain the pasta again, and set aside.

2. Preheat the oven to 450 degrees F.

3. For the topping, heat the butter and oil in a 12-inch skillet over medium heat. Stir in the panko and cook until it turns golden brown, about 4 minutes. Transfer the panko to a small bowl. Stir in the Parmesan, then season with salt and black pepper.

4. For the sauce, wipe out the skillet. Add the butter and let it melt over low heat. Whisk in the flour until smooth. Whisk in the milk and cream, a third at a time, whisking each time until smooth. Adjust the heat under the skillet so that the sauce barely simmers as it thickens. When the sauce has cooked for 7 to 8 minutes, turn off the heat and season the sauce with the nutmeg and cayenne. Add the cheeses, a bit at a time, stirring until all the cheese has melted. Taste the sauce and season with salt and black pepper.

5. Fold the pasta into the sauce. Wipe the edges of the skillet clean with a paper towel. If desired, place slices of fresh tomato on top of the pasta and sauce. Scatter the bread crumbs on top. Bake until the mac and cheese is bubbly and the topping is well browned, 10 to 12 minutes. Serve from the skillet.

PICADILLO STUFFED PEPPERS
with Quinoa

MAKES 6 SERVINGS / Prep: 35 minutes / Bake: 33 to 39 minutes

One of the most beautiful recipes to make in an iron skillet is stuffed peppers. The bright colors of the peppers contrast with the black skillet, and when the peppers cook and caramelize around the edges, they have a gorgeous "don't mess with me" appearance. You almost hate to disturb them to eat! My mother used to bake stuffed peppers with ground beef and rice, and this is a modern riff on that 1960s recipe, featuring quinoa, onion, zucchini, oregano, garlic, and raisins. Back then, everyone parboiled the peppers before baking. Now, we know that extra step isn't necessary, and you can get more flavor by letting the peppers roast at a high heat until tender.

2 tablespoons olive oil,
plus more for brushing

1 cup finely minced onion

1 cup finely minced zucchini

2 mild peppers (such as Jimmy Nardello), minced (about 2 tablespoons)

3 cloves garlic, peeled and minced

1 teaspoon dried oregano

½ teaspoon kosher salt

¼ teaspoon cayenne pepper

Freshly ground black pepper

1 (24- to 26-ounce) jar tomato-based pasta sauce

1 tablespoon Worcestershire sauce

½ cup golden or dark raisins

¼ cup sliced green olives or Kalamata olives

2 cups cooked quinoa (see Note)

6 large bell peppers, preferably a mix of different colors

¼ cup crumbled cotija or feta cheese (optional)

Fresh oregano leaves

1. Preheat the oven to 400 degrees F.

2. Heat the olive oil in a 12-inch skillet over medium heat. Add the onion, zucchini, mild peppers, and garlic and sauté until soft, 2 to 3 minutes. Add the oregano, salt, cayenne, and a few grinds of black pepper and stir to combine. Add the pasta sauce, Worcestershire sauce, raisins, and olives and cook until the mixture reduces slightly and the flavors come together, 7 to 8 minutes. Transfer the mixture to a large mixing bowl. Fold in the quinoa and set aside.

3. Wipe out the skillet. Remove the stem and slice off the top ½ inch of each bell pepper. Remove the seeds and ribs. If necessary, slice off a tiny bit from the curved bottom of each pepper so they can sit upright. Stand the bell peppers in the skillet. Brush the outsides of the peppers with olive oil. With a large spoon or dry measuring cup, fill each pepper with ½ to 1 cup of the quinoa mixture.

4. Place the skillet in the oven and bake until the peppers are soft and browned on the outside and the filling is bubbling, 30 to 35 minutes. Remove the pan from the oven. Sprinkle with the cheese, if desired, and return to the oven to let the cheese melt slightly, 3 to 4 minutes. Sprinkle the top with fresh oregano and serve.

NOTE: To cook quinoa, in a small saucepan, bring 1 cup water to a boil. Add a pinch of salt and ½ cup rinsed quinoa. Bring the water back to a boil, then reduce the heat, cover, and let simmer until all of the water has been absorbed, 10 to 12 minutes. Remove the lid from the pan and fluff the quinoa with a fork. This yields about 2 cups quinoa.

SEARED BROCCOLI ALFREDO
with Cavatappi

MAKES 6 SERVINGS / Prep: 30 minutes / Cook: 22 to 26 minutes

Whether it's date night or dinner with the kids, this recipe delivers with familiar flavors, all in one pan. First you sear the broccoli briefly over high heat in the skillet, then you make a fast cream reduction that turns into a cheesy Alfredo sauce. Choose a curvy pasta, or a pasta that has a hollow in it like shells or orecchiette, so you can be sure to get pasta, cheese sauce, and broccoli in every bite. Yum!

1 large bunch broccoli (about 1½ pounds)

3 tablespoons olive oil, divided use

½ cup thinly sliced onion

2 cups heavy cream

1½ cups shredded sharp white Cheddar cheese

½ cup grated Parmesan

Salt and freshly ground black pepper

12 ounces dried cavatappi (see Note)

1. Preheat the oven to 350 degrees F.

2. Trim off and discard the bottom ½ inch of the broccoli stem. Cut between the crown and stem to separate them. Peel the rest of the stem. Cut the stem into ¼-inch-thick slices, then slice those in half. Slice lengthwise through the crown to form flat spears. If any little florets break off, that's OK. Put the stems and florets in a large bowl and drizzle with 2 tablespoons of the olive oil. Toss to coat all the pieces.

3. Heat a 12-inch skillet over high heat until it smokes, 3 to 4 minutes. Add the broccoli and let char, 4 to 5 minutes, then turn with tongs and char the other side, 4 to 5 minutes. Scatter the onions over the top and use the tongs to nestle them into the broccoli. Place the pan in the oven and bake until the broccoli is just tender, 10 to 12 minutes.

4. Meanwhile, prepare the sauce. In a large saucepan, bring the cream to a boil over medium heat. Reduce the heat and let the cream simmer until it reduces by half, 7 to 8 minutes. Stir in the Cheddar and Parmesan cheeses and season with salt and pepper. Keep warm.

5. Check on the skillet of broccoli. Poke a small, sharp knife into one of the larger florets, and if it is tender, remove the skillet from the oven. If not, let it cook a little longer.

6. Bring a large pot of water to a boil over medium-high heat. Add the cavatappi and 1 teaspoon salt and cook until al dente, 8 to 9 minutes. Drain the cavatappi, reserving ½ cup of the cooking water. Drizzle the cavatappi with the remaining 1 tablespoon olive oil.

7. To serve—on a platter or on individual plates—begin with the pasta. If the sauce has thickened too much, whisk in some of the reserved pasta cooking water. Spoon the sauce over the pasta, and scatter the seared broccoli and onion on top.

NOTE: If you cannot find cavatappi—which is the corkscrew-shaped pasta—look for orecchiette or small shells.

FRENCH CHICKEN
in a Skillet

MAKES 6 TO 8 SERVINGS / Prep: 25 minutes / Cook: About 1 hour 35 minutes

The tradition of roasting chicken on top of bread to trap pan juices is old and belongs to many countries, not just France. I recall my resourceful grandmother doing this with roast beef. And the late chef Judy Rodgers created a legendary roasted chicken based on a similar idea—a salad of bread and currants was flavored with roasted chicken drippings. In this modern adaptation, after the chicken is bathed in lemon and olive oil, it roasts on top of the bread slices, which turn into croutons. If you like, replace the bread with quartered potatoes, adding them to the pan during the last 30 minutes. The spatchcock technique of removing the backbone from a whole chicken and flattening it is popular because it reduces the roasting time. For a complete meal, I add carrots and asparagus to the skillet.

1 whole chicken, preferably under 3 pounds (see Note)

Kosher salt and freshly ground black pepper

Grated zest and juice of 1 lemon

2 tablespoons olive oil

½ loaf French bread, cut on the diagonal into ½-inch slices

Fresh herb sprigs, such as rosemary or oregano (optional)

3 medium carrots, peeled and cut into matchsticks or thick slices

8 spears asparagus, trimmed

1. Preheat the oven to 375 degrees F.

2. In the sink, rinse the chicken inside and out and pat it dry with paper towels. With sharp kitchen shears or a boning knife, cut out the backbone of the chicken and discard. Lay the chicken out flat. With the heel of your hands, press down on the top of the chicken to flatten it. Place the chicken in a 13-by-9-inch glass casserole dish or on a rimmed baking sheet. Sprinkle both sides of the chicken generously with kosher salt and lightly with black pepper.

3. Scatter half of the lemon zest over the chicken and reserve the rest. Squeeze the lemon juice over the top of the chicken. Drizzle the chicken with the olive oil. Now flip the chicken with tongs, to collect pan juices and coat both sides with the zest, lemon juice, and olive oil.

4. Cover a 12-inch skillet completely with bread slices. If desired, place fresh herb sprigs on top of the bread. Place the chicken, breast-side up, on top of the bread.

5. Place the skillet in the oven and roast until the chicken is golden brown, about 1 hour 15 minutes. Pack the carrots around the edges of the pan and use a big spoon to ladle any pan juices over the carrots. Season with salt and pepper and sprinkle with the remaining lemon zest. Return the skillet to the oven and roast for 15 minutes, until the carrots are tender. Add the asparagus, ladling pan juices over them. Roast for 5 minutes more, until the asparagus is tender.

6. Remove the skillet from the oven. Let the chicken rest in the pan for 10 minutes. Slice and serve right from the skillet, including some vegetables and soaked bread croutons with each serving.

NOTE: It's not easy to find smaller chickens (that is, under 3 pounds) at the supermarket these days, but they are worth seeking out because they are more tender and cook more quickly.

STICKY CHICKEN THIGHS
with Ginger and Garlic

MAKES 6 SERVINGS

Prep: 20 minutes / Marinate: As little as 20 minutes or up to 4 hours / Cook: 55 to 60 minutes

The iron skillet loves recipes in which the marinade and sauce cook and caramelize in the pan. When this simple sauce of honey, soy sauce, garlic, and ginger simmers down, it gets syrupy and sticky. Chicken thighs are basted with these sticky pan juices, turning the chicken a gorgeous mahogany color. What's left of the sauce can be served over the chicken and rice and is even more delicious the next day.

2 pounds boneless, skinless
chicken thighs

½ cup honey (see Note)

½ cup reduced-sodium soy sauce

2 cloves garlic, peeled and minced

3 tablespoons grated fresh ginger

Steamed white rice, for serving

Green onion slivers, for garnish

1. Trim the chicken thighs of excess fat, and put them in a medium glass bowl or zipper-lock bag.

2. In a small bowl, whisk together the honey and soy sauce. Fold in the garlic and ginger. Pour the marinade mixture over the chicken thighs and turn to coat. Cover the bowl or seal the bag and let the chicken marinate at room temperature for 20 minutes or in the fridge for up to 4 hours.

3. Preheat the oven to 375 degrees F.

4. Pour the chicken and marinade into a 12-inch skillet. Tuck the edges of the chicken under to form rounded thighs that dome in the center. Place the skillet in the oven and bake for 20 minutes. Remove the skillet and turn the chicken, basting with the pan juices. Return to the oven for 20 minutes.

5. Remove the skillet from the oven and place it over medium-low heat. Let the chicken and marinade simmer, turning the chicken every 2 or 3 minutes, until the marinade thickens, 15 to 20 minutes. The chicken will have turned a mahogany color, and the juices will be syrupy and sticky. Serve with rice, and garnish with slivers of green onion.

NOTE: Spray a liquid measuring cup with vegetable oil before measuring honey. The oil keeps the honey from sticking to the cup.

Easy
PERI PERI CHICKEN

MAKES 6 TO 8 SERVINGS / Prep: 15 minutes / Bake: 35 to 40 minutes

This fast and fabulous recipe was created by accident. Last spring I bought rotisserie chickens to serve as a last-minute lunch for friends. When my husband and I were carving the birds, we noticed that some weren't cooked as much as we would like, so we decided to finish cooking them in the oven. But first I whipped up a quick, spicy blend of hot chiles, garlic, lemon, oregano, and olive oil, a riff on the peri peri chicken I had tasted in Portugal. In the oven, the seasoning glazed the chicken, and the chicken juices caramelized on the bottom of the skillet. When the crispy, flavorful chicken was served, everyone wanted the recipe! How could I tell them that I hadn't roasted the chicken? Serve with your favorite potato salad, grits, orzo salad, or couscous.

1 (4- to 5-pound) cooked rotisserie chicken

PERI PERI SEASONING

4 cloves garlic, peeled and minced

1 serrano or Thai red chile, chopped,
or ¼ teaspoon harissa seasoning

Grated zest and juice of 2 medium lemons

¼ cup olive oil

1 teaspoon dried oregano

¼ teaspoon paprika

Kosher salt and freshly ground black pepper

1. Preheat the oven to 375 degrees F.

2. Cut the leg and thigh portions off the chicken, and put them in a 12-inch skillet. Use sharp kitchen scissors or a boning knife to cut out the backbone; discard the backbone. Press down on the breast bone to flatten the breast halves, and cut between the two halves of the breast with the scissors to separate them. Put the breast halves with wings attached in the skillet.

3. In a small bowl, combine the garlic, chile, and lemon zest and juice. Whisk in the olive oil until well combined. Stir in the oregano and paprika and season with salt and pepper. Spoon this seasoning mixture over the top of the chicken pieces.

4. Place the pan in the oven and bake until the chicken is very tender and the skin has deeply browned, 35 to 40 minutes. Remove the skillet from the oven and let the chicken cool for 15 minutes before serving.

Mom's
CHICKEN TETRAZZINI

MAKES 8 TO 10 SERVINGS / Prep: 30 minutes / Bake: 25 to 30 minutes

In my childhood home, chicken Tetrazzini was for company. You stewed the hen, shredded it with warm vermicelli and a homemade Parmesan cream sauce, and then baked the casserole until bubbling around the edges. Just the sound of the name *Tetrazzini* evoked glamour and sophistication. The recipe was supposedly named for Italian opera soprano Luisa Tetrazzini, who toured America in the early 1900s. This comforting chicken casserole with the Italian name would become a part of the home recipe box and morph into the recipe I still prepare today in an iron skillet. You can cook the chicken the old-fashioned way, by simmering a whole chicken in water flavored with onion, bay leaves, salt, and pepper until done. Or, use leftover rotisserie chicken or roasted turkey after the holidays. Which means that chicken Tetrazzini is perfect any time of the year and for any occasion—with or without company.

8 ounces thin spaghetti or vermicelli

Salt and freshly ground black pepper

2 teaspoons olive oil

4 tablespoons unsalted butter

8 ounces mushrooms, sliced
(about 2 cups)

½ cup chopped onion

½ cup chopped celery

3 tablespoons all-purpose flour

2 cups reduced-sodium chicken broth

1 cup heavy cream

2 tablespoons dry sherry

1 cup grated Parmesan cheese,
divided use

¼ cup sliced green olives

3 cups chopped or shredded cooked chicken

¼ cup chopped pecans (optional)

1. Preheat the oven to 375 degrees F.

2. Bring a large pot of water to a boil over medium-high heat. Break the spaghetti in half. Stir the spaghetti and 1 teaspoon salt into the boiling water and cook until just done, 6 to 7 minutes. Drain the spaghetti well in a colander, shaking it to remove excess water. Toss it with the olive oil and set aside.

3. Melt the butter in a 12-inch skillet over medium heat. Add the mushrooms, onion, and celery and cook, stirring, until soft, 3 to 4 minutes. Reduce the heat to low and add the flour. Cook, stirring, for 1 minute. Add the chicken broth and cook, stirring, until it begins to thicken, 1 to 2 minutes. Add the cream and stir until combined. Add the sherry, season with salt and pepper, and cook, stirring, until the sauce comes just to a boil, about 2 minutes. Remove the pan from the heat and stir in ½ cup of the Parmesan and the olives. Fold in the chicken and the spaghetti. Smooth the top and sprinkle with the reserved Parmesan and the pecans (if using).

4. Place the skillet in the oven and bake the casserole until it is bubbling, 25 to 30 minutes. Remove from the oven, let it rest for 5 minutes, then serve.

MESSY CHICKEN
Enchiladas

MAKES 6 TO 8 SERVINGS / Prep: 40 minutes / Cook: About 1½ hours

Just the kind of recipe to show off how well an iron skillet goes from oven to table, these chicken enchiladas keep warm thanks to the skillet. And the skillet is a workhorse in this recipe. It goes from cooking the chicken to sautéing onions and peppers to simmering the enchilada sauce. This recipe comes from an old family friend. It's best if you cook your own chicken, but in a pinch you can use 4 cups shredded cooked rotisserie chicken and 1 cup canned chicken broth.

CHICKEN AND VEGETABLES

3 (8-ounce) bone-in, skin-on chicken breasts or 4 cups shredded cooked rotisserie chicken

1 bay leaf

Salt and freshly ground black pepper

2 tablespoons olive oil

1 medium onion, peeled and thinly sliced

2 medium or 1 large green or red bell pepper, cored, deveined, seeded and sliced (about 1 cup)

ENCHILADA SAUCE

2 tablespoons unsalted butter

½ cup finely chopped onion

1 (14.5-ounce) can diced Ro-Tel tomatoes, plain or with poblanos

1 cup chicken broth, homemade or canned

1 teaspoon ground cumin

1 cup sour cream or full-fat plain Greek yogurt

ASSEMBLY

1½ cups (6 ounces) shredded Cheddar cheese, divided use

1½ cups (6 ounces) shredded Monterey Jack cheese, divided use

8 (9-inch) flour tortillas

GARNISHES

Diced avocado

Sliced radishes

Shredded lettuce

Chopped tomato or pico de gallo

Cooked pinto beans

Fresh cilantro sprigs

1. For the chicken and vegetables, put the chicken breasts in a 12-inch skillet. Add the bay leaf, season with salt and pepper, and cover halfway with water. Cover the skillet and heat over medium-high heat until the water comes to a boil. Reduce the heat to low and let the chicken simmer until done, 40 to 45 minutes. Drain the chicken, discard the bay leaf, and reserve 1 cup of the broth. When the chicken is cool, shred it to yield about 4 cups meat. Discard the skin and bones.

2. Wipe out the skillet and heat the olive oil over medium heat. Add the onion and pepper and sauté until softened, 3 to 4 minutes. Transfer the onion and pepper to a plate. Wipe out the skillet.

3. Preheat the oven to 350 degrees F.

4. For the sauce, melt the butter in the skillet over medium heat. Add the onions and sauté until soft, 3 to 4 minutes. Add the tomatoes with their juices, chicken broth, and cumin and simmer until the sauce reduces slightly, 5 minutes. Transfer the contents to a large bowl and stir in the sour cream or yogurt. Wipe out the skillet.

5. Combine the shredded cheeses in a bowl. Lay out the tortillas on a work surface. Divide the chicken, sautéed onion and pepper, and 2 cups of the mixed cheese between the tortillas. Roll up each tortilla and place it seam-side down in the skillet to completely fill the skillet. Pour the sauce over the tortillas and sprinkle with the remaining 1 cup cheese.

6. Place the skillet in the oven and bake the enchiladas until they are bubbling and cooked through, 30 to 35 minutes. Remove the skillet from the oven, garnish as you like, and serve warm from the skillet.

CHICKEN AND RICE SKILLET SUPPER
Blueprint

MAKES 4 SERVINGS / Prep: 25 minutes / Bake: About 1 hour

Baked chicken and rice is one of those dishes that seems like it doesn't really need a recipe because it has so few ingredients. But because it's so simple, you've got to choose your ingredients carefully. Buy the best-quality chicken you can find—both organic and kosher chicken have good flavor. Use kosher or sea salt when seasoning. Use fresh bay leaves, not those dried-up, splintered leaves at the bottom of the spice jar, and cook the chicken and rice covered so that the juices—and real flavor—stay in the skillet. If you get this right the first time, then by all means, change it up the second. Add a pinch of saffron when you add the rice. Add some red pimentos. Add a tablespoon of tomato paste. Craving Cajun? Add slices of andouille sausage. The world is your baked chicken and rice skillet, so go for it!

2 bone-in, skin-on chicken breasts

2 bone-in, skin-on chicken thighs

Kosher salt and freshly ground black pepper

Creole seasoning

2 tablespoons vegetable oil

1 medium onion, peeled and quartered

4 carrots, peeled and cut into 2-inch matchsticks

2 large fresh bay leaves

½ cup dry white wine or water

¾ cup basmati or other long-grain white rice

¾ cup water

1 cup frozen peas (optional)

1. Preheat the oven to 350 degrees F.

2. Pat the chicken dry and season it with salt, pepper, and Creole seasoning.

3. Heat the oil in a 12-inch skillet over medium heat. When the oil is shimmering, add the chicken pieces, skin-side down. Let them cook until they are golden brown, 3 to 4 minutes. With tongs, turn the chicken to the other side and let cook until golden, 3 to 4 minutes. If desired, pick up the chicken with the tongs and sear the sides. Transfer the chicken to a plate and pour off the oil in the skillet, but do not scrape the bottom of the skillet.

4. Return the chicken to the skillet. Add the onion and carrots to the skillet and place the pan over medium heat to let the onion brown lightly, about 2 minutes. Add the bay leaves. Turn off the heat. Pour in the wine and use a wooden spoon to loosen any browned bits from the bottom of the skillet. Cover the skillet and place it in the oven.

5. Bake until the chicken is done, about 40 minutes. Remove the lid and scatter the rice around the chicken. Pour in the water. Replace the lid and return the skillet to the oven. Bake until the rice is done, 18 to 20 minutes.

6. Remove the skillet from the oven and place it, uncovered, over low heat for a few minutes, if desired, to evaporate any excess liquid in the pan. Turn off the heat. Add the frozen peas, replace the lid, and let the peas cook in the heat of the skillet. After 3 to 4 minutes, taste for seasoning and adjust with salt and pepper. Remove and discard the bay leaves. Serve.

CHICKEN CURRY
in a Hurry

MAKES 4 SERVINGS / Prep: 25 minutes / Cook: 10 to 15 minutes

Even when my children were young, they loved the exotic taste of curry. Maybe it was the apple and coconut sweetness or the aromatic basmati rice, or its bright come-get-me color that looked so fresh on the plate. Chicken curry became part of our weeknight dinner rotation, usually following a whole roasted chicken the night before. If I was in a hurry, I would begin the recipe with boneless chicken tenders or thighs. In this recipe I brown onions in the iron skillet and then add the chicken pieces, and finally pour in coconut milk, apples, and seasonings to quickly cook into a sauce. It's my unrefined, fast but fabulous version of korma, the northern Indian cooking sauce. To garnish, add toasted almond slices, fresh cilantro, coconut flakes, and mango chutney.

1 pound chicken tenders (about 12)
or boneless, skinless chicken thighs,
cut into 1-inch pieces

2 teaspoons curry powder

2 teaspoons ground cumin

Pinch cayenne pepper

Pinch kosher salt

2 tablespoons vegetable oil

1 medium onion, peeled and sliced

1 cup canned coconut milk (see Note)

1 tablespoon tomato paste
or tomato sauce

1 cup diced peeled apple

1 cinnamon stick

1 cup hot water, divided use

1 tablespoon heavy cream

Steamed basmati rice, for serving

GARNISH

2 tablespoons toasted almond slices

Fresh cilantro sprigs

Sweetened flaked coconut

Mango chutney

1. Put the chicken pieces in a small bowl and sprinkle on the curry powder, cumin, cayenne, and salt. Toss to coat well.

2. Heat the oil in a 12-inch skillet over medium heat. Add the onion and cook, stirring, until lightly browned, 3 to 4 minutes. Add the chicken and spices and cook, stirring, until golden, 3 to 4 minutes. Add the coconut milk, tomato paste, apple, cinnamon stick, and ½ cup of the hot water. Let simmer until the chicken is cooked through, 2 to 3 minutes. Add the cream and remaining ½ cup hot water and increase the heat to medium-high. Cook until the sauce thickens, about 2 minutes. Remove the cinnamon stick.

3. Serve with steamed basmati rice, garnished with almonds, cilantro, coconut, and chutney, if desired.

NOTE: When you open the can of coconut milk, the milk might have separated from the fat at the top. Pour the milk into a glass measuring cup, add a tablespoon of the fat, and stir until creamy.

SUSAN'S CHICKEN POT PIE
Blueprint

MAKES 6 TO 8 SERVINGS / Prep: 40 minutes / Cook: 32 to 38 minutes

I adapted my sister Susan's famous chicken pot pie recipe to the iron skillet. Through the years this recipe has become a blueprint of how to make pot pie. I found that the bottom crust needs to be pre-baked to keep it crisp, but if you are short on time, you can skip this step. What you get by baking pot pie in the skillet is a crispy, crusty top and a main dish that goes straight from oven to table.

3 (9-inch) pie crust rounds, fresh or frozen (You can double the Food Processor Pie Crust recipe, page 247.)

4 tablespoons unsalted butter

3 cups chopped fresh or frozen vegetables (see Note)

4 cups shredded cooked chicken

6 tablespoons all-purpose flour

Salt and freshly ground black pepper

5 cups reduced-sodium chicken broth

1 large egg, beaten slightly

1. Preheat the oven to 450 degrees F.

2. Place two pastry rounds in a 12-inch skillet, overlapping the crusts on the bottom of the skillet. Press the crusts across the bottom and up the sides of the skillet. Let any excess pastry hang over the top edge. Prick the bottom of the crust a few times with a fork. Cover the crust with a square of parchment paper, then top with pie weights or 1 cup dried beans. Bake the pastry until it is very lightly browned, 6 to 7 minutes. Carefully remove the parchment paper and pie weights and set the skillet aside. Reduce the oven temperature to 350 degrees F.

3. While the crust bakes, melt the butter in a second large skillet over medium heat. Add the vegetables and cook, stirring, for 1 minute. Add the chicken and cook, stirring, for 1 minute more. Sprinkle the flour over the vegetables and chicken, then season with salt and pepper. Cook, stirring, until the flour is incorporated, about 1 minute longer. Add the broth to the skillet, increase the heat to medium-high, and cook, stirring constantly, until the mixture thickens slightly, 1 to 2 minutes. Pour the chicken mixture into the baked crust.

4. Cut the remaining pastry round into 1-inch strips. Lay out half of the strips horizontally over the chicken mixture, and lattice the remaining strips vertically to make a basket-weave pattern. Fold the overhanging prebaked edges back onto the strips to seal the top and bottom crusts. Crimp the crust with your fingers, and stamp the edges with the tines of a fork. Brush the top with the beaten egg.

5. Bake the pie until the crust is golden brown and the juices are bubbling, 25 to 30 minutes. If the pie seems done but the top is not brown, run the pie under the broiler briefly. Let rest for 10 minutes, then serve.

NOTE: Use peas, carrots, green beans, asparagus tips, mushrooms, leeks, and squash. Cut the larger veggies into smaller pieces so everything cooks evenly.

SMOTHERED GRUYÈRE
Chicken

MAKES 4 TO 6 SERVINGS / Prep: 35 minutes / Cook: 53 to 58 minutes

We've been assembling this nearly one-dish meal of breaded chicken cutlets for years. I'll admit that when we first started making it for company, we used ordinary Swiss cheese, and we dirtied every pan in the kitchen. But now that we've adapted it to the skillet, our kitchen cleanup is minimal, and since the upgrade to Gruyère, well, there is no comparison in flavor! For a truly one-dish meal, increase the amount of arugula on top and offer crusty bread on the side.

4 boneless, skinless chicken breasts

Kosher salt and freshly ground black pepper

2 large eggs

1 cup panko bread crumbs

½ cup vegetable oil

3 tablespoons unsalted butter

¼ cup all-purpose flour

2½ cups whole milk

½ cup dry white wine

1 cup (4 ounces) shredded Gruyère cheese

1 medium tomato, cut into thin wedges

1 avocado, peeled, pitted, and sliced

2 cups arugula

1. Preheat the oven to 350 degrees F.

2. Put one chicken breast in a gallon-size zipper-lock bag or between sheets of waxed paper and pound with a rolling pin or flat meat mallet to ¼-inch thickness. Sprinkle with salt. Repeat with the remaining chicken breasts. Beat the eggs in a shallow dish and put the panko in another shallow dish. Dip each chicken cutlet in the eggs, then dredge on both sides in the panko. Set the breaded chicken breasts aside.

3. Heat the oil in a 12-inch skillet over medium-high heat. When the oil is hot enough to sizzle a few of the bread crumbs, add two chicken breasts and brown for 2 minutes per side. Transfer the chicken breasts to paper towels to drain. Repeat with the remaining two chicken breasts. Pour off the oil from the skillet and wipe out the skillet.

4. Melt the butter in the skillet over medium-low heat. Whisk in the flour until smooth. Season with salt and pepper. Gradually whisk in the milk and cook until the sauce has thickened. Turn off the heat. Whisk in the wine.

5. Spoon half of the sauce into a small bowl and reserve. Place the chicken breasts on top of the sauce in the skillet, overlapping them as needed. Spoon the reserved sauce on top and smooth the top with a spatula.

6. Place the skillet in the oven and bake until the sauce bubbles and the chicken has cooked through, 45 to 50 minutes. About 5 minutes before you take the chicken out of the oven, sprinkle the cheese on top to melt. Let the chicken cool for 10 minutes. Top with the tomato wedges, avocado slices, and arugula and serve.

CHICKEN KATSU

MAKES 3 TO 4 SERVINGS / Prep: 25 minutes / Cook: 4 to 5 minutes

Traditionally made with pork in Japan, this recipe is also delicious with chicken breast or thighs, pounded until thin. It is similar to Smashed Chicken Scaloppine (page 157), but the prep differs. Here we dredge this chicken in flour, dip in egg, then coat in panko, which creates a very crisp outer layer that seals in the juices of the chicken and keeps it moist. When frying chicken cutlets in a cast-iron skillet, don't let the oil get too hot. When you see the chicken breading browning too quickly, turn the heat down a bit. The skillet retains heat so well that you've got to keep an eye on the oil while you fry. Katsu is traditionally served with a ketchup-based sauce called tonkatsu. Serve with steamed rice and spinach.

TONKATSU SAUCE

½ cup ketchup

2 tablespoons reduced-sodium soy sauce

1 tablespoon dark brown sugar

1 tablespoon grated fresh ginger

1 tablespoon mirin (Japanese rice wine) or dry sherry

2 teaspoons Worcestershire sauce

1 clove garlic, peeled and minced

CHICKEN

3 boneless, skinless chicken breasts

1 teaspoon kosher salt

½ cup all-purpose flour

2 large eggs

2 cups panko bread crumbs

1 cup vegetable oil

1. For the sauce, whisk together the ketchup, soy sauce, brown sugar, ginger, mirin, Worcestershire sauce, and garlic in a medium-size bowl. Cover with plastic wrap and let it rest at room temperature until ready to serve.

2. For the chicken, slice each breast two or three times with a sharp paring knife a third of the way through. Place the breasts in a shallow glass dish and sprinkle with the kosher salt. Cover with plastic wrap and refrigerate for 2 hours. The salt acts as a brine and tenderizes the chicken breasts.

3. Put one chicken breast in a gallon-size zipper-lock bag or between sheets of waxed paper and pound with a rolling pin or flat meat mallet to ¼-inch thickness. Repeat with the remaining chicken breasts. Put the flour in one shallow dish. Put the eggs in a second shallow dish and lightly beat with a fork. Put the panko in a third shallow dish. Dredge each chicken cutlet first in flour, then dip in egg, and then coat on both sides with panko.

4. Pour the oil into a 12-inch skillet and heat over medium-high until 350 degrees F. Add one or two pieces of chicken to the skillet, so they fit but have room around them, and fry until golden and crispy, 1½ to 2 minutes. Turn the chicken to cook on the other side for another 1½ to 2 minutes. Transfer to paper towels or brown paper to drain. Repeat with the remaining chicken.

5. Serve the chicken warm with the tonkatsu sauce.

SMASHED CHICKEN
Scaloppine

MAKES 4 TO 6 SERVINGS / Prep: 15 minutes / Cook: 4 to 5 minutes

This recipe has been a mainstay of my kitchen through the years. We pound chicken breasts with a heavy rolling pin or meat mallet until they are about ¼ inch thick. Then we dip them into beaten egg white and press both sides into bread crumbs, either homemade or straight from the box. After shallow frying in the skillet, these golden chicken cutlets are ready to serve with a fabulous salad of tomatoes and arugula on top. Leftovers—should you be so fortunate to have them—go onto tomorrow's sandwiches or turn into a quickie chicken parm with the addition of pasta sauce, Parmesan, and mozzarella, plus a little time in a hot oven.

4 boneless, skinless chicken breasts

1 large egg white

1 cup panko bread crumbs

1 large clove garlic, peeled and minced

2 tablespoons grated Parmesan

Pinch dried oregano (optional)

Salt and freshly ground black pepper

1 cup vegetable oil

SALAD TOPPING

2 cups arugula

1 cup chopped fresh tomatoes

¼ cup shaved Parmesan

Pinch grated lemon zest

Good olive oil

1. Put one chicken breast in a gallon-size zipper-lock bag or between sheets of waxed paper and pound with a rolling pin or flat meat mallet to ¼-inch thickness. Repeat with the remaining chicken breasts. Put the egg white in a wide, shallow dish and beat lightly with a fork. Combine the panko, garlic, Parmesan, and oregano (if using) in another wide, shallow dish and season with salt and pepper. Dip each chicken breast in the egg white. Press the breast into the crumbs to coat both sides.

2. Heat the oil in a 12-inch skillet over medium-high heat. When the oil is hot, slide one cutlet into the hot oil and fry until golden, about 2 minutes, then turn with tongs and brown the other side for 2 minutes. Transfer to a platter to keep warm. Repeat with the remaining chicken, straining the dried bread crumb bits from the oil as needed between batches.

3. To serve, top each chicken cutlet with a little arugula, chopped fresh tomatoes, Parmesan shavings, lemon zest, and olive oil and season with salt and pepper.

Think Ahead

Pound the chicken breasts in the plastic bags and then tuck the bags in your freezer until you are ready to cook. These breasts thaw in under 30 minutes, so you can come home, let them thaw while you are getting everything else ready for dinner, then cook.

PAN-FRIED CHICKEN

MAKES 6 TO 8 SERVINGS
Prep: 20 minutes / Soak: 1 hour / Cook: 26 to 33 minutes

When my mother fried chicken in the 1960s, she used an electric skillet, not the cast-iron skillet her mother had used. It was the latest invention and acted as a skillet and oven in one. Nowadays we don't cook as much with electric skillets. We've returned to cast iron! But we can re-create that fried chicken of my memory—crispy outside and moist inside—by using the cast-iron skillet to brown the chicken and the oven to cook it to doneness. Fried chicken purists may consider this heresy, but they obviously haven't tested as many ways to cook fried chicken in a skillet as I have. I have browned chicken on both sides, then covered the skillet with the lid and let it steam until done. I have inverse-fried the chicken, covering it first until nearly done and then uncovering until it fried to doneness. But these methods were messy and cumbersome and resulted in underdone or overdone chicken. I settled on my favorite method, this recipe. It has the perfectly browned crust and tender chicken that I remember from my mother's kitchen, a new-fashioned iron skillet chicken.

1 whole chicken, preferably under
3 pounds, cut into 8 pieces

1 tablespoon plus 1 teaspoon kosher salt

2 cups all-purpose flour

½ teaspoon freshly ground black pepper

¼ teaspoon Creole seasoning (optional)

2 cups peanut oil

1. Put the chicken pieces in a large bowl and cover with ice water. Add 1 tablespoon salt and stir to combine well. Let sit at room temperature for 1 hour. (This old-school method was used to draw out the blood of freshly cut-up chicken, and it still makes the fried chicken taste better.)

2. Preheat the oven to 350 degrees F.

3. Combine the flour, 1 teaspoon salt, pepper, and seasoning in a large brown grocery sack. Drain the chicken from the ice water, and add a few pieces of chicken at a time to the seasoned flour. Shake the bag to coat each piece well. Set aside on a baking rack. Repeat with the remaining chicken pieces.

4. Heat the oil in a 12-inch skillet over medium-high heat. When the oil reaches 350 degrees F, place the chicken thighs and breasts, skin-side down, in the oil. Let cook, undisturbed, for 3 to 4 minutes, until the skin is deeply browned and crisp. Turn with tongs to cook on the other side until browned, 3 to 4 minutes. Transfer the chicken to a plate to rest. Repeat the process with the drumsticks and wings.

5. When all the chicken has cooked, pour off the oil from the skillet. Return the chicken to the skillet and place the skillet in the oven. Bake until the chicken has cooked through (165 degrees), 20 to 25 minutes. Serve.

How to Make Gravy for Fried Chicken

A country-style gravy that covers the accompanying mashed potatoes or rice is as important a part of the fried chicken meal as the chicken itself. Old-timers know there are two types of gravy for fried chicken: the summer gravy (tomato) and the rest of the year gravy (milk). And never, ever pour the gravy over your beautifully fried chicken. It goes on the side.

Tomato Gravy: Heat 2 tablespoons chicken cooking fat and drippings in the skillet and add ¼ cup finely chopped onion. Sauté over low heat until soft. Add 2 tablespoons seasoned flour left from dredging the chicken and stir just until combined, about 30 seconds. Add 2 cups peeled, seeded, chopped tomatoes. If the mixture seems dry, add ½ cup chicken broth. Add a pinch of sugar and season with salt and pepper. Stir and simmer until the mixture is thickened.

Milk (or Cream) Gravy: Heat 2 tablespoons chicken cooking fat and drippings in the skillet. Add 2 tablespoons seasoned flour left from dredging the chicken and stir just until combined, about 30 seconds. Add 2 cups whole milk and season with salt and pepper. Stir and cook until the mixture is thickened. Add crumbled cooked sausage or diced fried country ham if you like.

NASHVILLE HOT CHICKEN

MAKES 3 TO 4 SERVINGS

Prep: 35 minutes / Chill: At least 2 hours / Cook: 5 to 6 minutes

It seems like Nashville hot chicken is popping up everywhere on restaurant menus. And while spicing up fried chicken has been around for a long time and, in fact, there are Caribbean recipes for fried chicken in which you stuff onions, garlic, and spices into slits in the chicken before frying, Nashville hot chicken is off-the-charts hot. It involves soaking the chicken in a hot pepper sauce and then dunking the fried chicken in a spicy oil. This recipe uses chicken tenders, and it is based in part on Hattie B's restaurant recipe and in part on the way the Anchor Bar in Buffalo prepares its chicken wings.

CHICKEN

1 pound chicken tenders (about 12)

Kosher salt and freshly ground black pepper

4 cups peanut oil

1 large egg

½ cup milk or buttermilk

1 tablespoon hot pepper sauce

1 cup all-purpose flour

HOT PEPPER DIP

¼ cup melted margarine, lard, butter, or vegetable oil

1 tablespoon cayenne pepper

1 tablespoon light brown sugar

¼ teaspoon paprika

Pinch garlic powder

Kosher salt and freshly ground black pepper

FOR SERVING

Ranch dressing

Soft white bread

Dill pickles

1. Put the chicken tenders in a medium bowl and sprinkle all over with salt and black pepper. Cover the bowl with plastic wrap and refrigerate for at least 2 hours.

2. Pour the oil into a 12-inch skillet and heat over medium-high until the oil reaches 330 degrees F.

3. While the oil is heating, whisk together the egg, milk, and hot sauce in a large bowl. In another large bowl, whisk together the flour, ½ teaspoon salt, and a few grinds of black pepper. Pat the chicken tenders dry. Dip each tender first in the flour mixture, then in the egg mixture, and then back in the flour mixture. Place them on a baking sheet.

4. Add four or five tenders at a time to the hot oil and fry, turning occasionally, until deeply golden brown, 5 to 6 minutes. Use tongs to transfer the chicken tenders to a rack to drain.

5. To make the hot pepper dip, combine the melted margarine, cayenne, brown sugar, paprika, and garlic powder in a large bowl. Season with salt and black pepper. Dip the fried chicken tenders in the mixture and serve at once with ranch dressing, soft white bread, and dill pickles.

SKILLET-ROASTED TURKEY
with Garlic and Herbs

MAKES 12 SERVINGS / Prep: 25 minutes / Cook: 2½ hours

If you've avoided roasting turkey because you don't own the right pan, well, I am happy to say you are able to roast a turkey in a 12-inch skillet. You probably don't want to roast one larger than 12 pounds—it won't fit if you go larger! But for friend gatherings and small families and that busy holiday weekend when you think it would be nice to have roasted turkey on hand for sandwiches, a bird 12 pounds and under fits nicely and serves 12 to 16 people. In the skillet the turkey gets golden brown and develops a lot of flavor. Begin with a good turkey; in the sink, rinse it well and remove all the packets of necks and innards. (While I am not a fan of the innards, I do make turkey stock from the neck by covering it with cold water in a saucepan, adding some onion, bay leaf, and salt and pepper, and simmering it for an hour.) If you'd like to stuff the turkey, make my stuffing on page 162 and stuff it into the body and neck cavities. For best results, insert an instant-read thermometer into the thigh meat, not hitting the bone. It needs to register 165 degrees F for doneness. Then just let the turkey rest, slice and serve with homemade gravy.

1 (10-pound) whole turkey, neck and giblets removed (see Note)

3 to 4 tablespoons unsalted butter, at room temperature

Kosher salt and freshly ground black pepper

1 small onion, peeled and cut in half

2 ribs celery, cut into 4-inch pieces

2 bay leaves

1 head garlic

2 small apples, cored and cut into quarters

Fresh rosemary or thyme sprigs

1. Preheat the oven to 325 degrees F.

2. In the sink, rinse the turkey well with cold water inside and out and pat it dry with paper towels. Place the turkey in a 12-inch skillet. Smear the butter over the top and sides of the turkey. Season the cavity with salt and pepper. Put the onion halves, celery, and bay leaves in the cavity. (This turkey is small enough to fit snugly enough in the skillet, so you do not need to truss it to keep the wings close to the body.) Break apart the garlic into cloves and coarsely chop the cloves (skins still on); scatter them around the turkey in the skillet. Place the apple quarters around the turkey. Stick a few herb sprigs around the turkey or inside the cavity. Tie the legs together with kitchen twine.

3. Place the skillet in the oven and roast the turkey until it is golden brown and an instant-read thermometer inserted in the center of the thigh registers 165 degrees F, about 2½ hours. If the turkey gets to the desired brownness before it is cooked through, tent the skillet with aluminum foil and keep roasting until you reach 165 degrees F.

4. Remove the skillet from the oven and let the turkey rest for 30 minutes. Carefully transfer it to a serving platter and tent with foil to keep it warm. Discard the bay leaves. Prepare gravy, if desired (see box on page 162). Carve the turkey and serve with the gravy.

NOTE: Save the turkey neck to make stock: Put it in a saucepan, cover with water, and add salt, pepper, a small onion, and a bay leaf. Simmer for 1 hour. Remove and discard the bay leaf.

Continued

MY FAVORITE TURKEY STUFFING

MAKES ENOUGH TO STUFF A 10-POUND TURKEY
Prep: 20 minutes / Cook: 4 hours (if cooking in turkey),
1 hour (if cooking separately)

3 tablespoons unsalted butter, divided use

1 cup chopped onion (1 medium onion)

1 cup chopped unpeeled apple (1 medium apple)

½ cup chopped celery

3 cups crumbled French bread
or sandwich bread

1½ cups crumbled cornbread or muffins

½ teaspoon dried thyme leaves
(or 1 teaspoon fresh thyme)

½ cup chopped fresh parsley

1 large egg, lightly beaten

Salt and freshly ground black pepper

About 1 cup turkey or chicken broth

1. If you are going to stuff your turkey, preheat the oven to 325 degrees F. If you will bake your stuffing separately, preheat it to 375 degrees F.

2. Melt 1 tablespoon of the butter in a 12-inch skillet over medium heat. Add the onion and cook, stirring, until softened, 4 to 5 minutes. Transfer the onion to a large mixing bowl, and place the skillet back over the heat.

3. Add 1 tablespoon of butter to the skillet and when it melts, add the apple and cook, stirring, until lightly colored but not mushy, 5 to 6 minutes. Transfer the apple to the mixing bowl with the onion.

4. Melt the remaining 1 tablespoon butter in the skillet. Add the celery and cook, stirring, until it softens, 5 to 6 minutes. Transfer the celery to the mixing bowl.

5. Add the crumbled French bread and cornbread, thyme, parsley, and egg to the bowl and stir just to combine. Season with salt and pepper to taste. Pour in enough broth to really moisten.

6. To stuff the turkey: Spoon the stuffing into the cavity of the turkey and bake the turkey and stuffing at 325 degrees F to doneness (see page 161 for instructions), about 3 to 3½ hours.

7. To make the stuffing separately, bake it in a buttered casserole dish or 12-inch skillet, uncovered, at 375 degrees F until it browns lightly on top and is firm to the touch, about 40 minutes. Let it cool 5 minutes, then cover with foil to keep warm.

How to Cook a Turkey Breast in a Skillet

Preheat the oven to 325 degrees F. Heat a little vegetable oil in a 12-inch skillet over medium-high heat. Sear a 5- to 7-pound turkey breast, skin-side down, in the oil. Surround the breast with sliced garlic and onion and fresh herbs. Season with salt, pepper, and seasonings. Turn seared-side up, then season the top with salt and pepper. Place the skillet in the oven and roast until an instant-read thermometer inserted in the center of the breast registers 165 degrees F, about 1 hour 15 to 30 minutes, depending on the size of the turkey breast. Tent with aluminum foil if the turkey reaches the desired brownness before the breast is cooked through.

How to Make Gravy for Turkey

Drain all but ¼ cup pan drippings from the skillet. Remove the apple quarters and herbs. Squeeze some of the roasted garlic into the drippings, if desired. Heat the drippings over medium-low heat and whisk in ¼ cup all-purpose flour until smooth. Pour in 2 cups chicken broth or stock from cooking the turkey neck and whisk until smooth. Season with salt and pepper.

Marian's
FISH AND POTATO PIE

MAKES 4 SERVINGS / Prep: 20 minutes / Bake: 55 to 60 minutes

When we lived in England, our friend Marian Petrie made the most wonderful fish pie. The fish was cod—fresh or frozen—and the potatoes were sliced and simmered in a garlicky cream sauce. There was no crust on this "pie," just a bubbly casserole of fish and potatoes. We have made this recipe in all sorts of pans over the years, but my favorite way to bake it so far is in the cast-iron skillet. The edges get crispy, and it remains the ultimate comfort food.

2 pounds russet potatoes, peeled and sliced

4 tablespoons plus 2 teaspoons unsalted butter, at room temperature, divided use

½ cup all-purpose flour

⅛ teaspoon ground mustard

⅛ teaspoon ground nutmeg

2 cups whole milk

2 cloves garlic, peeled and minced

½ cup grated Parmesan or shredded Gruyère cheese

Salt and freshly ground black pepper

1 pound white fish fillets, such as cod or haddock, fresh or frozen, cut into bite-size pieces

2 tablespoons fresh lemon juice

2 tablespoons minced fresh flat-leaf parsley or chives

1. Preheat the oven to 350 degrees F.

2. Put the potato slices in a medium saucepan and cover with water. Bring the water to a boil over medium-high heat, then cover the pan and remove it from the heat. Leave the potatoes in the hot water while you prepare the rest of the pie.

3. Melt 4 tablespoons of the butter in a 12-inch skillet over medium-low heat. Whisk in the flour, mustard, and nutmeg and cook until thickened, 1 minute. Whisk in the milk and garlic and bring to a boil. Reduce the heat to low and continue stirring until thickened. Fold in the cheese. Season with salt and pepper. Pour the sauce into a medium bowl and wipe out the skillet. Spread the remaining 2 teaspoons soft butter all over the bottom of the skillet.

4. Drain the potatoes and spread out half of the potatoes in the skillet. Put the fish on top of the potatoes. Sprinkle the lemon juice over the fish. Season with salt and pepper. Place the remaining potato slices on top. Season with salt and pepper again. Pour the sauce over the potatoes, making sure the potatoes are covered.

5. Place the skillet in the oven and bake until the potatoes are tender and the pie is golden brown, 55 minutes to 1 hour. Sprinkle with minced parsley or chives before serving.

FISH AND CHIPS FOR TWO
(or Three)

MAKES 2 TO 3 SERVINGS

Prep: 35 minutes / Cook: 3 to 5 minutes for the fish, 5 to 7 minutes for the potatoes

One of the great delicacies in life is freshly fried fish and chips (French fries). It took me by surprise to learn a few years ago that British fried fish and chips was originally a Sephardic Jewish delicacy. Post Inquisition, Jews who fled Portugal brought their way of battering fish with flour, olive oil, and egg with them to England. As the skillet is such a great vehicle for frying, I wanted to create an authentic version of fish and chips for this book. So, I used fresh cod, battered the Sephardic way, and added potatoes, cut into matchsticks. If you can't find cod, use any other firm white fish, such as haddock. This recipe serves two or three, depending on how hungry you are.

1½ pounds fresh cod

4 cups vegetable oil

4 medium-size yellow potatoes, scrubbed

BATTER

2 large egg whites

1 cup unbleached all-purpose flour

1½ tablespoons olive oil or
1 large egg yolk

¼ teaspoon kosher salt

Kosher salt and freshly ground black pepper

FOR SERVING

Chopped fresh flat-leaf parsley

Lemon wedges

Malt vinegar

Skillet Spa Treatment

There is nothing your skillet loves more than oil and heat. So, if you think about it, this recipe is like a trip to the spa for your skillet. In fact, if your skillet is new or if you haven't used it in a while, this is precisely the recipe to get it on the road to a shiny black patina. The heat and oil help build that nonstick polymer.

1. Preheat the oven to 300 degrees F.

2. Cut the cod into five or six even pieces and refrigerate while you prepare the potatoes.

3. Heat the oil in a 12-inch skillet over medium heat until it reaches 300 degrees F. Meanwhile, cut the potatoes into French fries, 2 to 3 inches long and about ⅓ inch wide. Put them in a bowl and cover with cold water.

4. When the oil is hot, drain the potatoes and pat them dry with paper towels. Fry the potatoes in three batches until they just take on color, 3 to 4 minutes. Transfer to brown paper to drain. Raise the heat under the skillet to bring the oil to 350 degrees F.

5. Meanwhile, make the batter. Beat the egg whites with an electric mixer on high speed until stiff. In another bowl, whisk together the flour and olive oil. Fold in the beaten egg whites and salt until nearly smooth.

6. Remove the fish from the fridge. Dunk the pieces of fish liberally in the batter and fry two fillets at a time, turning once, until golden brown, 3 to 5 minutes. Steam will rise from the fish when it is nearly done. Use tongs to transfer the fish to a rack set over a rimmed baking sheet. Season the fish with salt and pepper. Place the pan in the oven to keep warm. Repeat with the rest of the fish.

7. With the oil still at 350 degrees F, return the potatoes in batches to the skillet and fry until deeply golden, 2 to 3 minutes. Remove the potatoes with a slotted spoon to brown paper to drain. Season with salt and pepper.

8. Garnish the fish and chips with parsley and serve with lemon wedges and malt vinegar.

SKILLET-SEARED SHRIMP
with Lemon-Basil Potlikker

MAKES 4 SERVINGS / Prep: 30 minutes / Cook: 8 to 11 minutes

Someone once said there are only so many original recipes in this world, and the rest are variations. There is truth to this, and that's the case with this recipe, which is an offspring of the popular grilled shrimp wrapped in basil and prosciutto. And, it's also a twist on my husband's way of quick-cooking fresh shrimp. In this fun recipe, you sear the shrimp in the skillet, then remove them to keep from overcooking. Next, add chopped prosciutto and minced onion, let it cook down and develop some flavor in the pan, and then deglaze to create "potlikker"—or gravy—in which the shrimp gently poach to doneness. Serve with ribbons of fresh basil over rice. It's elegant but easy.

1 pound jumbo (20 count) fresh (or thawed frozen) shrimp, peeled, deveined, and tails removed

3 tablespoons olive oil, divided use

1 large clove garlic, peeled and minced

½ teaspoon sweet paprika

¼ teaspoon cayenne pepper

Kosher salt and freshly ground black pepper

4 ounces prosciutto, chopped

½ cup minced onion

Grated zest and juice of 1 medium lemon

1 cup reduced-sodium chicken broth or water

½ cup sliced fresh basil (see Note)

Steamed rice, for serving

1. In a large bowl, toss the shrimp with 1 tablespoon of the olive oil, the garlic, paprika, and cayenne, and season with salt and black pepper.

2. Heat the remaining 2 tablespoons olive oil in a 12-inch skillet over medium heat. When the oil shimmers, add the shrimp and sear on each side until they release from the skillet, about 30 seconds per side. Transfer the shrimp to a plate.

3. Add the prosciutto and onion to the skillet. Reduce the heat to medium-low and cook and stir until the prosciutto crisps and the onion softens, 4 to 5 minutes. Stir in the lemon zest and juice. Add the chicken broth or water and stir with a wooden spoon to scrape up the bits stuck to the skillet. Let the mixture simmer for 2 to 3 minutes to reduce slightly and to allow the flavors to mingle. Turn off the heat and return the shrimp to the skillet, and toss with the potlikker. The retained heat from the pan will finish cooking the shrimp in 1 to 2 minutes. Toss the basil into the skillet, and serve at once with rice.

NOTE: To create a chiffonade of fresh basil, stack 6 or 7 large basil leaves on top of each other, and roll them up into a cigar shape. Slice the cigar into thin crosswise slices to make ribbons. You will need about 16 basil leaves to yield ½ cup.

THE BEST SHRIMP
and Grits

MAKES 4 SERVINGS / Prep: 35 minutes / Cook: 16 to 20 minutes

Shrimp and grits started as a breakfast recipe enjoyed by coastal fishermen, and now it's one of the most well-loved recipes in the South. To make memorable shrimp and grits, something that will turn the head of a good cook from the Low Country, you need to follow rules. First, use fresh and preferably local shrimp. But if you don't have access to local shrimp, do the next-best thing and buy frozen Argentinian red shrimp from Trader Joe's. Thaw them and drain well. They are sweet and more lobster-like in flavor than most shrimp. Second, don't overcook the shrimp. With the method I share, you cannot overcook them because they are nestled raw right in the grits and baked to doneness. And last, use stone-ground grits. They have more texture and more corn flavor, and that makes a huge difference. I prefer white grits, but yellow are fine, too.

1 pound jumbo (20 count) fresh (or thawed frozen) shrimp, peeled, deveined, and tails removed

2 tablespoons olive oil

2 cloves garlic, peeled and minced

Pinch cayenne pepper or harissa seasoning

Kosher salt and freshly ground black pepper

2 tablespoons unsalted butter

1 cup finely chopped onion

½ cup finely chopped red bell pepper or green Jimmy Nardello pepper

3 cups water

1 cup heavy cream

½ teaspoon hot sauce, or to taste

1 cup white stone-ground grits

1 to 1½ cups shredded sharp Cheddar cheese

½ cup grated Parmesan cheese

1. Preheat the oven to 375 degrees F.

2. In a large bowl, toss the shrimp with the olive oil, garlic, and cayenne. Season with salt and black pepper. Set aside.

3. Melt the butter in a 12-inch skillet over medium heat. Add the onion and pepper and sauté until soft, 3 minutes. Add the water, cream, and hot sauce and stir to combine. Increase the heat to bring to a boil, then reduce the heat to a simmer and whisk in the grits. Stir and cook until the grits thicken, 5 to 7 minutes. Turn off the heat and stir in the Cheddar and Parmesan cheeses until melted.

4. Arrange the shrimp in the middle of the grits mixture, in a spoke pattern, pushing them down into the grits. Place the skillet in the oven and bake until the shrimp have just cooked through, 8 to 10 minutes. Serve warm.

Gluten-Free
SKILLET GUMBO

MAKES 4 SERVINGS / Prep: 35 minutes / Cook: About 50 minutes

A few years ago on a book tour, I was demonstrating gumbo on morning TV in—of all places—New Orleans! Who but a crazy cookbook author like myself goes to NOLA to tell people how to make gumbo? Fortunately, my recipe was gluten-free, and everyone was really intrigued how I could make a gumbo this way because the roux—which is what gives gumbo its characteristic flavor, color, and texture—is made from flour. But thanks to naturally gluten-free sweet rice flour, you can make gluten-free gumbo, which is what I shared on TV. I have always used the cast-iron skillet to brown sweet rice flour for the roux when making gumbo, and now I use it to make the entire gumbo, from start to finish.

1 tablespoon sweet rice flour
(see Note)

2 tablespoons unsalted butter
or vegetable oil

1 cup chopped onion

2 cloves garlic, peeled and minced

2 ounces sliced (about ½ cup) cooked
andouille sausage or smoked ham

1 cup sliced fresh okra

2 fresh thyme sprigs

1 bay leaf

1 tablespoon chopped fresh
flat-leaf parsley

1 (15-ounce) can diced tomatoes

Shrimp broth (see box) or
water, as needed

Kosher salt and freshly ground
black pepper

8 ounces large (24 count) shrimp,
shelled, deveined, and tails removed

8 ounces lump crabmeat, drained
and picked over for cartilage

1 pint shucked fresh oysters,
plus liquid (optional)

Steamed rice, for serving

1. Toast the sweet rice flour in a 12-inch skillet over low heat. Cook, stirring with a wooden spoon, until the rice flour turns from light brown to reddish-tan, 8 to 10 minutes. Transfer the browned flour to a small bowl and set aside.

2. Add the butter to the skillet and melt over medium heat. Add the onion, garlic, and sausage and cook until the onion softens, about 3 minutes. Add the okra, thyme, bay leaf, parsley, and tomatoes with their juice. Fill the tomato can 1½ times with shrimp broth and/or water and add to the skillet. Season with salt and pepper. Increase the heat and let the gumbo come to a boil, then reduce the heat to low and simmer for 15 minutes. Whisk in the browned sweet rice flour until it dissolves. Let the gumbo simmer, stirring occasionally, until slightly thickened, 25 to 30 minutes.

3. Just before serving, add the shrimp and crabmeat (and oysters, if using) and simmer until the shrimp are just cooked through, 2 minutes. Remove and discard the bay leaf. Serve at once with steamed rice.

NOTE: Look for sweet rice flour in grocery stores and online where gluten-free ingredients are sold.

Create Your Own Shrimp Broth

Put the shrimp shells in a small saucepan and cover with 2 cups water. Bring to a boil over medium heat, then reduce the heat and simmer until the shells are pink, about 15 minutes. Strain the liquid and reserve for adding to the gumbo.

SKILLET-SEARED HALIBUT
with Peas and Lemon

MAKES 4 SERVINGS / Prep: 25 minutes / Cook: 6 to 8 minutes

Firm, fresh fish like halibut is a natural for cooking in cast iron. You can season it as you choose, and then cook it as you would a beef steak, searing then roasting in the oven to cook through. For this one-pan recipe, use halibut steaks or a thick fillet. In order to get the sear you want when searing any protein in the skillet, you have to crank up the heat under the skillet before cooking. And although butter tastes best with fish like halibut, really accentuating its natural rich flavor, it will burn if added to the hot skillet. And olive oil will smoke. So, I use a little vegetable oil—it has a higher smoke point—to sear the halibut, and then once that is in the pan, I add butter for flavor. Frozen peas are handy to toss under any fish for roasting; if asparagus is in season, by all means use that instead.

1½ pounds halibut steaks or fillets

Kosher salt and freshly ground black pepper

Creole seasoning

1 tablespoon vegetable oil

2 tablespoons unsalted butter, cut into pieces

½ cup chopped onion

1 medium lemon, cut in half

12 ounces frozen or fresh peas

¼ cup chopped fresh mint or flat-leaf parsley

1. Preheat the oven to 425 degrees F.

2. Heat a 12-inch skillet over medium-high heat until it smokes, 4 to 5 minutes. Season the halibut on both sides with the salt, pepper, and Creole seasoning. When the skillet is hot, add the vegetable oil and tilt the pan to spread it out evenly. Place the halibut in the skillet and let it sear, undisturbed, until golden, 2 to 3 minutes. Run a metal spatula under the halibut and carefully turn it over. Turn off the heat, add the butter and onion to the skillet, and shake the skillet to disperse the butter and onion so they are evenly distributed around the skillet. Squeeze the lemon juice over the top of the fish. Finally, carefully lift up the fish and place the peas on the bottom of the skillet, then lay the halibut back down on top of the peas.

3. Place the skillet in the oven and roast the fish until it just flakes, 4 to 5 minutes. Season the fish with salt and pepper, if needed, and garnish with mint or parsley. Serve warm.

SKILLET SALMON
Two Ways

MAKES 4 SERVINGS

Salmon and the cast-iron skillet are the perfect partners, for each is better with the other. In the case of salmon, the skillet uses the natural fat in farm-raised salmon, and what results is a crispy exterior. When testing this book, I did not create a bad salmon recipe. But I did learn that when using wild salmon, it's important to add a little oil to the pan before searing, and to watch the time carefully because it easily overcooks. But with the fattier, farm-raised salmon, you can cook it one of two ways. The first is to just sear it on each side in the hot skillet. The second is to finish a thicker piece of salmon in the oven. So I offer the quick method first, followed by the oven method.

CRISPY STOVETOP SALMON

Prep: 8 to 10 minutes / Cook: 10 minutes

1½ pounds salmon (see Note)

Kosher salt and freshly ground black pepper

2 teaspoons vegetable oil

1 tablespoon unsalted butter, cut into pieces

2 tablespoons capers

1 medium lemon, cut in half

1 tablespoon chopped fresh flat-leaf parsley or chervil

1. Season the salmon liberally on both sides with salt and pepper.

2. Heat a 12-inch skillet over medium-high heat until it smokes, about 4 minutes.

3. Add the oil to the pan, and place the salmon in the skillet. Sear the salmon for 3 to 4 minutes, undisturbed. It will be deeply golden brown. Run a metal spatula under the salmon to loosen it, then carefully flip it to the other side and cook for 3 to 4 minutes more. Turn off the heat.

4. Add the butter to the skillet. When it melts, add the capers and toss the skillet to heat them. Squeeze the lemon halves over the salmon and let the juice reduce a bit. Shower the top of the salmon with parsley and serve.

NOTE: If the salmon has skin on one side, sear it first on the skinless side and finish skin-side down.

PLAN B: HOW TO COOK A THICKER PIECE OF SALMON IN THE OVEN

Prep: 10 to 13 minutes / Cook: 30 minutes (includes resting time)

1½ pounds salmon, 1½ to 2 inches thick

Kosher salt and freshly ground black pepper

¼ cup honey (see Note on p 145)

2 tablespoons reduced-sodium soy sauce

½ teaspoon chili powder, or 2 tablespoons shredded fresh ginger and 1 teaspoon minced garlic

1. Preheat the oven to 400 degrees F.

2. Season the salmon liberally on both sides with salt and pepper.

3. Heat a 12-inch skillet over medium-high heat until it smokes, about 4 minutes. Add the salmon, skin-side down, and let it sear, undisturbed, for 4 to 5 minutes, until very crispy. Turn off the heat.

4. Flip the fish onto the other side, and sear in the residual heat of the pan for 1 minute, or until you get the browning you like. Turn the fish back skin-side down.

5. For the glaze, whisk together the honey, soy sauce, and either chili powder or ginger and garlic. Drizzle the top of the salmon with the glaze and slide the skillet into the oven to bake until just done, 5 to 7 minutes. Let the salmon rest for 15 minutes before serving.

Classic
BLACKENED SNAPPER

MAKES 2 TO 4 SERVINGS / Prep: 25 minutes / Cook: 4 to 5 minutes

Cajun chef Paul Prudhomme changed the way we ate when he blackened redfish in a cast-iron skillet in the late 1970s. This was how his Louisiana family had cooked for generations, and Prudhomme naturally gravitated to cooking in cast iron. The redfish was first brushed with melted butter, then dredged in a hot and spicy seasoning before searing in the skillet. It became a national phenomenon and nearly depleted the Gulf of Mexico redfish population. Even today, it is hard to find redfish outside of the New Orleans area, which is why I am offering this snapper recipe instead. You can still dredge it in the intense cayenne and paprika blend and get the skillet smoking-hot to cook the fish, which is the hallmark of the recipe. It's a good recipe to take outdoors and cook on the grill because of the smoke that comes out of the skillet while blackening. At the very least, turn on the exhaust fan over your stove!

BLACKENED SEASONING

1½ teaspoons sweet paprika

1 teaspoon kosher salt

½ teaspoon onion powder

½ teaspoon garlic powder

½ teaspoon cayenne pepper

¼ teaspoon dried or fresh thyme

1 to 1¼ pounds red snapper or redfish (either 1 big piece or fillets)

6 tablespoons unsalted butter, melted

1 medium lemon, cut in quarters

1. In a small bowl, mix the paprika, salt, onion powder, garlic powder, cayenne, and thyme.

2. Heat a 12-inch skillet over high heat until it smokes. Brush the fish with some of the melted butter and sprinkle liberally with the seasoning mix. When the skillet is hot, place the fish in the skillet. Pour a little of the melted butter on top of the fish (to fan the flame!). Let the fish cook, undisturbed, until it looks blackened, about 2 minutes. Run a metal spatula under the fish and carefully turn it over. Drizzle the top with more butter and cook for 2 to 3 minutes more, until the fish is cooked through.

3. Serve the fish with extra melted butter and lemon quarters for squeezing at the table.

TUNA NIÇOISE
in a Skillet

MAKES 4 SERVINGS

Prep: 30 minutes / Chill: 1 hour / Cook: 25 to 30 minutes

This recipe screams dinner party. I love how convivial it is, and how it begs you to share it with friends. While there are a few components, you can manage the prep in stages. Begin by making the vinaigrette dressing, then prep the vegetables and extras for the garnish. Next, make the marinade and slide the tuna in it an hour before you plan to cook. Then sear the tuna. Everything can be done in advance, and once your guests arrive, you can enjoy their company, heat the bread, pour the wine, and then serve a skillet full of tuna Niçoise. Recipes that are called "Niçoise" imply that they originated in or around Nice, in southern France. They typically have the small, flavorful black olives of Nice as a garnish.

4 (6- to 9-ounce) tuna steaks

⅓ cup fresh lemon juice
(from 2 to 3 lemons)

⅔ cup olive oil

2 cloves garlic, peeled and minced

½ cup chopped fresh dill

1 to 2 tablespoons vegetable oil, to sear the tuna

Salt and freshly ground black pepper, to season the tuna

VINAIGRETTE

2 tablespoons white wine vinegar

1 tablespoon Dijon mustard

6 tablespoons olive oil

Kosher salt and freshly ground black pepper

1 large shallot, peeled and minced

1 tablespoon minced fresh flat-leaf parsley

GARNISH

1 cup tiny new potatoes

Salt

2 cups fresh thin green beans

2 medium-size ripe tomatoes, peeled and quartered

¼ cup Niçoise or Kalamata olives, pitted

2 hard-cooked eggs, peeled and quartered

1 cup watercress or small arugula leaves

4 anchovies (optional)

1 tablespoon capers, drained (optional)

1. Put the tuna in a 13-by-9-inch glass baking dish. In a small bowl, whisk together the lemon juice and olive oil. Add the garlic and dill. Pour the marinade over the tuna and turn the steaks to coat them well. Cover the dish with plastic wrap and refrigerate for 1 hour.

2. For the vinaigrette, whisk together the vinegar, mustard, and olive oil until smooth. Season with salt and pepper. Stir in the shallot and parsley. Set aside.

3. Put the potatoes in a medium saucepan and cover with water. Add a pinch of salt. Bring to a boil over high heat, then reduce the heat to medium-low and simmer until just tender, 10 to 12 minutes, depending on the size of the potatoes. Remove the potatoes with a slotted spoon, drain, and toss with a little of the vinaigrette in a bowl. Set aside.

4. Return the saucepan of water to a boil over medium-high heat and add the green beans. Let them cook until bright green, 3 to 5 minutes, then drain in a colander in the sink and run cold water over them. Let sit in the colander and drain well, then add to the bowl with the potatoes and toss with a little vinaigrette.

5. Heat a 12-inch skillet over medium-high heat until it is smoking, 4 to 5 minutes. Remove the tuna from the marinade, and pat it very dry with paper towels. Add the vegetable oil to the skillet. When it is hot, place the tuna in the skillet and let it sear until well browned, about 3 minutes. Turn the tuna and let it sear until well browned on the other side, about 3 minutes. Transfer the tuna to a plate and season with salt and pepper.

6. When you are ready to serve, cut the tuna into strips. Arrange the potatoes and green beans on a platter or in the center of the skillet. Place the tuna strips on top. Arrange the tomatoes, olives, and egg quarters around the edges. Pile the watercress on top and add anchovies and capers (if using). Pour a little vinaigrette over to moisten, and serve.

PAN-ROASTED MUSSELS
with Garlic Butter and Pommes Frites

MAKES 6 TO 8 SERVINGS AS AN APPETIZER; 4 SERVINGS AS A MAIN DISH
Prep: 15 minutes / Cook: 14 to 15 minutes

Mussels are shiny blue-black bivalves much beloved in Europe, whether cooked on top of a cast-iron stove for hungry fishermen or steamed with white wine and served with frites in a Brussels café. But they aren't cooked as much in America, which is a shame because these mollusks, with their sweet orange flesh, are easy to cook thanks to the iron skillet. I like to cook them at a high heat in the oven, where they will open quickly and have more intense flavor than if steamed in a pot of water. You have to begin with fresh mussels, which means get them from a reputable source. As they are living shellfish, be sure to buy them in netted bags instead of plastic.

3 to 4 pounds black mussels, cleaned (see box)

2 tablespoons olive oil

½ cup dry white wine

3 cloves garlic, peeled and minced

¼ teaspoon red pepper flakes (optional)

2 tablespoons unsalted butter, cut into pieces

Sea salt and freshly ground black pepper

2 tablespoons chopped fresh flat-leaf parsley

Crusty bread, for serving

1 recipe Pommes Frites (page 31), for serving

1. Preheat the oven to 400 degrees F.

2. Pile the mussels into a 12-inch skillet. In a small bowl, whisk together the olive oil, wine, garlic, and red pepper flakes (if using) and pour over the mussels. Toss to combine. Place the skillet in the oven and bake for 10 minutes. Add the butter to the skillet and return it to the oven. Bake until the mussels open, 4 to 5 minutes.

3. Remove the skillet from the oven, season with salt and pepper, and sprinkle with chopped parsley. Take the skillet right to the table. Serve with crusty bread for dipping into the broth and pommes frites alongside.

Cleaning Mussels

Scrub and rinse the mussels well under cold running water. If any do not close after rinsing, discard them. Partly open? Tap with your fingers, and if they close, they are still fresh. If not, throw them away. Put the mussels in a large bowl and fill with cold water, then swish them around and drain off the water. Repeat this process several times. Finally, pull out their beards, the fuzzy, seaweed-like string found on mussels that are not farm-raised.

Pan-Grilled
SUMMER TROUT

MAKES 2 SERVINGS

Prep: 30 minutes / Cook: 5 to 15 minutes, depending on butterflied or whole fish

I can't tell you how many times our family has grilled fish only to have the delicate trout or grouper fall through the grill grates and into the fire. We finally got one of those hinged fish baskets, and that helped keep everything intact, but honestly, it was a mess to clean. Enter the cast-iron skillet. My hero! Thankfully the skillet sears delicate fish right on top of an open fire or gas grill and protects it from tearing. You get the heat, the char, and the sear on the skin, which locks in flavor and makes the fish moist. And you get the cool factor of cooking your fish outside over fire, in your skillet, and it doesn't heat or smoke up your kitchen. You can cook the trout either whole or butterflied. The fish will cook more quickly and have more surface area to brown and get crispy if butterflied. But it will be more tender and delicate if left whole—your choice.

2 (1-pound) rainbow trout (see Note), cleaned and either butterflied or left whole

1 large lemon, juiced or sliced

2 cloves garlic, peeled and minced or sliced

Kosher salt and freshly ground black pepper

Chopped fresh chives and/or flat-leaf parsley

2 tablespoons olive oil

1. If butterflying the fish, sprinkle the lemon juice, minced garlic, salt and pepper, and fresh herbs all over the fish in a glass dish, and let the mixture soak into the trout for about 1 hour. If cooking the whole trout, season the inside of the fish with salt and pepper, then stuff lemon and garlic slices and herb sprigs inside the fish. Rub the outside of the whole fish with the olive oil. Drizzle the butterflied fish on both sides with a little olive oil.

2. Heat a 12-inch skillet on a grate over a hot fire or a gas or charcoal (gray coals) grill until it is smoking hot, 4 to 5 minutes. Slide the trout into the skillet—skin-side down first for butterflied fish—and let it cook, undisturbed, for 4 minutes. Run a metal spatula under the fish to loosen any bits of skin sticking to the pan, and carefully flip it onto the other side. For butterflied trout, cook for 2 minutes more, then remove the skillet from the fire and the fish from the skillet. For whole trout, let it cook for 4 to 5 minutes more on the second side. Test for doneness. If the fish has not cooked through, move the skillet to a place on the grate where the heat is indirect. Let the trout continue to cook, turning if needed, for 5 to 7 more minutes.

NOTE: Instead of trout, you can use 1 pound red snapper or grouper or any other delicate 1-inch-thick fish fillet such as Arctic char, preferably with skin on.

A Quick Pan Sauce for Fish

Remove the fish from the skillet and deglaze the pan over the fire with ¼ cup lemon juice or dry white wine. Scrape the sides and bottom of the skillet with a metal spatula to loosen any browned bits. Whisk in 1 to 2 tablespoons cold butter for a richer sauce. Season with salt and pepper, and add chopped fresh herbs, such as flat-leaf parsley, tarragon, or dill. Or add a tablespoon of capers. Pour over the fish, then serve.

SEARED RIB-EYE STEAK
with Red Wine Pan Sauce

MAKES 2 SERVINGS / Prep: 20 minutes / Cook: 30 to 35 minutes

When steaks are 1½ to 2 inches thick, it's best to use a "reverse sear" method of cooking them. This process begins in the oven and then moves to the top of the stove for the sear. This method keeps the thick steaks really moist and flavorful. An added bonus is the pan sauce, made possible since all the meat's juices stay in the skillet rather than falling through the grates of your grill! If your steaks are 1 inch thick or less, there is no need to reverse sear—you can just sear both sides on the stovetop and then serve (see box, opposite).

1 (1½- to 2-inch-thick) bone-in beef rib-eye steak (about 1 pound)

Kosher salt and freshly ground black pepper

1 tablespoon vegetable oil

1 tablespoon unsalted butter

PAN SAUCE

1 tablespoon minced shallot

1 teaspoon fresh thyme or rosemary leaves

½ cup dry red wine

1 tablespoon unsalted butter, chilled and cut into pieces

Kosher salt and freshly ground black pepper

Fresh thyme sprigs and/or capers, for garnish (optional)

1. Preheat the oven to 225 degrees F.

2. Season both sides of the steak with salt and pepper. Place the steak on a rack set in a rimmed baking sheet and bake until the steak comes to an internal temperature of 115 degrees F, about 30 minutes.

3. When the steak is nearly ready, heat a 12-inch skillet over medium-high heat until smoking, 4 to 5 minutes. Add the oil and butter; when the butter melts, place the steak in the pan to sear until deeply browned, about 45 seconds. Turn the steak over to the other side and sear until deeply browned, about 45 seconds. With tongs, turn the steak on its sides and brown them. Transfer the steak to a platter to rest while you make the pan sauce. (The steak should come up to an internal temperature of 130 to 135 degrees F for medium-rare. If not, place the steak back on the rack on the pan and bake until it does.)

4. Place the skillet back over medium heat. Add the shallot and thyme and sauté until softened, about 2 minutes. Add the wine. Let the mixture reduce for 1 minute. Whisk in the butter, season with salt and pepper, and pour over the steak. Serve at once, garnished with thyme sprigs and/or capers, if desired.

How to Pan-Sear a 1-Inch-Thick Boneless Rib-Eye Steak

1. Heat a 12-inch skillet over medium-high heat until it smokes, 4 to 5 minutes.

2. Pat the steak dry with paper towels and season both sides with salt and pepper or your favorite steak dry rub.

3. Drizzle 2 teaspoons vegetable oil into the pan, then place the steak in the skillet to sear, undisturbed, for 2 to 3 minutes. Using tongs, pick up the steak and hold it over the pan so that the pan has a minute to dry off from the heat. Let the steaks sear on the other side for 2 to 3 minutes. Add a pat of butter to the skillet if you like. Turn off the heat, but do not move the steak.

4. Insert an instant-read thermometer in the steak and let the steak rest in the skillet until the temperature comes to 130 to 135 degrees F for medium-rare, 5 to 10 minutes. Remove and serve.

Note on searing over electric versus gas heat: A gas burner heats up more quickly than an electric burner, so it may take a little longer to heat up your skillet if you are using an electric stove. You may want to heat the skillet on high instead of medium-high. Look for a visual sign, like the empty skillet beginning to smoke or, if you are using a little oil, seeing the oil shimmer. And the steak may take a little longer to cook through, so be sure to rely on your thermometer to determine doneness.

TWO-STEP SKILLET
Tenderloin

MAKES 2 TO 4 SERVINGS / Prep: 10 minutes / Cook: 10 to 11 minutes

The trick to perfectly cooked filets is a two-step process: Sear on top of the stove, then roast to doneness in the oven. It's incredibly easy—and given the price of filets at the supermarket versus the steakhouse, a lot thriftier, too. For the best results, cook just two filets at a time to allow for sufficient room around the steaks to promote browning. The best way to gauge internal cooking time and doneness is to use an instant-read thermometer. Stick the thermometer in the center of the steak and remove the steak from the heat a little bit before it reaches the desired temperature (medium-rare is 130 to 135 degrees F), because the temperature will rise a few degrees as the steak rests.

2 (12-ounce) beef tenderloin steaks (filets mignons), 1½ to 1¾ inches thick

4 teaspoons Montreal steak seasoning or other coarse steak rub, or just a mixture of kosher salt and freshly ground black pepper

2 teaspoons vegetable oil

1. Preheat the oven to 400 degrees F.

2. Heat a 12-inch skillet over medium-high heat until it smokes, 4 to 5 minutes. Pat the filets dry with paper towels and season them generously on both sides. When the skillet is hot, drizzle the oil into the pan. When it is hot, place the steaks in the skillet to sear, undisturbed, for 2 minutes. Using tongs, pick up the steaks and hold them above the pan so that the pan has a minute to dry off over the heat. Turn the steaks over and let them sear on the other side, undisturbed, for 2 minutes.

3. Immediately place the skillet in the oven and cook until an instant-read thermometer inserted in the center of the steaks reaches 130 degrees F, 6 to 7 minutes. Transfer the steaks to a serving plate set at the back of the stove to keep warm for 10 minutes. (The steaks will continue cooking as they rest, reaching 135 degrees F for medium-rare.) Serve.

How to Make Compound Butter

For an extra special entrée, you can top your filets with a blue cheese or herb compound butter. In a small bowl, mash together 2 tablespoons soft butter, a generous pinch of kosher salt, and either 1 tablespoon crumbled blue cheese or 1 tablespoon chopped fresh herbs (such as flat-leaf parsley and chives). Spread the mixture onto a small square of waxed or parchment paper and roll it up into a log. Chill until firm. Slice the log into 4 pieces and put one on top of each steak before it goes in the oven or just before serving. Reserve the remaining pieces wrapped in the fridge up to two weeks.

Sunday Night
CHEESEBURGERS

MAKES 6 SERVINGS / Prep: 35 minutes / Cook: 5 minutes

This diner-style burger is the best burger you will ever make at home. It is crispy around the edges and just the right size to layer on a bun or Homemade English Muffin (page 60) with loads of condiments. You can even stack two if you're really hungry. The beef is seasoned and then formed into a ball and chilled. Once the skillet is searing-hot, the chilled balls go into the pan and are flattened out with a big flat metal spatula (or a 10-inch cast-iron skillet, if you have one). It's important to keep pressing down on the burger as it cooks to keep it flattened out and to create the crispy diner-style edges. After a couple of minutes, turn the burger, top with cheese, and let it cook on the other side. Perfection! Thanks to Meathead Goldwyn for introducing me to this method, and thanks to my family for asking me to make burgers so I could perfect them.

1½ pounds ground beef chuck
or 80% lean ground beef

1 teaspoon seasoning salt

Freshly ground black pepper

1 tablespoon unsalted butter

6 burger buns or Homemade
English Muffins (page 60), split in half

6 slices mild cheese (such as
mild Cheddar or a melty-type American)

Condiments of your choice: mustard,
mayo, ketchup, pickles, sliced onion,
sliced tomato, lettuce, etc.

1. If you want to keep the cooked burgers warm between batches, preheat the oven to 275 degrees F.

2. Put the beef in a mixing bowl and use your hands to gently work in the seasoning salt and pepper until loosely combined. Do not overwork the meat, or this will make tough burgers. Divide the meat into six equal-size loose balls, wrap, and chill while getting everything else prepared.

3. When you're ready to cook, melt the butter in a 12-inch skillet over medium heat. Place the buns, cut-side down, in the skillet and griddle until lightly browned, about 30 seconds. Remove and keep warm.

4. Wipe out the skillet with a paper towel. Heat the skillet over medium-high heat until it smokes, 4 to 5 minutes.

5. Unwrap the meat and place three balls of meat in the skillet, spaced about 3 inches apart. Press down on them with a large metal spatula or a 10-inch iron skillet until they are about ⅓ inch thick. Let them cook, undisturbed, until well browned, about 3 minutes. Keep pressing down on the burgers as they cook to get the edges crispy and to flatten them. Flip the burgers to the other side, regulating the heat as needed so the burgers don't burn. Place a slice of cheese on each burger. After 2 minutes, transfer the burgers to a baking sheet and cover them with a large saucepan lid so the cheese melts. If desired, place the baking sheet in the oven to keep the burgers warm while you make the next batch. Wipe out the skillet and repeat with the remaining three burgers. Serve warm, with your favorite condiments.

NOTE: Instead of cooking in two batches, you can cook the burgers all at once in two skillets.

POT ROAST
with Sweet Onion Gravy

MAKES 8 SERVINGS / Prep: 15 minutes / Cook: 3 to 3½ hours

One day I got hungry for pot roast, and that was the beginning of my quest for the perfect pot roast formula. I had been raised on pot roast swimming in tomato sauce, and I knew I wanted something much more. Step one was the right cut of beef: chuck roast. Step two, a heavy pan in which to sear the beef and then let it braise to tender doneness. That's where the iron skillet comes in: It retains heat and lets the roast cook at a gentle 300 degrees F, and once the roast is done, you have a delectable onion gravy already in the pan. But truly the best part of creating this perfect pot roast formula is the aroma in my house when I am cooking it! I think pot roast trumps mulled spices at Christmas.

1 (3½- to 4-pound) boneless
beef chuck roast

¼ cup all-purpose flour

Salt and freshly ground
black pepper

Seasoning salt of your choice
(optional)

2 tablespoons vegetable oil

3 large Vidalia or other sweet onions,
peeled and cut in half crosswise

4 cups chopped peeled carrots

4 cups chopped peeled potatoes,
parsnips, or turnips

1. Preheat the oven to 300 degrees F.

2. Pat the roast dry with paper towels. Put the flour in a shallow dish and season with salt, pepper, and seasoning salt (if using). Dredge the roast on all sides in the seasoned flour and set it aside.

3. Heat the oil in a 12-inch skillet over medium heat until it shimmers, about 3 minutes. Add the roast and brown on each side until well seared, 3 to 4 minutes per side. Remove the skillet from the heat. Transfer the roast to a plate. Place the onion halves, cut-side down, in the skillet. Place the roast on top of the onions and cover the skillet.

4. Place the pan in the oven and bake for 2 hours, then add the root vegetables to the skillet. Spoon the pan juices over the vegetables to baste them. Put the lid back on the skillet and continue baking until the pot roast is tender and the juices have thickened, another 1 to 1½ hours.

5. Transfer the roast to a cutting board and slice it. Arrange slices of beef on plates with carrots, onions, and veggies. Spoon the pan gravy over the top and serve.

Day Two Beef Stew

The second best part of pot roast is the leftovers, which we turn into beef stew. Chop the remaining meat and vegetables, skim the fat off the cooking juices, and add a little beef broth or water to thin it all out. Heat and serve atop egg noodles or grits, or in warm bowls with toasted garlic bread.

CHUCK WAGON
Casserole

MAKES 6 TO 8 SERVINGS / Prep: 20 minutes / Cook: 22 to 25 minutes

Life isn't all about filet mignon and seared scallops. Sometimes it calls for down-home chow, as in the case of this recipe. It's named after the old "chuck wagons" of the late nineteenth century, which were traveling kitchens in the American West. The chuck wagon was invented by Texan Charles Goodnight, who created a cabinet to hold cooking ingredients and supplies, and it fit in the back of a horse-drawn wagon. It was to the "cookie" at the campsite what a food truck is today. But unlike this modern riff on a cowboy classic, there weren't onions and peppers on the cattle drive to flavor the beef—much less frozen biscuits or corn chips to pile on top of this one-skillet meal. But there would have been dried beef, and there would have been an iron skillet. This recipe feeds a crowd of Scouts or campers, or serves as a main dish for a cowboy-themed get-together. Dress it up with sliced avocado, cilantro, and salsa. Or dress it down with canned biscuits, American cheese, and pork and beans. Whatever your life calls for!

1 tablespoon olive oil or vegetable oil

1 pound lean ground beef

½ cup chopped onion

½ cup chopped red or green bell pepper

1 generous tablespoon chili powder

1 generous teaspoon ground cumin

1 teaspoon sweet paprika

½ teaspoon salt

3 ounces (half a 6-ounce can) tomato paste

1 cup water

1 (15- to 16-ounce) can pinto beans,
rinsed and drained

1 (8-ounce) can vegetarian baked beans

4 fresh or frozen biscuits, cut in half

1 cup shredded sharp Cheddar cheese

1 cup corn chips

1. Preheat the oven to 425 degrees F.

2. Heat the oil in a 12-inch skillet over medium heat. Crumble the ground beef into the skillet and sauté until the beef is cooked through, about 3 minutes. Add the onion and bell pepper and sauté until they soften, about 2 minutes. Reduce the heat to low and add the chili powder, cumin, paprika, and salt. Toss to coat the meat with the spices. Turn off the heat.

3. Add the tomato paste, water, pinto beans, and baked beans to the skillet. Stir to combine. Place the halved biscuits, cut-side down, in a ring around the edge of the skillet. Sprinkle the biscuits with the cheese.

4. Place the skillet in the oven and bake until the mixture is hot but the biscuits are not yet browned, about 12 minutes. Remove the skillet from the oven and scatter the corn chips over the middle of the skillet. Continue baking until the biscuits are golden brown, 10 to 12 minutes more. Serve at once.

OLD-FASHIONED SHEPHERD'S PIE

MAKES 8 SERVINGS / Prep: 50 minutes / Bake: 20 to 25 minutes

The first time I baked a shepherd's pie, I was unimpressed with my efforts. The meat and gravy layer underneath was boring, and the mashed potato topping turned out dry. But now I have figured it out, and using the skillet from stovetop to oven to table makes the process easier, too. If you want to be authentic, use ground lamb (beef is traditionally used for cottage pie). Russet potatoes make the fluffiest mashed potatoes for the topping. This recipe has the addition of an egg yolk, which gives it a warm color and makes it richer and more substantial, too. For a dazzling show, sweep the potato mixture into swirls using a teaspoon before baking.

POTATO TOPPING

1½ pounds russet potatoes, peeled and cut into 1-inch pieces

½ teaspoon kosher salt, plus a pinch

¼ cup whole milk, plus more if needed

4 tablespoons unsalted butter

¼ teaspoon freshly ground black pepper

1 large egg yolk

MEAT FILLING

2 tablespoons olive oil

1 small onion, peeled and chopped

3 small or 2 medium carrots, peeled and chopped

2 cloves garlic, peeled and minced

1½ pounds ground lamb or lean ground beef

1 teaspoon kosher salt

½ teaspoon freshly ground black pepper

2 tablespoons all-purpose flour

1 cup reduced-sodium chicken or beef broth

1 tablespoon tomato paste

1 teaspoon Worcestershire sauce

2 teaspoons fresh thyme leaves, plus more for garnish

½ cup fresh or frozen green peas

1. For the potato topping, put the potatoes in a saucepan, add a pinch of salt, and cover with cold water. Bring the water to a boil over medium-high heat, reduce the heat to low, cover, and let the potatoes simmer until they are tender, about 15 minutes. Drain the potatoes.

2. Meanwhile, warm the milk in a saucepan or in the microwave. Add the warm milk and butter to the pan with the potatoes. Season with the ½ teaspoon salt and the pepper, and mash the potatoes until they are smooth. Add a little more milk, if needed, to thin the mixture, but be sure it will still be thick enough to spread and hold its shape on top of the pie. Fold in the egg yolk and stir until it is well combined. Set the potatoes aside.

3. Preheat the oven to 400 degrees F.

4. For the meat filling, heat the olive oil in a 12-inch skillet over medium heat. When it is hot, add the onion and carrots and sauté until they soften, about 3 minutes. Add the garlic and stir to combine. Crumble the meat into the skillet and sauté until it is cooked through, about 4 minutes. Season with the salt and pepper. Sprinkle the meat with the flour and toss to coat the mixture well. Add the broth, tomato paste, Worcestershire, and thyme and stir to combine. Bring the mixture to a boil, then reduce the heat to low, cover, and simmer until the sauce thickens, 10 to 12 minutes. Fold in the peas.

5. Scoop the mashed potatoes on top of the meat filling and spread nearly to the edge but not all the way. Using a teaspoon, dip and swirl the potatoes to create a decorative effect. Place the skillet in the oven and bake until the potato topping browns, 20 to 25 minutes. Let the pie cool 10 minutes, then garnish with the thyme and serve.

GRANDMOTHER'S MEAT LOAF

MAKES 6 SERVINGS / Prep: 10 minutes / Bake: 45 to 50 minutes

Something about meat loaf lends itself to stories. I was speaking to a new neighbors' group several years back, and I don't know how we started talking about meat loaf or marriage, but we did. One woman said that she married the son of a minister, and on her wedding day, "He told me right then and there to never make meat loaf. He had seen enough of it at church suppers all his life." And thus she's had a happy marriage but hasn't tasted meat loaf in fifty years. I sure would miss the ease of meat loaf and the way it caramelizes in the pan and how it tastes the next day on sandwiches with pickles, lettuce, and a little mayonnaise. My mother-in-law, too, loved meat loaf. Her meat loaf recipe was written on a small piece of paper and attached to her refrigerator lest she forget it. It's delicious baked in an iron skillet.

1 large egg

1 medium onion, peeled and finely chopped

½ cup whole milk

10 Ritz crackers, crumbled

1 tablespoon Worcestershire sauce

1 cup ketchup, divided use

Kosher salt and freshly ground black pepper

1½ pounds ground beef sirloin

1. Preheat the oven to 350 degrees F.

2. In a large mixing bowl, lightly beat the egg. Add the onion, milk, crumbled crackers, Worcestershire sauce, and ½ cup of the ketchup and stir to combine. Season generously with salt and pepper. Crumble the ground beef into the bowl and use your hands to work the beef into the mixture until just combined—but not too much or the meat loaf will be tough.

3. Transfer the mixture to a 12-inch skillet and form it into a loaf shape. Drizzle the remaining ½ cup ketchup over the top of the meat loaf.

4. Place the skillet in the oven and bake until the top and sides of the meat loaf have browned and the meatloaf is cooked through, 45 to 50 minutes. Remove the skillet from the oven, and let the meat loaf rest in the skillet for 20 minutes, then slice and serve.

STIR-FRIED STEAK
with Broccoli and Ginger

MAKES 4 SERVINGS / Prep: 20 minutes / Cook: 8 to 12 minutes

There is nothing more delicious mid-week than stir-fry. And when the stir-fry is as substantial as this one—with sirloin steak—it can transition into weekend dinner party fare. The skillet is a natural for stir-frying because it retains heat and develops flavors in the pan. Some stir-fry recipes require a pantry full of ingredients, but for this recipe nearly everything is likely on hand, except perhaps the hoisin sauce. To make slicing the steak easier, freeze it until it's nearly frozen.

3 tablespoons reduced-sodium soy sauce

3 tablespoons dry sherry

2 tablespoons hoisin sauce

2 tablespoons water

1 teaspoon honey

2 teaspoons cornstarch

2 cloves garlic, peeled and minced

1 tablespoon grated fresh ginger

Pinch red pepper flakes

1 tablespoon vegetable oil, plus more if needed

2 cups broccoli florets

2 cups shredded cabbage mix for slaw

12 ounces boneless beef sirloin steak, trimmed and thinly sliced

Steamed rice or ramen noodles, for serving

1. In a small bowl, whisk together the soy sauce, sherry, hoisin sauce, water, honey, cornstarch, garlic, ginger, and red pepper flakes. Set aside.

2. Heat a 12-inch skillet over medium-high heat until nearly smoking, 3 to 4 minutes. Add the vegetable oil. When it is hot, add the broccoli florets and stir-fry for 2 minutes. Transfer the broccoli to a bowl. Add another teaspoon of oil to the skillet, if needed, and add the cabbage mix. Stir-fry until crispy, 1 to 2 minutes. Transfer to the bowl with the broccoli.

3. Add the steak to the skillet and stir-fry until the meat is cooked but still pink in the center, 2 to 3 minutes. Push the meat to one side of the pan. Add the sauce to the skillet and let it cook until bubbly, about 1 minute. Return the broccoli and slaw mix to the skillet and stir everything together to coat through. Serve at once with rice or noodles.

Dotty's
CHICKEN-FRIED STEAK

MAKES 2 TO 3 SERVINGS / Prep: 45 minutes / Cook: 4 to 5 minutes

I was going to call this recipe "How to Cook Chicken-Fried Steak like a Texan," but then I decided to name it after my friend, writer Dotty Griffith. Dotty grew up in Terrell, Texas, "the last small town east of Dallas," where she was raised by a mother who fried steak and served it with mashed potatoes and cream gravy. Dotty eagerly shared her family's secrets for cooking this Texas-loved delicacy, which is rooted in both the German settlers who schnitzeled the local beef and the South's "penchant for frying everything." The beauty of chicken-fried steak is that it cooks fast. "Frying is not a cool operation," says Dotty. "You go into a hot kitchen, and in Texas, you get it done and get out." Her special tricks are to soak the pounded beef in milk while you are prepping everything else. As a Texas extra, she adds pickled jalapeños to the soaking milk, then fries those peppers to garnish the top of the steak.

1 (1-pound) boneless beef round steak, ½ to 1 inch thick

1½ to 2 cups whole milk, divided use

2 large eggs

1 cup all-purpose flour

Salt and freshly ground black pepper

3 cups vegetable oil

CREAM GRAVY

¼ cup reserved pan drippings

¼ cup leftover seasoned flour from dredging, or fresh flour

Milk (listed above)

Salt and freshly ground black pepper

1 tablespoon drained, sliced pickled jalapeño peppers (optional; see Note)

1. Cut the steak into two or three pieces. Place on a cutting board and use a meat mallet to pound the pieces to ¼-inch thickness, turning them from side to side in this process. Put the meat in a large glass dish and pour ½ cup of the milk over them. With a fork, turn the pieces so they are covered with the milk. Set aside for 15 to 20 minutes.

2. In a shallow dish, whisk the eggs with a fork to break up the yolks. Put the flour in another shallow dish, and season it well with salt and pepper.

3. Remove the meat from the milk, pour the milk into the bowl with the eggs, and whisk to combine. Dredge each piece of meat in the flour mixture to coat both sides, dip it in the egg, then dredge it again in the flour. Place the meat on a wire rack set in a rimmed baking sheet to rest and dry out for 15 minutes. Reserve the seasoned flour.

4. Pour the oil into a 12-inch skillet and heat over medium-high heat until it reaches 375 degrees F. When the oil is hot, dredge the meat one more time in flour if the flour has dissolved. Carefully slide the meat in the skillet, being careful not to crowd the pieces. (This will ensure the meat cooks quickly and browns well.) Cook until well browned, about 2 minutes, then turn and cook on the other side until well browned and the meat is no longer pink inside, about 2 minutes. You may need to adjust the heat up or down to keep it at a constant 375 degrees F. Transfer the meat to brown paper to drain. Repeat with the remaining meat, making sure the oil is back up to 375 degrees F before frying. Once all the meat has been fried, keep it in a warm spot and cover it with a kitchen towel while you make the gravy.

5. To make the gravy, pour out all but ¼ cup drippings and fat from the skillet. Off the heat, whisk in ¼ cup of the seasoned flour (or use fresh flour). Place the skillet back over medium heat and whisk until smooth. Pour in 1 cup of the remaining milk and whisk until smooth. Add up to ½ cup more milk as needed to get to the right gravy consistency. Turn off the heat and season with salt and pepper. Top the fried steaks with the warm gravy and serve.

NOTE: Dotty likes to add pickled jalapeños to the milk soaking liquid. After frying the meat, dust them in the seasoned flour, dip in egg, then dust again in flour. Fry in the hot oil until well browned, 2 to 3 minutes. Serve on top of the chicken-fried steaks.

Stretching a Round Steak into Many Portions

The technique of stretching and pounding a round steak into many portions, then breading and frying it, economizes and makes a lot out of a little. Use the back of an iron skillet or a heavy meat tenderizer with spikes to pound the beef to ¼-inch thickness—or, as Dotty says in the Texas vernacular, "beat the crap out of it."

SEARED LAMB CHOPS
with Tomato and Mint Slaw

MAKES 3 TO 4 SERVINGS

Prep: 30 minutes / Cook: 6 to 8 minutes per batch

The iron skillet delivers big, bold flavors, and boy, is this recipe a great example. You season lamb chops with garlic, salt, pepper, and spicy harissa before searing. (Harissa not only comes in paste form, but also as a powdered seasoning blend that you can sprinkle on lamb, pork, and chicken before cooking.) The refreshing slaw of tomato and mint and a dollop of yogurt cools things off nicely.

8 small rib or loin lamb chops
(1¾ to 2 pounds total)

3 cloves garlic, peeled and minced

Kosher salt and freshly ground
black pepper

Harissa seasoning

3 tablespoons vegetable oil

TOMATO AND MINT SLAW

1½ cups halved red and yellow
cherry tomatoes or quartered
small plum tomatoes

Kosher salt and freshly ground
black pepper

½ cup packed fresh mint leaves,
bruised and roughly chopped

1 tablespoon fresh lime juice

¼ cup olive oil

¼ teaspoon red pepper flakes

GARNISH

Fresh mint sprigs

Plain full-fat yogurt

1. Put the lamb chops in a single layer in a 13-by-9-inch glass dish. Season both sides with the garlic, salt, pepper, and harissa.

2. Heat a 12-inch skillet over medium-high heat until nearly smoking, 3 to 4 minutes. Add the vegetable oil to the pan. When it is hot, sear 4 lamb chops until well browned, 3 to 4 minutes per side for medium-rare. Do not move the lamb chops while they sear on each side. With tongs, pick up each lamb chop and sear around the edges. Transfer to a plate and repeat with the remaining 4 lamb chops.

3. For the slaw, put the tomatoes in a mixing bowl and season with salt and pepper. Add the mint leaves and lime juice. Drizzle in the olive oil and add the pepper flakes. Toss to coat.

4. Garnish the lamb chops with fresh mint sprigs. Serve with the slaw alongside, plus a dollop of yogurt.

BUTTERMILK PORK CHOPS

MAKES 4 SERVINGS

Prep: 10 minutes / Soak: 30 minutes or up to 2 hours / Cook: 6 to 8 minutes per batch

Back when my mother fried pork chops, they were thin and crispy and irresistible. They just needed a soaking in buttermilk and a dredging in cornmeal and flour, and then a fast frying in the skillet. It was and still is the kind of pork chop you want to pick up and eat with your fingers. So, go ahead! Serve with green beans, coleslaw, and mashed potatoes.

8 (4-ounce) bone-in pork rib chops, less than ½ inch thick

2 cups buttermilk

1 cup white cornmeal

1 cup all-purpose flour

Creole seasoning

2 cups vegetable oil

Kosher salt and freshly ground black pepper

1. Put the pork chops in a single layer in a 13-by-9-inch glass dish. Pour the buttermilk over the pork chops and turn the chops to coat them in the buttermilk. Cover the dish with plastic wrap and refrigerate for at least 30 minutes or up to 2 hours.

2. When ready to fry, combine the cornmeal, flour, and Creole seasoning in a medium bowl. Remove the pork chops from the buttermilk and pat dry with paper towels. Dredge both sides in the seasoned flour mixture. Place on a rack set in a rimmed baking sheet.

3. Heat the oil in a 12-inch skillet over medium-high heat until it reaches 350 degrees F. Slide 2 pork chops into the oil and fry until golden, 3 to 4 minutes per side. Transfer the pork chops to brown paper to drain, and season with salt and pepper. Cover them with a kitchen towel and keep them in a warm spot while you repeat with the remaining pork chops. Serve at once.

SKILLET-ROASTED PORK
with Apples and Pears

MAKES 4 TO 6 SERVINGS / Prep: 30 minutes / Chill: 1 hour / Cook: About 1 hour 15 minutes

A pork loin roast, surrounded by apples, pears, onions, and garlic, smells heavenly when roasting in your oven. The trick is to find a pork roast with a layer of fat on top. Then, season the pork well with smoked paprika, salt, and pepper and sear it in the skillet. A 3-pound roast is just the right amount for two meals: the first with its own juices spooned over mashed potatoes, and the second on sandwiches smeared with Lemon-Fig Barbecue Sauce (page 261).

1 (3-pound) boneless pork loin roast

Creole seasoning

Kosher and freshly ground
black pepper

Smoked paprika

2 cloves garlic, peeled and minced

1 large onion, peeled and quartered

2 apples, cored and quartered

2 pears, cored and quartered

1. Rub the pork roast all over with Creole seasoning, kosher salt, pepper, paprika, and garlic. Place on a plate and refrigerate for 1 hour.

2. Preheat the oven to 350 degrees F.

3. Heat a 12-inch skillet over medium-high heat until nearly smoking, 3 to 4 minutes. Place the pork roast, fat-side down, in the skillet and cook until browned, about 3 minutes. Turn off the heat and turn the roast fat-side up. Scatter the onion, apples, and pears around the meat.

4. Place the skillet in the oven and bake until the pork reaches 160 degrees F, about 1 hour 15 minutes (if your roast is larger or smaller, figure on about 25 minutes per pound). Transfer the pork to a cutting board and let it rest for 20 minutes, then slice and serve with the skillet pan juices.

Desserts are a natural for the cast-iron skillet. Cakes bake up moist, and pie crusts get crispy. I knew pineapple upside-down cake was made for this skillet, but I had no idea just how good a strawberries and cream pound cake or sweet potato spice cake would taste baked in a skillet as well. Or that tortes, tarts, pies, and cookies could be baked in it, making this skillet the only pan you need in a small kitchen. The trick when baking in cast iron is to fully use the skillet—toast nuts in it first, or layer down some fruit and sugar before you add a cake batter so the fruit caramelizes while the cake bakes. The skillet bakes crust so crisp that most pies lift right out for easy slicing. Or serve dessert right from the skillet—bake a clafoutis or fruit crumble, or a big chocolate chip cookie topped with vanilla ice cream that melts into the warm cookie dough as you scoop it into bowls.

CHAPTER 6

SWEETS

SKILLET LOVE

The Cast-Iron
POUND CAKE

MAKES 12 TO 16 SERVINGS / Prep: 25 minutes / Bake: 1 hour 5 to 10 minutes

This is the recipe that inspired this book. I wanted to create a new twist on a Southern classic by baking a pound cake in cast iron. And I wanted this cake to take me back to simpler flavors. The recipe is a slight riff on the late John Egerton's pound cake, all butter with a cup of cream. After rubbing the skillet with a little soft butter, I poured in the batter and placed the pan in the oven. The cake baked to a glorious height, and the heavy pan created a crispy crust that released from the pan easily. And the creamy, moist interior? Perfection.

1 cup (2 sticks) plus 1 teaspoon unsalted butter, at room temperature, divided use

¼ teaspoon salt

3 cups sugar

6 large eggs, at room temperature

3 cups sifted all-purpose flour (see Note)

1 cup heavy cream

2 teaspoons vanilla extract

1. Preheat the oven to 325 degrees F.

2. Rub the bottom and sides of a 12-inch skillet with 1 teaspoon of the soft butter.

3. In a large mixing bowl, beat the remaining 1 cup soft butter and the salt with an electric mixer on medium-low speed until creamy, 1 minute. Beat in the sugar, a cup or so at a time. Increase the mixer speed to medium and beat until pale in color, 1 minute. With the mixer running, add the eggs, one at a time, beating each egg until thoroughly incorporated before adding the next. Scrape down the sides of the bowl with a silicone spatula.

4. With the mixer on low speed, add the flour and cream alternately, beginning and ending with the flour, and beat until combined. Blend in the vanilla, then scrape down the sides of the bowl. Transfer the batter to the prepared skillet, smoothing the top with the spatula.

5. Place the pan in the oven and bake the cake until the top is golden brown and crackly, 1 hour 5 to 10 minutes. Run a knife around the edges of the skillet and let the cake cool in the pan for 30 minutes. Give the pan a good shake, invert the cake onto a plate or your hand, then invert it again onto a wire rack. Let it cool for 1 hour before slicing. Wrap leftovers in aluminum foil and store at room temperature for up to 5 days or in the freezer for up to 6 months.

NOTE: Sift the flour before measuring.

BROWN SUGAR
Birthday Cake

MAKES 12 SERVINGS / Prep: 35 minutes / Bake: 40 to 45 minutes

We are fond of caramel, and so I loved the caramel-like flavor of brown sugar in this cake. It is a caramel cake without effort. One layer pops out easily from the iron skillet after cooling. No need to grease and flour layers, stack, and frost for that last-minute birthday cake. You just place it on a cake stand, pour over a quick icing, then light the candles!

1 cup (2 sticks) plus 1 teaspoon
unsalted butter, at room temperature

½ cup plus 1 teaspoon granulated sugar,
divided use

2 cups lightly packed light brown sugar

6 large eggs

1 teaspoon vanilla extract

3 cups unbleached all-purpose flour

1 teaspoon salt

1 teaspoon baking soda

1 cup sour cream

CREAM CHEESE ICING

4 ounces cream cheese,
at room temperature

4 tablespoons unsalted butter,
at room temperature

½ teaspoon vanilla extract

1¾ cups confectioners' sugar

How to Make a Two-Layer Caramel Cake

If caramel layer cake is what you're dreaming of, then let this brown sugar cake cool and slice horizontally in half using a long serrated knife. Prepare the Old-Fashioned Delta Caramel Icing (page 263) and slather it between, on top, and around the sides of the two cake layers.

1. Preheat the oven to 350 degrees F. Rub a 12-inch skillet with 1 teaspoon of the soft butter and sprinkle with 1 teaspoon granulated sugar. Set aside.

2. In a large mixing bowl, beat the remaining 1 cup butter, the brown sugar, and the remaining ½ cup granulated sugar with an electric mixer on low speed until well combined, about 2 minutes. Add the eggs, one at a time, beating each egg until thoroughly incorporated before adding the next. Add the vanilla and beat until combined.

3. In another large bowl, whisk together the flour, salt, and baking soda. Add a third of the flour mixture to the butter mixture and beat on low speed, then beat in a third of the sour cream. Repeat adding the flour mixture and then the sour cream two more times. Beat on low until smooth, 1 minute longer. Dump the batter into the prepared skillet.

4. Place the skillet in the oven and bake until the cake is firm to the touch when pressed in the center and has deeply browned, 40 to 45 minutes. Run a knife around the edges of the skillet and let the cake cool in the pan for 30 minutes. Give the pan a good shake, invert the cake onto a plate, then invert it again onto a wire rack. Let it cool for 1 hour before icing.

5. For the icing, in a medium mixing bowl, beat the cream cheese and butter with an electric mixer on low speed until combined, 30 seconds. Stop the machine and add the vanilla and confectioners' sugar. Blend on low speed until combined, 30 seconds. Increase the mixer to medium and beat until fluffy, about 1 minute.

6. Place the cooled cake on a cake stand. Pour the icing over the top, slice, and serve.

BLUEBERRY-LEMON
Ricotta Cake

MAKES 12 TO 16 SERVINGS / Prep: 35 minutes / Bake: 50 to 55 minutes

Ricotta cheese is both an old and new ingredient in cake baking. It's been used for centuries in Italian baking to impart richness and texture. I first made a cranberry-orange version of this sturdy cake, but one day when cranberries weren't in season, I subbed in blueberries and lemon zest instead. Now it has become my year-round favorite. The beauty of a versatile recipe is that it changes with the seasons. It's good with vanilla ice cream any time of year!

1¾ sticks (7 ounces) unsalted butter, at room temperature, divided use

2 cups unbleached all-purpose flour

1 cup yellow cornmeal

1 tablespoon baking powder

1 teaspoon salt

1½ cups sugar, plus 1 tablespoon for sprinkling

3 large eggs

¼ cup honey (see Note, page 145)

¼ cup vegetable oil or light olive oil

1 tablespoon vanilla extract

1 tablespoon grated lemon zest

2 cups (15 ounces) whole-milk ricotta cheese

2½ cups fresh blueberries, divided use

1. Preheat the oven to 350 degrees F. Lightly grease a 12-inch skillet with 1 teaspoon of the butter.

2. In a large mixing bowl, whisk together the flour, cornmeal, baking powder, and salt.

3. In another large mixing bowl, beat the remaining soft butter with an electric mixer on medium speed until creamy, about 30 seconds. Add the 1½ cups sugar and beat until the mixture is light and fluffy, 1 to 1½ minutes. Scrape down the sides of the bowl. Add the eggs, one at a time, beating each egg on medium speed until thoroughly incorporated before adding the next. Add the honey, oil, vanilla, and grated lemon zest and blend until well combined, 45 seconds.

4. With the mixer on low speed, add the flour mixture and ricotta alternately, beginning and ending with the flour, and beat until combined. Fold in 1½ cups of the blueberries and blend on low speed briefly, about 20 seconds, to break them up a bit. Dump the batter into the prepared skillet and smooth the top. Scatter the remaining 1 cup berries on top of the batter and sprinkle with the remaining tablespoon sugar.

5. Place the skillet in the oven and bake the cake until it is firm to the touch and golden brown, 50 to 55 minutes. Run a knife around the edges of the skillet and let the cake cool in the pan for 30 minutes. Give the pan a good shake, invert the cake onto a plate or your hand, then invert it again onto a wire rack. Let it cool for 1 hour before slicing.

NOTE: For the original cranberry-orange version, simply substitute chopped fresh cranberries for the blueberries and grated orange zest for the lemon.

PRUNE AND RYE CAKE
with Buttermilk Glaze

MAKES 12 SERVINGS / Prep: 25 minutes / Bake: 40 to 45 minutes

My mother used to bake prune cake with buttermilk glaze about the time the weather turned cool and you could feel fall in the air. I didn't know until I researched the history behind American cakes that the prune cake was brought to our country by Eastern European immigrants. It's now a favorite throughout the Midwest and South, and with my interest in trying new flours, I decided to give my mom's prune cake a bit of a face-lift by adding some rye flour. I found that rye's natural, subtle spice works well with the prunes and spices in this old family recipe.

1 teaspoon unsalted butter,
at room temperature

2 cups unbleached all-purpose flour

1 cup rye flour

2 teaspoons baking soda

2 teaspoons ground cinnamon

2 teaspoons ground allspice

2 teaspoons ground nutmeg

½ teaspoon salt

2 cups sugar

1½ cups vegetable oil

2 large eggs plus 4 large egg yolks

½ cup buttermilk

2 cups chopped pitted prunes
(see Note)

BUTTERMILK GLAZE

½ cup sugar

¼ cup buttermilk

2 teaspoons light corn syrup
or honey

2 tablespoons unsalted butter

¼ teaspoon salt

1 teaspoon vanilla extract
or rye whiskey

1. Preheat the oven to 350 degrees F. Grease a 12-inch skillet with the soft butter.

2. In a medium bowl, whisk together both flours, the baking soda, cinnamon, allspice, nutmeg, and salt.

3. In a large mixing bowl, blend the sugar and oil with an electric mixer on medium speed until combined, 30 seconds. Add the eggs and egg yolks and blend until combined and slightly thickened, about 1 minute.

4. With the mixer on low speed, add the flour mixture and buttermilk alternately to the creamed oil and sugar, beginning and ending with the flour, and beat until combined. Fold in the chopped prunes. Dump the batter into the prepared skillet, smoothing the top with a spatula.

5. Place the skillet in the oven and bake the cake until the top springs back when slightly pressed in the center, 40 to 45 minutes.

6. About 10 minutes before the cake is done, prepare the glaze. Combine the sugar, buttermilk, corn syrup or honey, butter, and salt in a medium saucepan and bring to a boil over medium heat, stirring. Reduce the heat to low and let the mixture simmer until smooth and thickened, about 2 minutes. Remove the pan from the heat and stir in the vanilla or rye whiskey.

7. When the cake is done, remove the skillet from the oven and immediately prick the top several times with a fork to create holes. Drizzle the glaze over the warm cake, then smooth the top of the cake with a small metal spatula so the glaze is nearly absorbed by the cake. Let the cake rest for 30 minutes for the glaze to set slightly, then slice and serve.

NOTE: Most prunes are sold pitted and soft. If not, remove the pits with a small paring knife. Put the prunes in a small saucepan and pour in ½ inch of water. Simmer over medium heat for 3 to 4 minutes, until they soften. Drain, cool, and chop.

STRAWBERRIES AND CREAM
Pound Cake

MAKES 12 TO 16 SERVINGS / Prep: 30 minutes / Bake: 1 hour 10 to 15 minutes

Pound cakes bake so beautifully in the iron skillet. And it's amazing how the simple addition of chopped strawberries turns my favorite pound cake into perfection. If you want to unmold these skillet cakes—versus slice and serve right from the pan—run a knife around the pan edges as soon as the cake comes out of the oven. This makes unmolding so much easier. And for the easiest process of all, line the bottom of the skillet with a round of parchment paper.

1 cup (2 sticks) plus 1 teaspoon unsalted butter, at room temperature, divided use

3 cups all-purpose flour

½ teaspoon salt

3 cups granulated sugar

6 large eggs, at room temperature

2 teaspoons vanilla extract

1 cup heavy cream

1 cup chopped strawberries (5 to 6 large, capped)

Confectioners' sugar, for dusting (optional)

Sweetened whipped cream and sliced fresh strawberries, for garnish (optional)

1. Preheat the oven to 350 degrees F. Grease a 12-inch skillet with 1 teaspoon of the soft butter.

2. In a small bowl, whisk together flour and salt.

3. In a large mixing bowl, beat the remaining 1 cup butter with an electric mixer on medium-low speed until creamy, 1 minute. Beat in the sugar, a cup or so at a time. Increase the mixer speed to medium and beat until pale in color, 1 minute more. Turn the mixer to low speed and add the eggs, one at a time, beating each egg until thoroughly incorporated before adding the next. Blend in the vanilla. Scrape down the sides of the bowl.

4. With the mixer on low speed, add the flour mixture and cream alternately, beginning and ending with the flour, and beat until combined. Scrape down the sides of the bowl. Dump the batter into the prepared skillet, smoothing the top with the spatula. Scatter the chopped strawberries over the top.

5. Place the skillet in the oven and bake until the cake is golden brown and crackly on top, and a toothpick inserted near the center of the cake comes out clean, 1 hour 10 to 15 minutes. Run a knife around the edges of the skillet and let the cake cool in the pan for 30 minutes. Give the pan a good shake, invert the cake onto a plate or your hand, then invert it again onto a wire rack. Let it cool for 1 hour before slicing. Serve with a dusting of confectioners' sugar or top with whipped cream and sliced strawberries. Wrap leftovers in aluminum foil and store at room temperature for up to 5 days or in the freezer for up to 6 months.

NOTE: In lieu of whipped cream and berries on top, you can top this cake with a simple glaze. Whisk together 1 cup confectioners' sugar and about 2 tablespoons lime juice or milk in a small bowl. Add a little grated lime zest, if desired, and drizzle the glaze over the cooled cake.

GEORGIA BURNT
Caramel Cake

MAKES 12 TO 16 SERVINGS / Prep: 30 minutes / Bake: 60 to 65 minutes

I spent almost 20 years in Georgia, attending college and also working as the food editor for the *Atlanta Journal-Constitution*. It was during these years that I developed a deep affection for peaches and pound cake. And I love how this recipe, which is a variation on one given to me decades ago by the late Jimmy Bentley, merges the two. A "conserve" of peach preserves, marmalade, and pecans is assembled and folded into the pound cake batter to give it a peach flavor. And my twist is to drizzle a quick caramel glaze that tastes like burnt sugar on top of the cake before serving.

2 cups (4 sticks) plus 1 teaspoon
unsalted butter, at room temperature,
divided use

2½ cups granulated sugar

8 large eggs

3¾ cups all-purpose flour

½ teaspoon salt

1 teaspoon vanilla extract

CONSERVE

½ cup peach preserves

¼ cup orange marmalade

¼ cup finely chopped pecans

BURNT CARAMEL GLAZE

4 tablespoons unsalted butter

¼ cup dark brown sugar

¼ cup light brown sugar

Pinch salt

2 tablespoons milk

1 cup confectioners' sugar

½ teaspoon vanilla extract

1. Preheat the oven to 325 degrees F. Grease a 12-inch skillet with 1 teaspoon of the soft butter.

2. In a large mixing bowl, beat the remaining 2 cups butter and the sugar with an electric mixer on medium–low speed until the mixture is well beaten and creamy, 1½ to 2 minutes. Add the eggs, one at a time, beating each egg on low speed until thoroughly incorporated before adding the next. Add half of the flour and beat until just incorporated, about 15 seconds. Add the salt, the rest of the flour, and the vanilla and beat until well incorporated, about 1 minute more. Scrape down the sides of the bowl.

3. To make the conserve, stir together the peach preserves, orange marmalade, and pecans in a small bowl.

4. Transfer about half of the batter to the skillet. Dollop about half of the conserve by teaspoonsful over the top. Dump the rest of the batter into the skillet, and dollop the top with the remaining conserve. Swirl the conserve into the batter with a dinner knife.

5. Place the skillet in the oven and bake the cake until it is well browned on the top, about 40 minutes. Tent the top of the cake with aluminum foil and continue to bake until a long toothpick inserted in the center comes out clean, 20 to 25 minutes more. Run a knife around the edges of the skillet and let the cake cool in the pan for 30 minutes. Give the pan a good shake, invert the cake onto a plate or your hand, then invert it again onto a wire rack. Let it cool for 30 minutes.

6. Meanwhile, prepare the glaze. Combine the butter and both brown sugars in the skillet used to bake the cake. Let the residual heat of the skillet melt the butter; if it doesn't melt, place the pan over low heat and stir with a wooden spoon until the sugars bubble up and the butter has melted. Sprinkle with the salt. Stir in the milk. Whisk in the confectioners' sugar and vanilla until smooth. Turn off the heat. Pour the glaze over the cake while it is warm. Let the cake and glaze rest for 30 minutes, then slice and serve.

FRESH PINEAPPLE
Upside-Down Cake

MAKES 12 TO 16 SERVINGS / Prep: 35 minutes / Bake: 40 to 45 minutes

The original "skillet cake," pineapple upside-down cake was born in a publicity campaign from Dole pineapple nearly a century ago. The company was eager to build awareness for its brand, so it asked American cooks to submit their favorite recipes using canned pineapple. As the recipes rolled in, a majority were for a pineapple cake baked in an iron skillet, then flipped upside-down to serve. The name stuck. I had never been a huge pineapple upside-down fan because the cake was often dry, but I was determined to create a recipe for a moist cake that could live up to the caramelized brown sugar, butter, and pineapple wonderfulness on the bottom of the skillet. Here it is. The cake is essentially a hot milk sponge cake. Feel free to use a 20-ounce can of sliced pineapple rings, but if you are going to make this cake for a special birthday dinner or potluck, try fresh, ripe pineapple!

TOPPING

1 (2- to 3-pound) ripe pineapple

6 tablespoons unsalted butter

¾ cup firmly packed light brown sugar

CAKE

1 cup whole milk

4 tablespoons unsalted butter

2 teaspoons vanilla extract

2 cups unbleached all-purpose flour

2 teaspoons baking powder

1¼ teaspoons salt

2 cups granulated sugar

4 large eggs

⅓ cup vegetable oil

Dark rum, for drizzling (optional)

Whipped cream, for serving (optional)

1. To make the topping, cut off the top of the pineapple and then cut off the skin, taking care to remove all the "eyes" of the pineapple. Quarter the pineapple lengthwise and cut away the core. Cut the pineapple quarters crosswise into ⅜-inch slices.

2. Melt the butter in a 12-inch skillet over medium heat. Stir in the brown sugar until the mixture bubbles, about 4 minutes. Pull the skillet off the heat. Arrange the pineapple slices in concentric circles on top of the butter and sugar, beginning at the edges of the pan and overlapping the pieces slightly (see Note). Set the pan aside.

3. For the cake, heat the milk and butter in a small saucepan over medium heat until the butter melts, about 2 minutes. Stir in the vanilla and remove the pan from the heat.

4. In a small bowl, whisk together the flour, baking powder, and salt.

5. In a large mixing bowl, beat the sugar and eggs with an electric mixer on medium speed until the mixture is thick and lemon-colored, 2 to 3 minutes. Add the oil and blend to combine. With the mixer on low speed, add the flour mixture and hot milk mixture alternately, beginning and ending with the flour, and beat until smooth. The batter will be runny. Pour the batter over the pineapple in the skillet.

6. Place the pan in the oven and bake until the cake is golden and springs back when lightly pressed on the center, 40 to 45 minutes. Let the cake rest in the skillet for 5 minutes, then run a knife around the edges of the skillet to loosen it. Place a flat platter, board, or plate over the skillet and invert the skillet so the pineapple ends up on top. Replace any pineapple still stuck to the bottom of the skillet. If desired, drizzle the top of the cake with dark rum. Let the cake cool for 30 minutes, then slice and serve with whipped cream, if desired.

NOTE: If desired, sprinkle ground cinnamon or drizzle lavender honey or dark rum on the pineapple slices before pouring the cake batter over them.

MISSISSIPPI MUD CAKE
with Chocolate Fudge Icing

MAKES 12 TO 16 SERVINGS / Prep: 30 minutes / Bake: 30 to 35 minutes

The South is home to all sorts of wacky chocolate cakes like the Coca-Cola cake and this Mississippi mud cake—so named because the color resembles the deep, dark soil along the Mississippi River. What makes this recipe perfect for the skillet is that it can be made entirely in one pan, from stirring the batter to baking the cake. The marshmallows are scattered on the hot cake so they melt, and then the chocolate icing is poured over. What results is a gooey chocolate, decadent mess of a cake, intended to be spooned onto plates and served warm with a glass of cold milk.

CAKE

2 cups all-purpose flour

1¾ cups granulated sugar

⅓ cup unsweetened cocoa powder

1 teaspoon baking soda

½ teaspoon salt

½ cup (1 stick) unsalted butter

1½ cups buttermilk

2 large eggs, beaten

1 teaspoon vanilla extract

1½ cups miniature marshmallows

CHOCOLATE FUDGE ICING

½ cup (1 stick) unsalted butter

4 tablespoons unsweetened cocoa powder

⅓ cup whole milk

Big pinch salt

3 to 3½ cups confectioners' sugar

1. Preheat the oven to 350 degrees F.

2. In a large bowl, whisk together the flour, sugar, cocoa, baking soda, and salt.

3. Melt the butter in a 12-inch skillet over medium-low heat. Remove the skillet from the heat. Pour the buttermilk into the skillet and stir to combine with the melted butter. Add the beaten eggs and vanilla and stir to combine. Add the flour mixture to the skillet and stir until smooth, about 2 minutes. Run a wet paper towel around the edges of the pan to clean them up.

4. Place the skillet in the oven and bake until the cake springs back when lightly pressed with a finger, 30 to 35 minutes. Remove the skillet from the oven and immediately scatter the marshmallows over the top of the cake. Set the skillet aside.

5. To make the icing, melt the butter in a medium saucepan over low heat. Stir in the cocoa powder and milk. Cook, stirring, until the mixture thickens and just begins to come to a boil, about 1 minute. Remove the pan from the heat. Stir in the salt and 3 cups confectioners' sugar, a little at a time, whisking until smooth. Add up to ½ cup more confectioners' sugar if needed to make an icing that is pourable and spreadable.

6. Pour the hot icing over the top of the marshmallows. Let the cake rest for 30 minutes, then serve.

CRANBERRY AND ALMOND TART

MAKES 12 TO 16 SERVINGS / Prep: 15 minutes / Bake: 35 to 40 minutes

This Nashville cake-meets-pie recipe has made the rounds at dinner parties because it is good and easy. All you need to do is scatter cranberries and almonds (or pecans) in the bottom of the skillet before pouring over a pound cake batter. It is chewy like a bar, and yet it feels like a crustless pie. For a dessert that can't decide what exactly it is, all I can say is—it's delicious! Serve with whipped cream.

1 cup plus 2 tablespoons (2¼ sticks) unsalted butter

3 cups fresh cranberries, rinsed and drained

2¼ cups sugar, divided use

½ cup finely chopped almonds or pecans

1½ cups all-purpose flour

3 large eggs, lightly beaten

1 teaspoon almond extract

Whipped cream or ice cream, for serving

1. Preheat the oven to 350 degrees F.

2. Melt the butter in a medium saucepan over low heat. Brush about a teaspoon of the melted butter over the bottom of a 12-inch skillet. Scatter the cranberries in the skillet. Sprinkle ¾ cup of the sugar and all of the nuts over the cranberries.

3. Pour the melted butter into a large mixing bowl, add the flour, eggs, almond extract, and remaining 1½ cups sugar, and stir with a wooden spoon to combine. Pour the batter over the cranberry mixture and smooth the top.

4. Place the skillet in the oven and bake until the tart is lightly golden brown and the center is firm and has set, 35 to 40 minutes. Let the tart cool for 30 minutes, then slice and serve warm with whipped cream or ice cream.

PEAR SKILLET GINGERBREAD

MAKES 12 SERVINGS / Prep: 20 minutes / Bake: 35 to 40 minutes

Many a gingerbread has baked in a cast-iron skillet, dating back to a time when cakes were baked in iron Dutch ovens over an open fire or in a "bake oven" fueled by wood. This recipe reunites the iron pan and gingerbread in a modern way, with the inclusion of pears and pear preserves. It's a perfect combo! I have learned that while molasses is most often used in baking gingerbread, you can substitute the milder sorghum if you have it. Both are acidic ingredients that react with the baking soda to help the cake rise.

½ cup (1 stick) plus 2 tablespoons unsalted butter, at room temperature, divided use

½ cup pear preserves

3 ripe pears, peeled, cored, and cut into 8 slices each, plus an extra pear for slicing as garnish

2¾ cups all-purpose flour

2 tablespoons ground ginger

1 teaspoon baking soda

1 teaspoon cream of tartar

1 teaspoon ground cinnamon

½ teaspoon ground nutmeg

½ teaspoon salt

½ cup firmly packed light brown sugar

1 cup molasses

½ cup milk or orange juice

¼ cup brandy, pear brandy, or coffee

3 large eggs, lightly beaten

1 teaspoon grated lemon zest (optional)

Vanilla ice cream, for serving

1. Preheat the oven to 325 degrees F.

2. Melt 2 tablespoons of the butter in a 12-inch skillet over medium heat. Remove the pan from the heat. Stir the pear preserves into the melted butter. Arrange the 24 pear slices across the bottom of the pan.

3. In a medium bowl, whisk together the flour, ginger, baking soda, cream of tartar, cinnamon, nutmeg, and salt.

4. In a large bowl, beat the remaining ½ cup butter with a wooden spoon or electric mixer on medium speed until creamy. Add the brown sugar and molasses and beat until smooth, 1 to 2 minutes. Fold in the flour mixture, along with the milk, brandy, eggs, and lemon zest (if using). Beat until smooth, about 2 minutes. Pour the batter over the pears in the skillet.

5. Place the skillet in the oven and bake until the top springs back when lightly pressed, 35 to 40 minutes. Remove the skillet from the oven. Spoon the hot cake into bowls and top with vanilla ice cream.

How to Make Your Own Brown Sugar

If you have granulated sugar and molasses in the pantry, you can make your own brown sugar in minutes. Here's how: Put 2 cups granulated sugar in a food processor fitted with a steel blade. With the motor running, pour in 3 tablespoons molasses through the feed tube and process until the molasses is incorporated and the white sugar turns brown, about 1 minute. This deeply flavored brown sugar can be used in recipes calling for light or dark brown sugar. Store in an airtight container at room temperature for up to 3 months.

SWEET POTATO SKILLET CAKE
with Pecan Crust

MAKES 8 TO 12 SERVINGS / Prep: 20 minutes / Bake: 45 to 50 minutes

Sweet potatoes just might be one of the most versatile ingredients, perfect for roasting and frying, for mashing and souffléing, and also for turning into this skillet spice cake. On the bottom of the skillet are finely chopped pecans, lightly toasted in the oven before the batter is poured in. And when the cake bakes, those pecans form a crispy crust. This cake is moist and full of spices, and it gets better on day two, so there's only one question: ice cream or whipped cream on top?

1¼ pounds sweet potatoes, peeled and cut into 1-inch pieces

1 cup pecan halves

2 cups all-purpose flour

1½ teaspoons baking soda

1½ teaspoons ground cinnamon

1 teaspoon ground nutmeg

1 teaspoon baking powder

1 teaspoon salt

½ teaspoon ground cloves

¼ teaspoon ground ginger

1½ cups vegetable oil

1¾ cups sugar

2 teaspoons vanilla extract

4 large eggs

Whipped cream or vanilla ice cream, for serving

Burnt Caramel Glaze (page 211), optional

1. Put the sweet potatoes in a large saucepan and cover with water. Bring the water to a boil over medium-high heat, then reduce the heat to low, cover, and let simmer until the potatoes are tender, about 15 minutes. Drain and mash. You should have about 2 cups mashed sweet potatoes. Set aside.

2. Preheat the oven to 325 degrees F. Scatter the pecan halves in a 12-inch skillet and place the skillet in the oven to lightly toast the pecans while the oven preheats, 6 to 8 minutes. Transfer the pecans to a cutting board. When the pecans are cool enough to handle, finely chop them and scatter the pieces in the bottom of the skillet.

3. In a large bowl, whisk together the flour, baking soda, cinnamon, nutmeg, baking powder, salt, cloves, and ginger.

4. In another large bowl, beat the oil and sugar with an electric mixer on medium-low speed until well combined, about 1 minute. Add the vanilla and eggs, one at a time, beating each egg on medium speed until thoroughly incorporated before adding the next. The mixture should be thickened and smooth. Stop the mixer, add the sweet potatoes, and blend to combine. Add the dry ingredients and beat on low until just combined and smooth, about 1 minute. Scrape down the sides of the bowl, then pour the batter over the pecans in the skillet.

5. Place the skillet in the oven and bake until the cake springs back when lightly pressed in the center, 45 to 50 minutes. Run a knife around the edges of the skillet and let the cake cool in the pan for 30 minutes. Slice and serve warm with whipped cream or vanilla ice cream. Or, pour the burnt caramel glaze on top, if desired.

Brown Sugar
SNICKERDOODLE BITES

MAKES ABOUT 4 DOZEN (1-INCH) SQUARES
Prep: 20 minutes / Bake: 25 to 30 minutes

Snickerdoodles—those irresistible cinnamon- and sugar-dusted cookies—were first baked as bars. So, honoring history, I made the cookie batter in my skillet and created small bites of that same beloved cookie. What the skillet does so well with bars and squares is crisp them up around the edges. And to keep the edges of these bites nice and clean, I score them with a knife straight out of the oven. If you want to present this as a giant cookie, perhaps a birthday cookie, do not score it. Stick candles in the still-warm cookie and slice it right at the table. Snickerdoodle pairs well with cinnamon, vanilla, or peach ice cream.

1 cup granulated sugar

½ cup lightly packed light brown sugar

½ cup (1 stick) unsalted butter, at room temperature

½ cup vegetable shortening (see Note)

1 teaspoon vanilla extract

2 large eggs

2¼ cups all-purpose flour

1 teaspoon baking soda

½ teaspoon salt

TOPPING

2 tablespoons granulated sugar

2 teaspoons ground cinnamon

1. Preheat the oven to 375 degrees F.

2. In a large mixing bowl, beat both sugars, the butter, and the shortening with an electric mixer on medium speed until creamy, about 2 minutes, scraping down the side of the bowl once. Add the vanilla and the eggs, one at a time, continuing to beat on medium speed for about 30 seconds.

3. In a small bowl, whisk together the flour, baking soda, and salt. Add the flour mixture to the butter mixture and beat on low speed until incorporated, scraping down the side of the bowl as needed. Dump the batter into a 12-inch skillet, smoothing the top.

4. To make the topping, stir together the sugar and cinnamon in a small bowl. Sprinkle the topping over the batter.

5. Place the skillet in the oven and bake until deeply golden brown, 25 to 30 minutes. Score the big cookie into 1-inch squares and let cool in the pan for 20 minutes. With a small metal spatula, transfer the squares to a rack to cool completely.

NOTE: Vegetable shortening makes a chewier cookie. If you want more butter flavor, use 1 cup (2 sticks) of butter instead of half butter and half shortening.

WARM CHOCOLATE CHUNK COOKIE
to Share

MAKES 12 SERVINGS / Prep: 20 minutes / Bake: 25 to 30 minutes

Hands-down, this is the one-pan skillet dessert that brings everyone to the table. I don't care how many of your guests say they are not eating dessert. If you pull this warm cookie from the oven, place it on a trivet in the middle of the table, then pile on ice cream, it's just too hard to resist! The trick is not to overbake the cookie. You want to bake it until "medium-rare" so the edges are crispy but the center is still soft and spoonable.

1 cup (2 sticks) unsalted butter

¾ cup firmly packed dark brown sugar

¾ cup granulated sugar

2 large eggs, lightly beaten

1 teaspoon vanilla extract

2 cups all-purpose flour

1 teaspoon baking soda

1 teaspoon salt

1 cup (6 ounces) semisweet chocolate chips

10 ounces bittersweet chocolate chunks

½ cup coarsely chopped walnuts or pecans

Vanilla ice cream, for serving

1. Preheat the oven to 375 degrees F.

2. Melt the butter in a 12-inch skillet over low heat. Turn off the heat. Stir both sugars into the melted butter. Fold in the eggs and vanilla.

3. In a small bowl, whisk together the flour, baking soda, and salt. Add the flour mixture to the butter-sugar mixture and stir until smooth. Fold in the chocolate chips and chocolate chunks. Run a wet paper towel around the edges of the pan to clean them up. Scatter the nuts over the top of the batter.

4. Place the skillet in the oven and bake until the edges are lightly browned and the center is still a little soft to the touch, 25 to 30 minutes. Remove the pan from the oven. Serve warm with vanilla ice cream.

SKILLET BROWNIE
on a Caramel Puddle

MAKES 12 TO 16 SERVINGS / Prep: 15 minutes / Bake: 35 to 40 minutes

Nothing is better than a skillet brownie—except, perhaps, a skillet brownie that bakes on a puddle of caramel and toasted walnuts or pecans. These sticky, wickedly delicious brownies are irresistible hot from the skillet. We spoon them straight into bowls and top with ice cream! Or, if you have more self-control, you can let them rest for an hour in the skillet and cut into bars to serve later.

2 cups chopped walnuts
or pecans

1 cup caramel sauce
(see Note)

4 ounces unsweetened
chocolate, chopped

1 cup (2 sticks) unsalted butter

2 cups sugar

4 large eggs, lightly beaten

1 teaspoon vanilla extract

½ cup all-purpose flour

½ teaspoon salt

1. Preheat the oven to 325 degrees F. Scatter the nuts in a 12-inch skillet and place the skillet in the oven to lightly toast the nuts while the oven preheats, 6 to 8 minutes. Remove the skillet from the oven and pour the caramel sauce over the nuts. Set the skillet aside.

2. Combine the chocolate and butter in a large, heavy saucepan. Cook over low heat, stirring, until the chocolate and butter melt, 4 to 5 minutes. Remove the pan from the heat and stir in the sugar. Add the eggs and vanilla and stir to combine well. Add the flour and salt. Stir just to combine. Pour the batter over the nuts and caramel in the skillet.

3. Place the skillet in the oven and bake until a toothpick inserted in the center comes out with moist, fudgy crumbs, 35 to 40 minutes. Place the pan on a rack to cool completely, about 1 hour. Cut into bars or squares and serve.

NOTE: Any good jarred caramel sauce works here. I like the one from Trader Joe's.

CLASSIC CHERRY
Clafoutis

MAKES 8 SERVINGS / Prep: 25 minutes / Bake: 35 to 40 minutes

This much-loved, rustic French dessert was designed to use the fruit of the season. Cherries are the classic addition, but you can use fresh apricots as well. Scatter the fruit on the bottom of the buttered skillet, then pour in a pancake-like batter. The result isn't eggy like a flan; it's more like a Dutch baby in texture. Old-timers believed you should leave the pits in your cherries because they impart an almond-like flavor to the recipe. But I think it's a lot easier to pit the cherries ahead of time! Serve warm right from the skillet.

2 teaspoons unsalted butter,
at room temperature

2 tablespoons sliced or
slivered almonds

12 ounces sweet pitted cherries

3 large eggs

½ cup plus 2 tablespoons
granulated sugar (see Note)

1 cup all-purpose flour

¼ teaspoon salt

1¼ cups whole milk

1 teaspoon vanilla extract

Pinch grated nutmeg (optional)

1. Preheat the oven to 375 degrees F.

2. Grease a 12-inch skillet with the soft butter. Scatter the almonds and cherries in the bottom of the skillet.

3. In a medium-size bowl, whisk together the eggs and ½ cup sugar. Fold in the flour and salt. Whisk in the milk, vanilla, and nutmeg (if using). Pour this batter over the almonds and cherries in the skillet. Sprinkle 2 tablespoons sugar over the top.

4. Place the skillet in the oven and bake until the clafoutis lightly browns and puffs up, 35 to 40 minutes. It should still shake a little in the pan. Serve warm.

NOTE: The granulated sugar sprinkled on top makes a nice crispy topping. If you wish to omit it, you can dust the baked clafoutis with confectioners' sugar before serving.

LULA'S TOASTED
Coconut Pie

MAKES 8 TO 12 SERVINGS / Prep: 20 minutes / Bake: 25 to 30 minutes

One of the easiest pies in the world just got more delicious thanks to the iron skillet. This is a family favorite recipe, given to me by the late Lula Estes, a Nashville artist and all-around wonderful person. She used to make this recipe in little tart shells, then freeze them and reheat for unexpected dinner guests. I took Lula's recipe one step further—and utilized my skillet—first by toasting the coconut and then by baking her pie.

2 cups unsweetened flaked coconut (see Note)

4 large eggs

2 cups sugar

¼ cup heavy cream

2 teaspoons vanilla extract (or 1½ teaspoons vanilla extract plus ½ teaspoon coconut extract)

1 recipe Food Processor Pie Crust (page 247)

1. Place a rack in the lower third of the oven. Preheat the oven to 375 degrees F. Scatter the coconut in a 12-inch skillet and place the skillet in the oven to lightly toast the coconut while the oven preheats, 5 to 7 minutes. Remove the skillet from the oven and transfer the coconut to a bowl or plate.

2. In a medium mixing bowl, whisk together the eggs, sugar, cream, and vanilla until smooth. Fold in the coconut.

3. When the skillet is cool enough to touch, press the pie crust dough into the bottom and up the sides, then crimp the top edges. Prick the bottom of the crust with a fork six or seven times. Pour the filling into the crust.

4. Bake until the pie crust and filling are golden brown, 25 to 30 minutes. Let the pie cool for 1 hour before slicing and serving.

NOTE: If you use sweetened coconut, you may want to reduce the sugar by a couple tablespoons. And when you toast sweetened coconut, be forewarned that it burns easily, so watch it closely and remove it when it is just light brown.

Our Favorite
BUTTERMILK PIE

MAKES 12 SERVINGS / Prep: 10 minutes / Bake: 50 to 55 minutes

I was able to wrangle this buttermilk pie recipe from my server at the Shaker Village restaurant in Kentucky. She handed over a massive, foodservice–size recipe that would have fed the entire first Shaker community. But with the aid of my calculator, and some testing, I was able to scale it down. Pies like this were first baked when cooking thrifty was a way of life. You didn't order ingredients from Amazon or drive to the supermarket—you just made a pie from what was at hand!

1 recipe Food Processor
Pie Crust (page 247)

3 cups sugar

6 large eggs

1 cup full-fat buttermilk

10 tablespoons (1¼ sticks)
unsalted butter, melted

½ teaspoon salt

1 teaspoon vanilla extract

1. Place a rack in the lower third of the oven. Preheat the oven to 350 degrees F.

2. Press the pie crust dough into the bottom and up the sides of a 12-inch skillet, and prick the crust with a fork about eight times.

3. In a large mixing bowl, beat the sugar, eggs, buttermilk, melted butter, salt, and vanilla in with a wooden spoon 40 to 50 strokes to combine well. Pour the batter into the pie crust.

4. Bake the pie until it is well browned and mostly firm to the touch but still a little jiggly, 50 to 55 minutes. Let the pie cool for at least 30 minutes—or, for best results, several hours—before slicing.

RUM-ROASTED PEACHES

MAKES 4 SERVINGS / Prep: 20 minutes / Bake: 20 to 25 minutes

This recipe comes with a disclaimer: Do not use fully ripe, in-season fruit. Because really, the best thing to do with gorgeous ripe peaches is to eat them out of hand and let the juices run down your arm. This dessert is for those other peaches—the ones that don't taste as sweet as promised, the ones that are a little firmer than you would like. These less-than-perfect peaches are just right for roasting and keep their shape beautifully!

2 tablespoons unsalted butter

½ cup lightly packed light brown sugar

3 tablespoons water

1 cinnamon stick

5 whole cloves

Pinch ground nutmeg

2 tablespoons dark rum, bourbon, or rye whiskey

4 large peaches, cut in half and pitted

Vanilla ice cream, for serving

1. Preheat the oven to 375 degrees F.

2. Melt the butter in a 12-inch skillet over medium heat. Add the brown sugar, water, cinnamon stick, cloves, and nutmeg and stir until the sugar dissolves, about 4 minutes. Stir in the rum. Place the peaches, cut-side down, in the skillet, and spoon some of the cooking juices over them.

3. Place the skillet in the oven and bake until the peaches are tender, 15 to 20 minutes. Remove the skillet from the oven and let the peaches cool in the juices until you can handle them, about 20 minutes. Peel away their skins. Spoon vanilla ice cream into bowls and slice the peaches on top of the ice cream. Spoon the cooking juices over, discarding the cinnamon stick and cloves, and serve.

BLACK AND BLUEBERRY
Crumble

MAKES 12 SERVINGS / Prep: 20 minutes / Bake: 40 to 45 minutes

Summer berries mean crumbles at our house. It's just so easy to pile fresh berries into the skillet, sprinkle with sugar and cinnamon, and top with an easy oat and flour crumble. The crumble is a sweet dough that is just that: crumbly. You want this mixture to hold its shape so that when it bakes it stays on top and gets browned and crispy. Serve warm—always—with vanilla ice cream. And, if there are leftovers, remove them from the skillet before storing. The natural acidity of the fruit is not good for the finish on your skillet.

1 teaspoon unsalted butter, at room temperature

4 cups fresh blueberries

3 cups fresh blackberries or raspberries

⅓ to ½ cup granulated sugar

¼ teaspoon ground cinnamon

CRUMBLE TOPPING

1¼ cups packed light brown sugar

1¼ cups unbleached all-purpose flour

½ teaspoon salt

¼ teaspoon ground cinnamon

¾ cup (1½ sticks) unsalted butter, chilled and cut into 24 pieces

1 cup rolled oats

Vanilla ice cream, for serving

1. Preheat the oven to 375 degrees F.

2. Grease a 12-inch skillet with the butter. Scatter the berries in the skillet. Sprinkle the sugar and cinnamon on top. Heat the skillet over medium heat, stirring and tossing the fruit until the sugar dissolves, 3 to 4 minutes. Pull the pan off the heat and set it aside.

3. For the crumble, combine the brown sugar, flour, salt, and cinnamon in the bowl of a food processor fitted with a steel blade. Pulse a few times to combine. Distribute around the work bowl. With your fingers, toss the butter with the flour mixture so it doesn't stick together, carefully avoiding the blades of the processor. Pulse 10 to 15 times, until the mixture just begins to pull together. Transfer to a mixing bowl and use your fingers to knead in the oats until the butter softens and the mixture gets crumbly. Drop the crumble mixture in big pieces on top of the fruit.

4. Place the skillet in the oven and bake until the crumble topping is dark golden-brown and the fruit mixture is bubbling around the edges, 40 to 45 minutes. Remove the skillet from the oven and let the crumble rest for 30 minutes, so the juices have a chance to thicken. Serve warm with ice cream.

APPLE TARTE TATIN

MAKES 8 TO 10 SERVINGS / Prep: 40 minutes / Bake: 30 to 35 minutes

The tarte Tatin was originally an upside-down apple pie baked by two sisters in the Loire Valley region of France. It was nothing but caramelized apples and thin pastry, but since then, the variations on this original pie look less like the original. So, I wanted to get back to basics and create a skillet version that feels authentic. (Although the optional cinnamon is not authentic, it is delicious!) In order to have good, tart apple flavor, I use Granny Smith apples, which you can find year-round. This tart is a little tricky to unmold, so if any apple pieces stick to the skillet, just patch them into place on top of your beautiful apple tart!

6 tablespoons unsalted butter

¼ cup granulated sugar

¼ cup firmly packed light brown sugar

¼ teaspoon ground cinnamon (optional)

2 pounds tart apples, peeled, cored, quartered, and each quarter cut into 3 slices

1 recipe Food Processor Pie Crust (page 247)

Vanilla ice cream or crème fraîche, for serving

1. Preheat the oven to 400 degrees F.

2. Melt the butter in a 12-inch skillet over medium-low heat. Add both sugars and the cinnamon (if using) and stir to combine. Spread out the butter–sugar mixture, then arrange the apple slices in concentric circles in the bottom of the pan. Cook, undisturbed, so the apples develop a golden brown color underneath but do not stick, 20 to 25 minutes.

3. Roll out the pie crust dough to a ⅓-inch thickness and cut out a 12-inch circle. Place the circle of dough on top of the apples, tucking the edges under so the pastry fits in the skillet.

4. Place the skillet in the oven and bake until the pastry is lightly browned, 30 to 35 minutes. Remove the skillet from the oven. Place a large, flat platter on top of the skillet. Invert the hot skillet onto the platter and carefully hit the skillet with your hand (in an oven mitt!) to release any apples that might stick. Let the tart fall onto the platter, and replace any stuck apples. Serve warm, topped with vanilla ice cream or crème fraîche.

FRESH BERRY CROSTATA
Blueprint

MAKES 8 TO 12 SERVINGS / Prep: 35 minutes / Bake: 25 to 30 minutes

I fell in love with crostatas when I was just too busy with young children to slow down and make a real pie. I'd just make crust, pat it out into a big round, fill it with fresh fruit of the season, and add sugar to sweeten. This freeform dessert saved me for many a dinner party. Now I have adapted the crostata recipe for the skillet, where it bakes up crispy all around. There's quite a bit of butter in this dough, so if you make it ahead of time, keep it chilled until you're ready to pat it out and bake. Use any mix of fresh berries you like—blueberries, blackberries, or raspberries. And add a few peaches, too. The fruit filling can truly be a delicious rainbow of colors and flavors.

DOUGH

2 cups unbleached all-purpose flour

¼ cup granulated sugar

½ teaspoon salt

1 cup (2 sticks) unsalted butter, cut into ½-inch cubes

¼ cup ice water

FILLING

3 cups fresh raspberries or other fresh berries

⅓ cup granulated sugar

¼ teaspoon ground nutmeg or cinnamon or 1 teaspoon grated lemon zest

1 teaspoon confectioners' sugar

1. For the dough, combine the flour, granulated sugar, and salt in the bowl of a food processor fitted with a steel blade. Process for 5 to 10 seconds, until blended. Scatter the butter cubes around the processor bowl and toss with the flour, being careful not to cut your fingers on the blades. Pulse for 15 to 20 seconds, until the mixture is the size of small peas. Pour in the ice water and process until the dough pulls together, 10 to 15 seconds. Remove the dough, wrap in plastic wrap, flatten into a disk, and refrigerate until ready to bake.

2. Preheat the oven to 425 degrees F.

3. On a floured work surface, roll the dough into a 12-inch circle, then drape the dough in a 12-inch skillet. Place the raspberries or other berries in the center of the dough, leaving a 1½- to 2-inch border around them. Sprinkle the granulated sugar over the berries. If desired, sprinkle the nutmeg or cinnamon or lemon zest over the sugar. Pull the dough up and over the raspberries, forming pleats. There will be an opening in the middle where the berries show through. Press down slightly on the pleats.

4. Place the skillet in the oven and bake until the fruit is bubbly in the center of the crostata and the dough has lightly browned, 25 to 30 minutes. Remove the skillet from the oven and let the crostata rest for 15 minutes. With a metal spatula, transfer the crostata to a platter and dust with confectioners' sugar. Slice and serve warm.

ATLANTIC BEACH PIE

MAKES 12 TO 16 SERVINGS / Prep: 35 minutes / Bake: 42 to 51 minutes

Key lime pie has always been a family favorite dessert, but this pie from coastal North Carolina caught my imagination because of the unique buttery crust. It is made from either all saltine crackers or, as I prefer, a blend of saltines and Ritz crackers. When baked in an iron skillet, this crust is substantial and crispy. The cool, refreshing filling is a lemon version of the Key lime, topped with a glorious meringue. You can lift the pie straight out of the skillet and onto a plate for a dramatic summertime dinner party dessert.

CRUST

30 saltine crackers

30 Ritz crackers

3 tablespoons sugar

½ cup (1 stick) unsalted butter, at room temperature

FILLING

8 large eggs, separated

2 (14-ounce) cans sweetened condensed milk

1 cup fresh lemon juice (from 8 to 10 lemons)

MERINGUE

½ cup sugar

1. Preheat the oven to 350 degrees F.

2. For the crust, crumble the crackers into the bowl of a food processor fitted with a steel blade. Add the sugar and soft butter and pulse until the mixture is nearly combined, about 20 seconds. The cracker crumbs should still be coarse. Pat the mixture into the bottom and up the sides of a 12-inch skillet. Bake until the crust turns golden brown, 15 to 18 minutes. Remove the skillet from the oven. Keep the oven on.

3. For the filling, whisk together the egg yolks, condensed milk, and lemon juice in a large bowl. Pour the filling into the crust and bake until the filling sets, 20 to 25 minutes. Remove the skillet from the oven. Keep the oven on.

4. For the meringue, in a large bowl, beat only 5 of the egg whites with an electric mixer on high speed until soft peaks form, 2 to 3 minutes. (Discard the remaining 3 egg whites or reserve for another use.) Gradually add the sugar and continue beating until stiff peaks form, 1 to 2 minutes more. Spread the meringue over the top of the filling (see Note). Bake until the meringue is golden brown, 7 to 8 minutes. Remove the skillet from the oven and let the pie rest for 30 minutes, then slice and serve.

NOTE: When spreading meringue over a baked filling and returning the pie to the oven, there are two camps on how to proceed: You can spread it all the way to the crust to seal the meringue to the crust—this prevents the meringue from "weeping" on day two and shrinking back from the crust. Or you can allow for a little margin of the filling to peek through all around the edge of the crust, which, in my opinion, is a more beautiful presentation.

Secrets to Perfect Skillet Pies

Here are some tips for adapting your favorite pie recipes to the iron skillet:

Use a pie crust recipe that makes enough for a 12-inch skillet, such as Food Processor Pie Crust (page 247).

Or, make a half recipe of Food Processor Pie Crust, roll it out, and cut it into strips to lattice on top of a crust-less pie.

Or, go without a crust completely. For fruit pies and cobblers, you can toss an easy crumble or topping on the fruit in the skillet before baking.

Flute the top of your pie crust just inside the rim of the skillet, not outside it.

Adjust the oven rack before baking: Lower it for crusts on the bottom of the skillet. Bake on the center rack if you need more browning on top of the pie.

PUMPKIN BOURBON TART
with Pecan Crumble

MAKES 8 TO 10 SERVINGS / Prep: 40 minutes / Bake: 38 to 45 minutes

Pumpkin pies and tarts seldom cross our minds most of the year, but when fall rolls around and Thanksgiving looms, we are on a search for the best pie with pumpkin. This skillet recipe is a big step above the recipe on the side of the pumpkin can, and it has a festive pecan and brown sugar crumble on top. The addition of bourbon really sets off this pumpkin tart as special-occasion fare.

1 recipe Food Processor Pie Crust (page 247)

½ cup (1 stick) unsalted butter, at room temperature

¾ cup lightly packed light brown sugar

1 (15-ounce) can pumpkin purée

3 large eggs, separated

¾ cup whole milk

¼ cup bourbon

½ teaspoon ground cinnamon

¼ teaspoon ground nutmeg

¼ teaspoon ground cloves

¼ teaspoon salt

CRUMBLE

¼ cup chopped pecans

2 tablespoons light brown sugar

1 tablespoon unsalted butter, at room temperature

1 tablespoon all-purpose flour

1. Place a rack in the bottom third of the oven and preheat the oven to 375 degrees F.

2. Roll the pie crust dough to a ⅓-inch thickness and press it into the bottom and up the sides of a 12-inch skillet. Prick the bottom of the crust six or seven times with a fork and crimp the top edge.

3. In a large bowl, beat the soft butter and brown sugar with an electric mixer on medium speed until the mixture is creamy and fluffy, about 1 minute. Add the pumpkin and blend on low speed to combine. Add the egg yolks, milk, bourbon, cinnamon, nutmeg, cloves, and salt and blend until well combined, about 1 minute.

4. In another large bowl, with clean beaters, beat the egg whites on high speed until stiff peaks form, 1 to 2 minutes. Fold a third of the egg whites into the pumpkin mixture to lighten it, then fold in the remaining egg whites until combined. Pour the mixture into the pie crust.

5. Bake until the filling is nearly set, 30 to 35 minutes. Remove the skillet from the oven. Keep the oven on.

6. For the crumble, combine the pecans, brown sugar, butter, and flour in a small bowl. Crumble this mixture around the outside edges of the pie and return the skillet to the oven. Bake until the crumble is golden brown, 8 to 10 minutes. Remove the skillet from the oven and let the pie rest in the skillet for 20 minutes, then slice and serve.

LITTLE FRIED HAND PIES

MAKES ABOUT 3 DOZEN HAND PIES / Prep: 1 hour / Cook: 2 minutes per batch

Depending on where you call home, these miniature pies are known as turnovers or hand pies. Whatever you call it, it's a small pastry round folded over a fruit filling—and also easy to make! You can use your own biscuit dough, or do as I do and thaw frozen biscuit dough. Vary the filling with any dried fruit you like.

6 ounces dried apricots

3 ounces dried Montmorency tart cherries

2 cups water

½ cup granulated sugar

36 (2- to 2½-inch) frozen biscuit rounds, thawed, or refrigerator biscuits

4 cups peanut oil

1 tablespoon confectioners' sugar

1. Put the dried apricots and cherries in a medium saucepan and add the water. Stir in the sugar. Bring the water to a boil over medium-high heat, then reduce the heat to a simmer and cook, stirring occasionally, until the fruit is very soft, 45 to 50 minutes. Turn off the heat and let the fruit filling cool in the pan. You should have about 2 cups filling.

2. Press the thawed biscuit rounds out to 3 inches in diameter and set aside.

3. Heat the peanut oil in a 12-inch skillet over medium-high heat to 350 degrees F. You can test the oil to see if it is ready for frying by placing a small piece of biscuit dough in the oil. It should sizzle and brown.

4. While the oil heats, place a rounded teaspoon of filling in the center of each biscuit round. Fold the round in half to make a semicircle. Seal the edges of the dough with a fork so the filling doesn't ooze out.

5. When the oil is hot, add four or five little pies and fry until golden on both sides, about 1 minute per side. With a slotted spoon, transfer them to brown paper to drain. Dust with the confectioners' sugar. Repeat with the remaining little pies. Serve hot or at room temperature.

The Delicious Science Behind Fried Pies

In Appalachia, where fried pies are a way of life and apple farmers dry fresh apple slices so they can use them later in baking, the filling is perfected to a science. A fresh fruit filling is just too runny to use in frying. But a filling that begins with dried fruit has just the right firmness to stay inside the pie. Plus, dried fruit has much more concentrated flavor, making the filling inside these pies all the better.

BANANAS FOSTER

MAKES 4 SERVINGS / Prep: 15 minutes / Cook: 4 to 5 minutes

When the late Ella Brennan created bananas Foster at Brennan's Restaurant in the early 1950s, she was trying to impress Richard Foster, chairman of a New Orleans crime commission. It was one of those shoot-from-the-hip moments in American food history, as Ella grabbed ripe bananas, brown sugar, butter, and rum and turned on the heat of her big kitchen stove. That dessert became a Brennàn's signature offering and still lives on, more than a half century later. We've all got ripe bananas in our kitchen, and there is nothing better than this combination of ingredients sizzled in cast iron and spooned over vanilla ice cream.

4 tablespoons unsalted butter

⅔ cup firmly packed dark brown sugar

¼ cup dark rum

1 teaspoon vanilla extract

½ teaspoon ground cinnamon

Big pinch salt

2 large or 3 medium bananas, peeled, cut in half lengthwise and again in half crosswise

Vanilla ice cream, for serving

1. Melt the butter in a 12-inch skillet over medium heat. Stir in the sugar, rum, vanilla, cinnamon, and salt. When the mixture sizzles and the sugar has dissolved, 3 to 4 minutes, add the banana quarters to the pan, cut-side down.

2. Cook until the bananas caramelize and lightly brown, about 2 minutes. With tongs, carefully turn the banana pieces so as not to break them, and cook on the rounded side until lightly browned, about 1 minute. The trick is to let the bananas caramelize but not cook so much that they get mushy.

3. Scoop vanilla ice cream into bowls, spoon the warm bananas and sauce over the top, and serve.

BUTTER PECAN SKILLET
Ice Cream

MAKES ABOUT 1 QUART (6 TO 8 SERVINGS)

Prep: 30 minutes / Chill: 1 hour 15 minutes / Freeze: 30 to 35 minutes, depending on the ice cream freezer

Our friend Jay is a butter pecan ice cream fanatic, so I wondered what homemade butter pecan ice cream would taste like. It must have originated at home, with someone cooking the pecans in butter and then turning them into ice cream. So, one Saturday, I tried making it. I pulled out my iron skillet, tossed in pecans and butter, and toasted them until crunchy and browned. Then, I made a simple vanilla ice cream custard right in the same skillet. When the ice cream had nearly finished churning, I added the skillet-toasted pecans and churned until the machine stopped. Jay was thrilled! We all were!

1 generous cup coarsely chopped pecans

2 tablespoons unsalted butter

¼ teaspoon kosher salt, plus more if needed

1 cup granulated sugar

¼ cup firmly packed dark brown sugar

3 tablespoons cornstarch

2 cups whole milk

2 teaspoons vanilla extract

2 cups heavy cream

1. Combine the pecans and butter in a 12-inch skillet. Cook over medium heat, stirring, until the butter has melted and the pecans have deeply browned, 3 to 4 minutes. Transfer the pecans and butter to a small bowl and sprinkle with the salt. Taste a pecan—it should taste a bit salty. If not, add a little more salt.

2. In the same skillet, off the heat, whisk together both sugars and the cornstarch. Whisk in the milk, a little at a time, until the mixture is smooth. Turn the heat to medium-low. When the mixture comes to a boil, reduce the heat to the lowest setting and simmer, whisking constantly, until thickened like custard, about 4 minutes. Turn off the heat. Whisk in the vanilla.

3. Transfer the custard mixture to a large heatproof bowl and refrigerate, uncovered, until fully chilled, about 1 hour 15 minutes.

4. When the custard has chilled, whisk in the cream. Pour the mixture into an ice cream maker and freeze according to the manufacturer's directions. About 15 minutes before it is done, add the salted, buttered pecans and resume freezing. Serve at once, or pack the ice cream into a plastic container and store in the freezer for up to 1 week.

FOOD PROCESSOR PIE CRUST

MAKES ENOUGH DOUGH TO FILL A 12-INCH SKILLET
Prep: 10 minutes / Chill: 2 hours

This crust is easy to prepare in the food processor, and you can transfer the dough right to the skillet or chill it for later use. The mix of butter and shortening makes for just the right flakiness. Be sure to measure and freeze the butter and shortening until firm, about 30 minutes. For the ice water, fill a measuring cup with water and ice, and then measure out the needed tablespoons.

1½ cups unbleached all-purpose flour

¼ teaspoon salt

¼ teaspoon sugar

4 tablespoons unsalted butter, frozen and cut into ½-inch pieces

4 tablespoons vegetable shortening, frozen and cut into ½-inch pieces

3 to 4 tablespoons ice water

1. Combine the flour, salt, and sugar in a food processor fitted with a steel blade. Pulse 2 or 3 times, until combined. Scatter the frozen butter and shortening pieces around the bowl of the processor. With your fingers, toss the butter and shortening with the flour mixture so it doesn't stick together, carefully avoiding the blades of the processor. Pulse 20 to 25 times, until big pea-size crumbs form.

2. Add the ice water and process until the mixture comes together into a ball, about 10 seconds. Use immediately, or transfer the dough to a sheet of wax paper and flatten it into a 6-inch disk. Wrap it up in the paper and refrigerate for at least 2 hours (see Note).

NOTE: If you prep the crust and place it immediately in the skillet, the dough will be soft, so you can gently press it into the skillet. But if you chill the dough, you will need to gently roll it out to a 14-inch circle on a floured surface. Carefully drape the circle of dough in the skillet, then decoratively crimp the edges so that the top of the dough is slightly below the top of the skillet.

This chapter is all about those extra touches that make salads, mains, desserts, appetizers, and even breakfast a whole lot more interesting. I knew the iron skillet was versatile, but I did not know how versatile until this chapter was complete. I discovered that I could bake crunchy croutons from day-old bread. I could make my own granola. I could roast chickpeas to top salads, slow-cook pecans for entertaining friends at cocktail hour, and let fresh cranberries roast alongside jalapeño peppers to make a sweet-meets-hot salsa that is perfect for roasted pork or barbecued ribs. I love how the skillet transforms something as simple as cherry tomatoes into a gourmet spread. And when given the chance to simmer down peach preserves to top cheese in an interesting way, or assemble a barbecue sauce of lemon and figs for pork, or make bacon-onion jam, the iron skillet cooks, caramel-izes, and proves, once again, just how indispensable it is in the kitchen.

CHAPTER 7

THE PANTRY

SKILLET-ROASTED
Chickpeas

MAKES ABOUT 1½ CUPS / Prep: 5 minutes / Cook: 20 to 25 minutes

Chickpeas—aka garbanzo beans—are a staple in the pantry at my house. I simmer them in soups, purée them into hummus, and even roast them in my skillet. It could not be easier! Use these crunchy chickpeas as you would croutons, on every salad imaginable.

1 (15-ounce) can chickpeas, drained

1 tablespoon olive oil

Kosher salt and freshly ground black pepper

Creole seasoning, ground cumin, or dried oregano (optional)

1. Preheat the oven to 425 degrees F.

2. In a 12-inch skillet, toss the chickpeas with the olive oil and season as desired. Go light on the seasoning; you can always add more later.

3. Roast the chickpeas, shaking the pan occasionally to toss them, until they are crispy, dark, and slightly shrunken, 20 to 25 minutes.

4. Remove the skillet from the oven and let the chickpeas cool in the pan. Taste and season as needed. Store in an airtight container at room temperature for up to 1 week.

SKILLET PEPPERS
and Garlic

MAKES ABOUT 2 CUPS
Prep: 30 minutes / Cook: About 1 hour

When it comes to tuna melts, grilled cheese sandwiches, pizza, baked potatoes, or fresh goat cheese, there is no better garnish than roasted red peppers. In fact, I can't think of a dish that doesn't improve from a spoonful of these skillet peppers. The foundation is six large red bell peppers, but you should add some slightly hot chiles—particularly if you have access to the fabulous Hatch chiles from New Mexico! It is that balance of hot versus sweet that makes this pepper mélange so intriguing. It surprises the mouth at first bite, but you just keep eating. And if you don't have any hot peppers on hand, simply add a good sprinkle of red pepper flakes instead.

6 large red bell peppers, cored, deveined, seeded, and cut into 1-inch strips

4 small serrano chiles or 1 large Hatch chile, seeded and thinly sliced, or ½ teaspoon red pepper flakes

12 cloves garlic, peeled and thinly sliced

⅓ cup olive oil

1. Preheat the oven to 400 degrees F.

2. Combine the bell pepper strips and hot chiles in a 12-inch skillet. Scatter the garlic over the peppers, then pour in the olive oil. Cover and bake until the peppers are nearly soft, 35 to 40 minutes.

3. Remove the lid and continue to bake until the peppers turn brown and quite soft, 30 to 35 more minutes. Transfer the pepper mixture to a bowl or other container and set aside to cool to room temperature, about 2 hours. Cover and store in the fridge for up to 1 month. Keep the peppers covered in oil, adding more olive oil as needed.

SLOW-ROASTED
Pecans

MAKES 1 POUND
Prep: 5 minutes / Cook: 1 hour 15 minutes

In the South, from Thanksgiving to Christmas, it's common to see a bowl of roasted, salted pecans on the table. It's something I was raised on, and we roast a pound of Desirables—our favorite variety of pecans—every year. My mother used her big turkey roasting pan to roast her pecans and Nuts and Bolts (page 33), but I find that the iron skillet is the perfect vehicle in which to slowly, evenly roast pecans or walnuts so that the nut cooks all the way through and has that characteristic crunch. The seasoning is up to you: My preferred choice is sea salt, with Creole seasoning blend a close second. Sometimes, I go for a little of each. Be sure to salt the pecans after roasting, and not before.

2 tablespoons unsalted butter

1 pound pecan halves

Fine sea salt and/or Creole seasoning

1. Preheat the oven to 200 degrees F.

2. Combine the butter and pecans in a 12-inch skillet. Heat, stirring, over medium heat until the butter melts. Once it has melted, turn off the heat.

3. When the oven has preheated, place the skillet in the oven. Roast the pecans, stirring every 15 minutes, until they are deeply golden brown, about 1 hour. Raise the temperature to 250 degrees F and continue roasting until the pecans are deep chestnut brown, 15 more minutes.

4. Transfer the pecans to paper towels and season as desired. Let cool, then serve. Store leftovers in an airtight metal container for up to 3 weeks.

NOTE: If your oven runs hot, the pecans may be fully roasted in 1 hour. Look for the chestnut brown color and no darker.

MINDY'S ROASTED
Cranberries and Jalapeños

MAKES ABOUT 2 CUPS / Prep: 20 minutes / Cook: 30 to 35 minutes

Not long ago, our friends Mindy and RB invited us over for roasted duck and completely blew us away with the side dishes of crisp, fresh coleslaw and this relish of roasted cranberries and jalapeños. I had never thought about adding heat to cranberries, and now I find it hard to eat cranberries without hot peppers! The skillet is the perfect vehicle for this condiment because it lets it cook down until nice and syrupy.

3 cups fresh cranberries

¼ cup finely chopped onion

3 jalapeño peppers, seeded and finely chopped

1 tablespoon vegetable oil

1 cup sugar

Pinch kosher salt

1. Preheat the oven to 400 degrees F.

2. Combine the cranberries, onion, and jalapeños in a 12-inch skillet and drizzle them with the oil. Add the sugar and salt and toss to coat.

3. Place the skillet in the oven and roast until the cranberries pop and are soft, and the juices thicken and cook down, 30 to 35 minutes.

4. Serve warm or transfer to a heatproof bowl to cool. Store in an airtight container in the fridge for up to 2 weeks.

ALLISON'S HOME-BAKED GRANOLA
Blueprint

MAKES 6 GENEROUS CUPS / Prep: 15 minutes / Bake: 25 to 30 minutes

Years ago, my friend Allison Greiner shared her granola recipe with me. She told me that her young son called it "squirrel food"—and I can't tell you how many meals and gifts I have made from this delicious, naturally gluten-free "squirrel food" over the years! It is a blueprint recipe, ready to be customized to whatever is in your pantry—use any nuts and dried fruit you like. The iron skillet is the perfect way to cook granola because it bakes evenly and allows the oats and nuts to toast along the edges of the pan.

4 cups extra-thick rolled oats

1 cup sliced almonds

½ cup unsweetened flaked coconut

¼ cup unsalted pepitas (hulled pumpkin seeds) or chopped walnuts

½ cup maple syrup

2 tablespoons vegetable oil

½ teaspoon kosher salt

½ teaspoon ground cinnamon

1 cup dried fruit, such as cherries, cranberries, raisins, and/or currants

1. Preheat the oven to 350 degrees F.

2. Toss the oats, almonds, coconut, and pepitas in a 12-inch skillet. Drizzle the maple syrup and oil over the oat mixture, then stir in the salt and cinnamon. Stir to combine well.

3. Bake the granola, tossing it once or twice with a spatula, until the oats and almonds are golden brown, 25 to 30 minutes. Stir in the dried fruit and let the granola cool in the skillet for 2 hours. Store in an airtight container at room temperature for up to 3 weeks.

HOMEMADE CROUTONS

MAKES 5 TO 6 CUPS

Prep: 15 minutes / Cook: About 2 minutes per batch

The best croutons start with a day-old loaf of bread. When the bread has dried out, it doesn't act like a sponge and soak up the oil in the skillet. My favorite is a baguette or any dense, hearty French loaf. Add just salt and pepper, or go all out with dried oregano, minced garlic, and grated Parmesan.

½ to ¾ cup olive oil

6 (2-inch-thick) diagonal slices day-old French bread, cut into ¾- to 1-inch cubes

Kosher salt and freshly ground black pepper

Dried oregano, minced garlic, and/or grated Parmesan (optional)

1. Heat ½ cup olive oil in a 12-inch skillet over medium heat until warmed, then add enough bread cubes to nearly fill the skillet. Fry on all sides until golden, about 2 minutes, using tongs to turn the cubes in the oil. Use a slotted spoon to transfer the fried croutons to brown paper to drain. Season while hot with salt, pepper, and any other seasonings you like.

2. Repeat with the remaining croutons, adding the remaining ¼ cup olive oil to the skillet as needed. Store in an airtight container at room temperature for up to 3 days.

BOURBON PEACH
Preserves

MAKES ABOUT 3 CUPS
Prep and cook: 20 minutes

This is one of those recipes I dream of: peach preserves cooked down in a skillet until syrupy. Oh, and a dash of bourbon, too. This is delicious stuff to pile onto warm ham biscuits, as we do in the South. It is also what we like to spoon into a small ceramic bowl and place on the cheese or pastry platter to create excitement and elevate the ordinary to the extraordinary.

3 cups good-quality peach preserves

1 tablespoon bourbon

¼ teaspoon ground cardamom

Pinch ground cinnamon

1. Heat the peach preserves in a 12-inch skillet over medium-low heat and cook, stirring, until the preserves begin to stick to the pan, 3 to 4 minutes. Stir in the bourbon, cardamom, and cinnamon. Let the mixture come to a simmer again, then turn off the heat.

2. Let the preserves cool in the skillet for about 10 minutes, then spoon into a bowl and serve, or store in an airtight container in the fridge for up to 1 month.

LEMON-FIG
Barbecue Sauce

MAKES ABOUT 1½ CUPS / Prep: 10 minutes / Cook: 18 to 20 minutes

Some of my favorite sauces started as last-minute creations. This recipe certainly qualifies! I had jars of homemade fig jam in my fridge, needing to be used or given away, and I had pork roasting that needed to be glazed. So I combined the jam with ketchup, some lemon, balsamic vinegar, brown sugar, and a hint of curry. This is a yummy barbecue sauce for chicken wings or to spread on turkey sandwiches.

1 cup fig jam or preserves

½ cup ketchup

Grated zest and juice of ½ lemon
(1 tablespoon juice and 1 teaspoon zest)

1 tablespoon balsamic vinegar

1 tablespoon brown sugar
(optional; see Note)

¼ teaspoon curry powder

1. Combine the fig jam, ketchup, lemon zest and juice, vinegar, brown sugar (if using), and curry powder in a 12-inch skillet. Bring to a boil over medium heat, stirring, then reduce the heat to very low and simmer until thickened, stirring occasionally, 18 to 20 minutes.

2. Transfer the jam to a heatproof bowl to cool. Store in an airtight container in the fridge for up to 2 weeks.

NOTE: Because fig jams and preserves vary in sweetness, you need to taste yours and determine if it needs the added brown sugar.

BACON-ONION JAM

MAKES ABOUT 1 CUP

Prep: 10 minutes / Cook: About 1 hour 20 minutes

I knew that bacon and cast-iron are natural together, so I thought, why not take this one step further and throw together a batch of jam made from bacon, onions, sugar, and balsamic vinegar? This is just the right spread for grilled cheese sandwiches, cheeseburgers, or a wedge of soft and runny Brie on the cheese tray. And it stores well in your fridge. The trick is to cook the bacon over low heat to render the fat, which you drain off to keep this wildly decadent spread just a little bit healthier.

8 ounces thick-cut bacon slices, cut into 1-inch pieces

2 cups chopped Vidalia or other sweet onions

3 tablespoons light brown sugar

¼ cup balsamic vinegar

3 to 7 tablespoons water

1 teaspoon Dijon mustard

1 teaspoon fresh thyme leaves (optional)

Kosher salt and freshly ground black pepper

1. Cook the bacon in a 12-inch skillet over medium-low heat, stirring, until the fat renders and the bacon crisps, 12 to 15 minutes. Use a slotted spoon to transfer the bacon pieces to paper towels or a bowl. Drain off all but 1 tablespoon of the bacon grease from the skillet.

2. Add the onion to the skillet and cook over medium-low heat until it begins to soften, 2 to 3 minutes. Return the bacon to the skillet. Add the brown sugar, vinegar, 3 tablespoons water, mustard, and thyme (if using) and stir to combine. Reduce the heat to low, cover the skillet, and cook until the onions are soft, 20 minutes.

3. Stir, partially cover the skillet, and let the jam cook down until it is dark brown, 45 to 50 minutes. If the mixture becomes dry as it cooks, add 1 tablespoon additional water at a time to keep it from sticking. Taste and season with salt and pepper.

4. Transfer the jam to a heatproof bowl and let it cool completely. Store in an airtight container in the fridge for up to 1 week.

OLD-FASHIONED DELTA
Caramel Icing

MAKES 4 CUPS; ENOUGH TO FROST A TWO- TO THREE-LAYER CAKE
Prep and Cook: 35 to 50 minutes

Here is the famous icing that can be used on a Two-Layer Caramel Cake (page 202). It's a special-occasion icing made in two pans: First, you caramelize the sugar in a cast-iron skillet, then you simmer the icing in a saucepan. It's a bit tedious but oh-so-delicious, a true labor of love!

3 cups sugar, divided use

1 cup evaporated milk

¼ teaspoon salt

½ cup (1 stick) unsalted butter

1 teaspoon vanilla extract

1. In a large, heavy saucepan, combine 2½ cups of the sugar, the evaporated milk, and the salt. Cook over medium heat, stirring constantly, until the mixture boils and the sugar has dissolved, then continue to stir and let the mixture boil for 3 minutes. Remove the pan from the heat.

2. Heat the remaining ½ cup sugar in a 12-inch skillet over medium heat. Cook the sugar, undisturbed, until it caramelizes and turns a deep golden brown, 4 to 5 minutes. Do not let it reach dark brown or it will burn from the residual heat in the skillet. Remove the pan from the heat.

3. Stir about ½ cup of the evaporated milk mixture into the hot caramelized sugar in the skillet to bring the heat down. Then pour the contents of the skillet into the saucepan with the remaining evaporated milk mixture. Stir until incorporated. Add the butter and vanilla and stir until the butter melts and the mixture is smooth.

4. Place the saucepan in a large bowl filled with 2 inches of ice water. Stir the icing with a wooden spoon until it cools and thickens, 4 to 5 minutes. You don't want the icing to thicken too much or it will be difficult to spread. When it is of a spreadable consistency, remove the pan from the ice water bath. Frost your cake quickly, as the icing will harden as it cools.

Roasted
CHERRY TOMATOES

MAKES ABOUT 4 CUPS
Prep: 10 minutes / Cook: 50 to 53 minutes

This gorgeous and versatile condiment sauce is perfect with just about anything! I like to eat it all by itself, spooned onto crusty bread, or add it to my favorite pizza. And it's just the right topper for soft goat cheese or Boursin when making Skillet Tartines (page 22). If you add a pinch of saffron as the sauce simmers down, it pairs perfectly with grilled fish.

¼ cup olive oil

4 cups red and yellow cherry tomatoes

5 to 6 cloves garlic, peeled and sliced

4 or 5 fresh oregano, rosemary, and/or thyme sprigs, plus more for garnish (optional)

Kosher salt and freshly ground black pepper

1. Preheat the oven to 350 degrees F.

2. Heat the olive oil in a 12-inch skillet over medium heat. Add the tomatoes, garlic, and herb sprigs and toss until the oil is hot and the garlic begins to brown, 4 to 5 minutes. Place the skillet in the oven and roast the mixture until the tomatoes pop and lightly brown, 45 to 48 minutes. Let the mixture cool in the pan for 10 minutes. Season with salt and pepper and garnish with additional fresh herbs, if desired. Serve warm or store in an airtight container in the fridge for up to 1 week.

How to Skillet-Roast Fish with Roasted Cherry Tomatoes

About 10 minutes before the tomatoes are done, nestle two or three fillets of grouper or red snapper in the pan. Spoon the pan juices over. Increase the oven temperature to 375 degrees F and roast until the fish flakes, about 20 minutes. Garnish with capers and a handful of chopped fresh flat-leaf parsley.

ACKNOWLEDGMENTS

Cookbooks begin with a thought planted in your mind. The thought turns into an idea and the idea into an outline, and out of that springs chapters and recipes and prose that grow into a living, breathing book when you're done with it.

An oversimplification, yes, but it's the process I used to write about the 12-inch cast-iron skillet. The subject intrigued me not only because of the skillet's unique place in our country's food history, but also, selfishly, because of my own iron skillets and wanting to learn how to cook with them in a more modern way. Not only is the iron skillet heirloom and authentic, but it is a naturally nonstick workhorse that appeals to cooks today. I could not have written this book as you see it now without the help of many others.

First, I would like to say thank you to the unknown former owner of my 12-inch Griswold skillet. You cherished this pan as much as I do now.

Thank you to my husband, John, for embracing this project with your usual wit and charm and traveling down this road with me. Thank you to my children, Kathleen, Litton, and John, and to my son-in-law, Hugh, for seeing this book as something your generation needs to cook and live well.

A big thank-you to my literary agent, David Black, and his team, for being curious as you always are and for seeing the value in a book like this.

Thank you to my editors Karen Murgolo and Morgan Hedden, who embraced this project, and cooked from it, too—the best compliment. Thanks to the hardworking team at Grand Central—Tareth Mitch, Amanda Pritzker, Tiffany Sanchez, Matthew Ballast, Karen Wise, Albert Tang, and publisher Ben Sevier, who understand the love you can have for a cast-iron skillet. Thanks also to Gary Tooth for bringing his beautiful design to these pages.

Thankfully, Danielle Atkins, my photographer and friend, is a skillet devotee. Her eye and lens bring the black cast-iron skillet to life in rich, mouthwatering color. To food stylist Teresa Blackburn and prop stylist Jessie Pickren, many thanks for creating photos that are original, fresh, and true to my recipes.

Posthumously, I would like to thank my mother, Bebe; my mother-in-law, Flowerree; and my grandmothers, Dee and Mur, for affecting the way I cook today. Your memories are rich and alive, and they never go away.

As a journalist, I have been influenced by the people around me, my travels, and what I read and hear and see. I am surely forgetting someone, but I would like to thank the following people because they are lovers of cast iron and helped me with the research on this book and on other articles I have written about it: Mollie Katzen, Lydie Marshall, Kelly Fields, Rebekah Turshen, Lisa-Marie White, and Nathalie Dupree. Thanks to Connie Carter at the Library of Congress for making me hungry to learn. Also thanks to Mark Kelly, Michael Whitfield, and Larry Raydo at Lodge; Isaac Morton at Smithey Ironware; and Dennis Powell of Butter Pat. I would also like to thank the late Bill Neal, wise sage of Southern cooking whose books I adore and continue to consult on projects like this.

The following people shared a recipe or good advice, and I'd like to thank them as well—Joan Nathan, Clarke Gallivan, Karen Vanarsdel, Ginger Moldrem, Francesca Bruzzese, Sara Zaban Franco, Nancy Vienneau, Lisa Dunn, Susan Anderson, Marian Petrie, Dotty Griffith, Allison Greiner, and Mindy Merrell.

And to all the readers of my cookbooks through the years, for your emails, enthusiasm, and loyalty, I thank you. I am happy to introduce *Skillet Love*, the newest member of the family.

INDEX

ABOUT THE AUTHOR

Anne Byrn is the bestselling author of more than a dozen cookbooks, including the *Cake Mix Doctor* and *American Cake*. Formerly food editor of the *Atlanta Journal-Constitution* and a graduate of École de Cuisine La Varenne in Paris, Byrn is a frequent contributor to *Food 52*, *The Local Palate*, and *The Bitter Southerner*. She is the mother of three grown children and lives with her husband in Nashville, Tennessee, in an old limestone home built by her grandfather in 1928.